FIREFLY
Encyclopedia
of Dinosaurs
and Prehistoric Animals

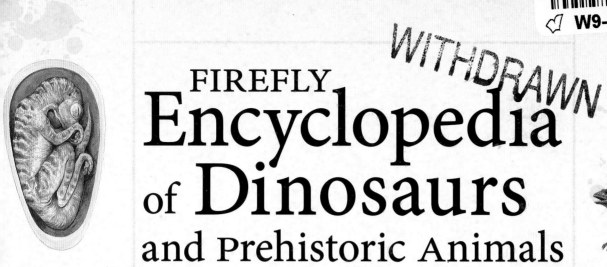

A Firefly Book

Published by Firefly Books Ltd. 2014

First printing

Publisher Cataloging-in-Publication Data (U.S.)

Palmer, Douglas.
Firefly encyclopedia of dinosaurs and prehistoric animals / Douglas Palmer.
[256]pages : col. ill. ; cm.
Includes index.
Summary: An illustrated who's who of the prehistoric world that includes
special features on the world in which these animals lived, their behavior and
why they disappeared.
ISBN-13: 978-1-77085-460-4 (pbk.)
1. Paleontology – Juvenile literature. 2. Animals, fossils – Juvenile literature.
3. Dinosaurs – Juvenile literature. I. Title. II. Encyclopedia of dinosaurs
and prehistoric animals.
566 dc 23 QE842.P345 2014

Library and Archives Canada
Cataloging in Publication

A CIP record for this title is available
from Library and Archives Canada

Published in the United States by
Firefly Books (U.S.) Inc.
P.O. Box 1338, Ellicott Station
Buffalo, New York 14205

Published in Canada by
Firefly Books Ltd.
50 Staples Avenue, Unit 1
Richmond Hill, Ontario L4B 0A7

Printed in China
by Toppan Leefung Printing Ltd

Created by Tall Tree Ltd.
Editors: Emma Marriott, Jon Richards
Designers: Marisa Renzullo, Malcolm Parchment
Art Director: Susi Martin
Publisher: Zeta Jones

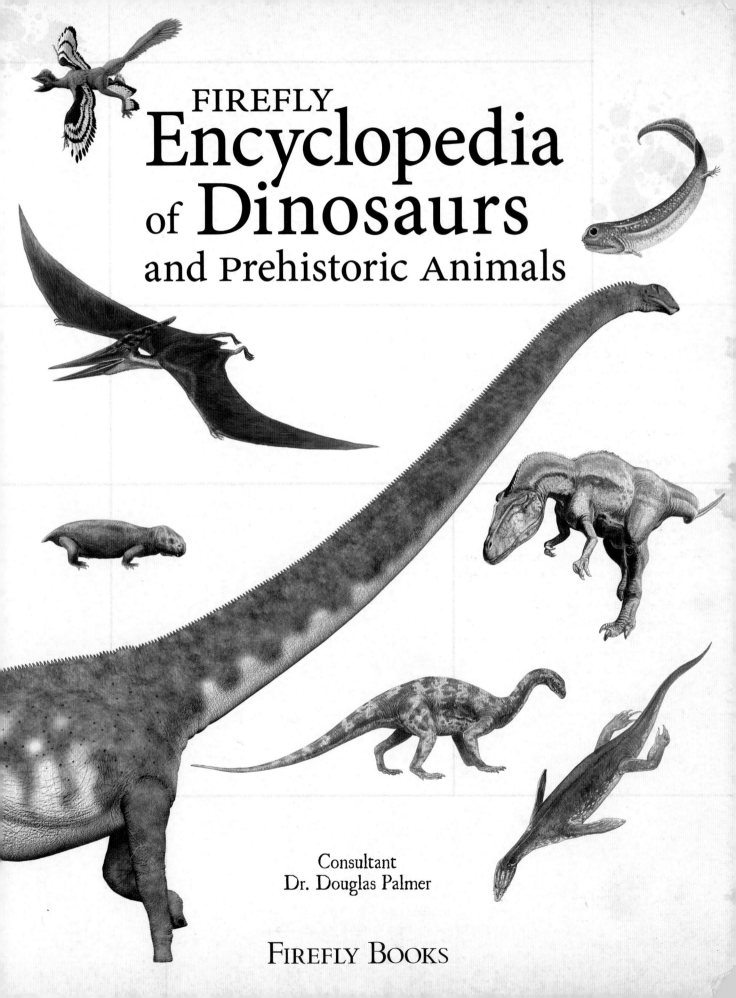

FIREFLY
Encyclopedia
of Dinosaurs
and Prehistoric Animals

Consultant
Dr. Douglas Palmer

FIREFLY BOOKS

CONTENTS

AVIAN DINOSAURS

SYNAPSIDS

MAMMALS

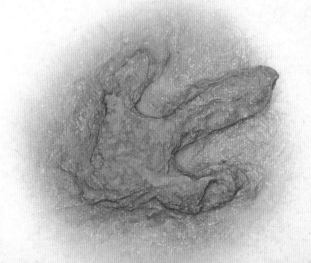

ANCIENT WORLDS

Since it was formed more than 4.5 billion years ago, the Earth has changed from an amalgamation of rock and space debris to the blue ocean planet we know today. These changes — the appearance of an atmosphere and water, the first stirrings of microscopic life, the evolution of complex organisms including plants and animals — have left their mark on the Earth, particularly in the rocks. Over the past 200 years, scientists have been able to reconstruct and map the ancient geological and biological history of our planet.

GEOLOGICAL TIMELINE

Throughout its long geological history, the Earth has undergone vast changes that have affected its life forms. Scientists divide the history of the Earth into different blocks of time. These include eons, which are divided into eras, which in turn are divided into periods. The Phanerozoic Eon dates from the time when life began to thrive on the Earth and the dates below show how many millions of years ago (MA) each began.

Fossilized shells of the sea creatures Brachiopods.

Early relatives of the mammals, such as this *Lystrosaurus*, dominated the Earth.

PERIOD	Cambrian	Ordovician	Silurian	Devonian	Carboniferous	Permian
	541 MA	485 MA	443 MA	419 MA	359 MA	299 MA
ERA	PALEOZOIC ERA					
EON	PHANEROZOIC					

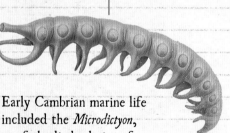

Early Cambrian marine life included the *Microdictyon*, a soft-bodied relative of the arthropods.

Amphibians, similar to the modern salamander, began to appear.

A rock contains the fossilized fronds of a fern. During the Carboniferous Period, ferns were very common.

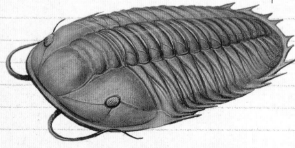

Trilobites, an extinct group of arthropods, were common occupants of ancient Palaeozoic seabeds.

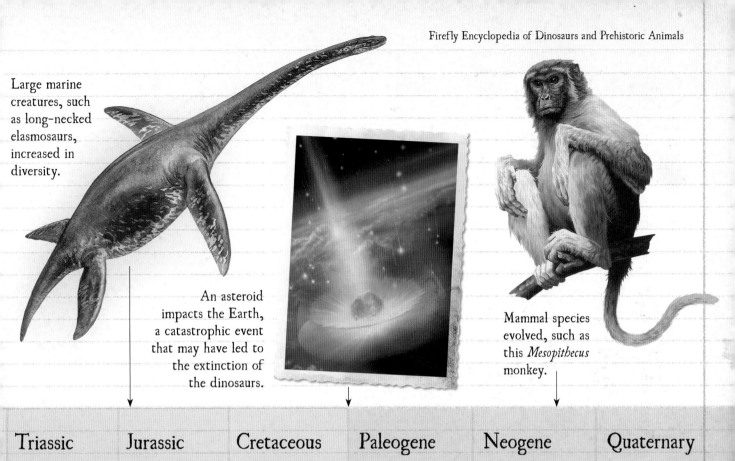

Large marine creatures, such as long-necked elasmosaurs, increased in diversity.

An asteroid impacts the Earth, a catastrophic event that may have led to the extinction of the dinosaurs.

Mammal species evolved, such as this *Mesopithecus* monkey.

Triassic	Jurassic	Cretaceous	Paleogene	Neogene	Quaternary
252 MA	201 MA	145 MA	66 MA	23 MA	2.5 MA

MESOZOIC ERA   CENOZOIC ERA

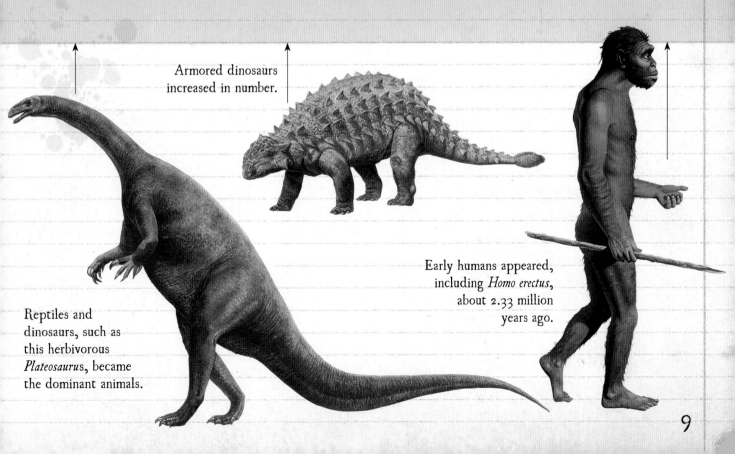

Armored dinosaurs increased in number.

Reptiles and dinosaurs, such as this herbivorous *Plateosaurus*, became the dominant animals.

Early humans appeared, including *Homo erectus*, about 2.33 million years ago.

FORMATION OF THE PLANET

The early history of the Earth is a story of slow but dramatic change, as its fiery surface cooled and produced the first signs of microscopic life. During the formation of our Solar System, the Earth was created by the coalescence of large fragments of rock and ice, along with dust and gas. As these pieces collided 4.6 billion years ago, they released enormous amounts of energy, heating the Earth to 9,000°F (5,000°C). A "meltdown" followed, lasting 100 million years, during which the Earth's interior assumed its present form.

The planets of the Solar System may have been formed by pieces of orbiting dust and rock colliding and joining together.

Hydrothermal vents have been found on the seabed of the Atlantic Ocean, pumping out mineral-rich water. Early bacteria fed on these minerals.

Scientists believe the universe began with the "Big Bang" about 12 billion years ago, when an infinitely small volume of matter with an infinitely large density exploded.

ATMOSPHERE

Large-scale volcanic eruptions of gas and steam formed the early atmosphere and the first surface water on the Earth. About 3.9 billion years ago, the Earth had cooled sufficiently for an early oxygenless atmosphere to form.

LAND AND SEA

About 4.5 billion years ago, it is thought that a planet the size of Mars may have crashed into the Earth.

Geologists are still not sure how the land or continental crust grew. The lighter silicate rocks of the crust may have risen high enough to form land "islands" about 4 billion years ago. Collisions between these islands are believed to have formed the first large landmasses about a billion years later.

By 4 billion years ago, the crust had cooled sufficiently for microscopic life to appear.

BEGINNING OF LIFE

The oldest known fossil remains of life on Earth have been found in rocks deposited on the seabed about 3.5 billion years ago. These microscopic organisms existed in an environment devoid of oxygen and subject to extremes of temperature and acidity. Although the earliest body fossils are 3.5 billion years old, rocks dating back another 200 million years may reveal traces of even older organisms. These rocks formed when the Earth was still relatively young and so were subjected to the high temperatures and pressures that existed at the time.

STROMATOLITES

The earliest fossil remains visible to the naked eye are stromatolites, curious laminated structures that grew in shallow, lime-rich seas. The first stromatolites are more than 3 billion years old and were built by layers of bacteria and sediment forming mounds up to 3 feet (1 m) high and 1 foot (30 cm) wide. Similar mounds are still being built today in warm tropical waters.

Volcanic hills

Stromatolites

Seabed sediment

EARLY SIGNS OF LIFE

By 3.5 billion years ago, primitive algae and bacteria had extensively colonized the margins of shallow, warm seas, growing as mats over the surface of the seabed sediment. When these mats were periodically covered by sediment, the primitive organisms migrated upward toward the light, creating a new mat at a higher level. This process eventually formed distinctive "stromatolitic" mounds.

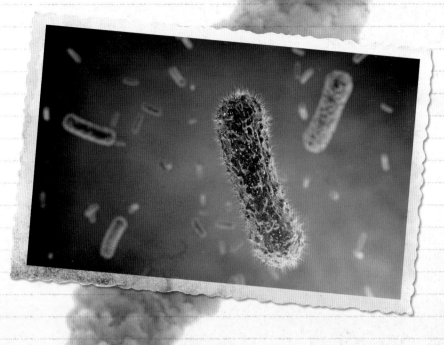

Stromatolitic mounds would have been the only visible sign of life in the bare and volcanic environment of Earth about 3.5 billion years ago.

Pyroclastic eruption

THE EDIACARAN PERIOD

Fossil evidence shows that complex organisms came into existence in the oceans of Precambrian times. The Ediacaran Period, the last section of the Precambian Age, ended 541 million years ago. It was a long period of Earth's history, a time of shifting continents and changing atmosphere and oceans. It was once regarded as a geological wasteland of complex and barren rocks, devoid of life. That complex life developed and diversified in the Ediacaran oceans is now clear both from direct fossil evidence and from the diversity of life forms found in rocks from the subsequent early Cambrian Period. This must have been the result of a long period of evolution of organisms in Ediacaran times.

DICKINSONIA

The flat disks of *Dickinsonia* grew to 2 feet (60 cm) long, making it one of the first "large" creatures. The body has a ribbed surface divided in two by a midline. Its body tissue may have been denser than that of jellyfish or worms.

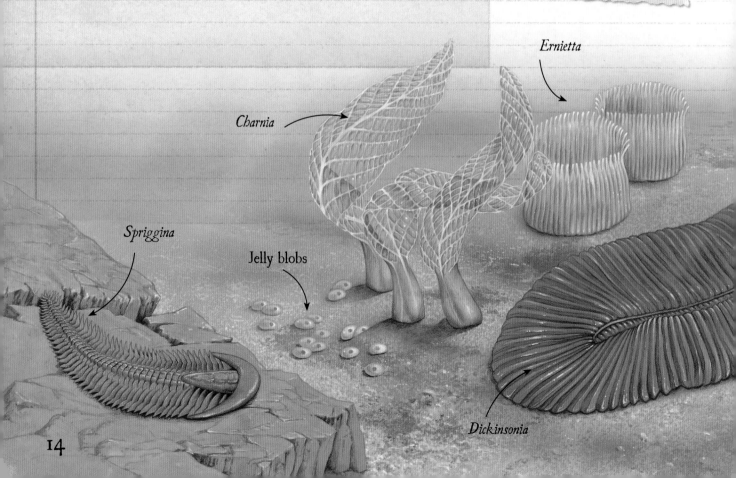

Ernietta

Charnia

Spriggina

Jelly blobs

Dickinsonia

CHANGING CONTINENTS

Most of the continents were clustered in the southern hemisphere. Toward the end of the Ediacaran Period the continental plates came together to form a short-lived supercontinent, which has been called Pannotia.

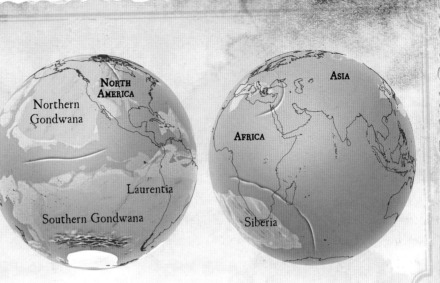

NORTH AMERICA

Northern Gondwana

Laurentia

Southern Gondwana

ASIA

AFRICA

Siberia

The organisms that lived in the shallow-water seas of Ediacaran times were all completely soft-bodied. Once considered to be jellyfish or wormlike creatures, it is now thought they were made of tougher material.

THE FIRST LARGE LIFE

Current research suggests that most groups of complex multicelled organisms, apart from the higher plants, must have come into existence in the Ediacaran oceans. Unfortunately, however, the majority of these animals have left no trace in the fossil record. The great exception is the Ediacarans, the first larger organisms of which traces have been found, fossilized in seafloor sediments.

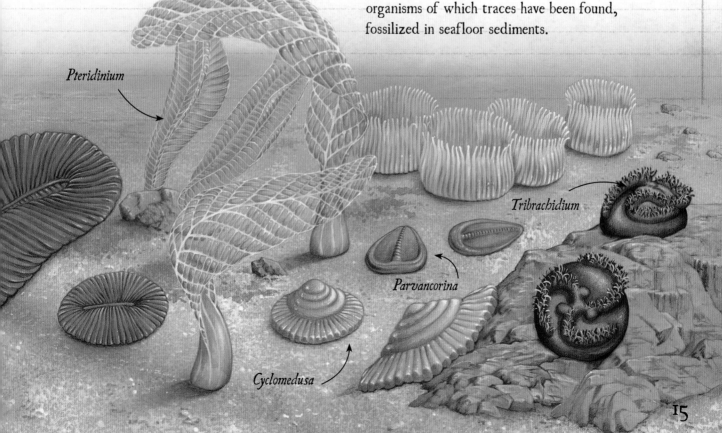

Pteridinium

Tribrachidium

Parvancorina

Cyclomedusa

CAMBRIAN EXPLOSION

Early Cambrian times brought a defining moment in the history of life on Earth — a burst in the evolution of marine life. The Cambrian Period, beginning 541 million years ago and lasting for around 50 million years, marks the beginning of a major division of geological time, known as the Paleozoic (meaning "ancient life"). It witnessed the rapid growth of an amazing diversity of life forms. A range of fossil forms, unknown in earlier rocks, suddenly appeared in sedimentary rocks in the sea. The Cambrian Period saw miniscule creatures inhabiting a curious submarine world and organisms became significantly smaller. The first fossil shells also appeared, as well as a variety of fossilized spines, studs and scalelike plates, all defensive devices that imply that life at this time became much more dangerous than in previous ages.

SEA LEVELS

The remarkable evolutionary events also coincided with major environmental changes. There was global warming and sea levels steadily rose. Seas flooded large areas of the continents, and in shallow equatorial waters small fossils were deposited.

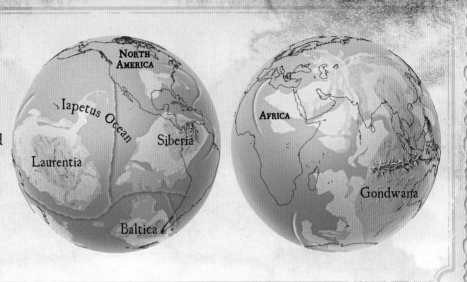

Latouchella

Tochelcionella

Brachiopods

EVIDENCE OF LIFE

The fossil record shows that organisms evolved and diversified, only to become extinct and be replaced by other organisms. Evidence of animal activity found in seabed sediment (called trace fossils) show that increasingly complex animals were evolving. Traces include scratch marks of animals with hardened skins (exoskeletons), which were probably the first arthropods — invertebrates with jointed limbs and segmented bodies.

A SMALL WORLD UNDER THE SEA

Tiny, mineralized fossil shells and plates from earliest Cambrian sediments show that seabed microcommunities thrived. They included many different kinds of animals that lived on, and perhaps in, the top layer of sediment.

Archaeocyathans

Microdictyon

Hyolithellus

Tommotia

LATE CAMBRIAN PERIOD

This period was marked by the continuing success of arthropods and the emergence of a possible ancestor of the vertebrates (animals with a spinal column). The warm, light-filled waters of the Cambrian Period were an ideal environment for life to expand and diversify, but progress was not smooth. This included a large-scale extinction event at the beginning of mid-Cambrian times, which contributed to 70 percent of species disappearing.

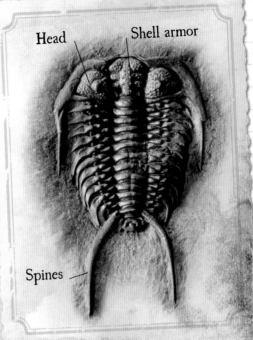

Head

Shell armor

Spines

TRILOBITE FOSSIL

Trilobites, such as *Olenoides*, were among the most successful arthropods of the time. Many had armored bodies and continued to develop and thrive. This Burgess Shale fossil shows *Olenoides*' spines in fine detail, projecting from underneath its hard, crablike covering.

Laggania

Fossils found in the 505-million-year-old mudstone of the Burgess Shale in British Columbia, Canada, have provided a vivid insight into life in the Cambrian seas. They show the wide variety of creatures that flourished in the sea at this time.

Marrella

Ottoia

Hallucigenia

Pirania

CHANGING CONTINENTS

As the world emerged from the "icehouse" state of the late glaciated Precambrian Era, the supercontinent of Pannotia continued to break up, creating the Iapetus Ocean, the forerunner of today's Atlantic Ocean.

MASS EXTINCTION

The mass extinction event that occurred halfway through the Cambrian Period seems to have been caused by fluctuating sea levels. As sea levels rose from the low levels of the late Precambrian Age, marine animals colonized the expanding shelf seas. Mid-Cambrian sea levels fell again, destroying the shallow-water environments and wiping out large numbers of marine species.

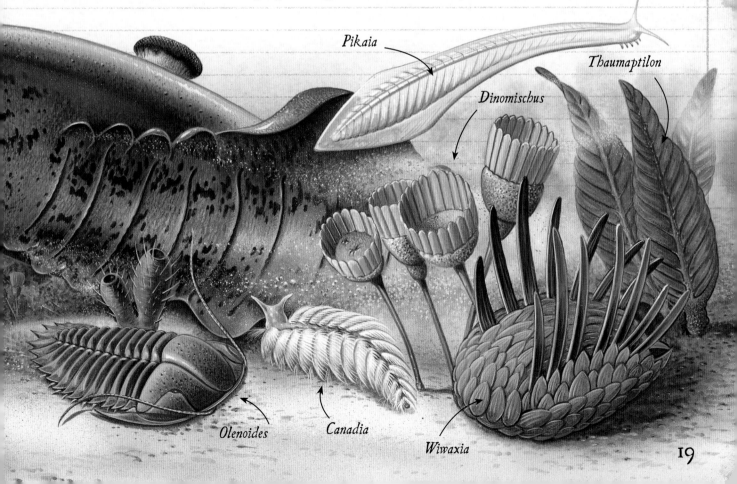

THE ORDOVICIAN PERIOD

Ordovician times saw the expansion of marine life, until climatic changes destroyed the environment on which so many species depended. The Ordovician Period marked a turning point in the evolution of marine life. Many organisms were increasing in size, strength and speed. Jawless organisms called conodonts were closely related to the first vertebrates. Fishlike jawless vertebrates were followed by the evolution of the first sharklike vertebrates, which had jaws and teeth. This diverse marine life was not to last, because an ice age drove many organisms into extinction.

BRACHIOPODS

The most common and successful Ordovician shellfish were the brachiopods. Most brachiopods, like these orthids, were permanently anchored to the seabed or to other shells by a short fleshy stalk called a pedicle, although some lay freely on the seafloor sediment. They lived by drawing seawater through their open shells and filtering out microscopic particles of food. Although they resemble clams, they are not related to them.

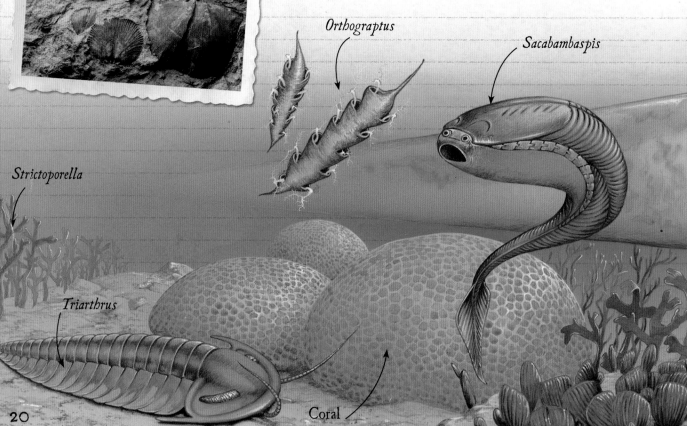

Orthograptus

Sacabambaspis

Strictoporella

Triarthrus

Coral

CONTINENTS

Throughout Ordovician times, the pace of global change quickened. Siberia and Baltica moved north, the Iapetus Ocean began to close, and the Rheic Ocean gradually opened to the south. The supercontinent of Gondwana continued to dominate the southern hemisphere.

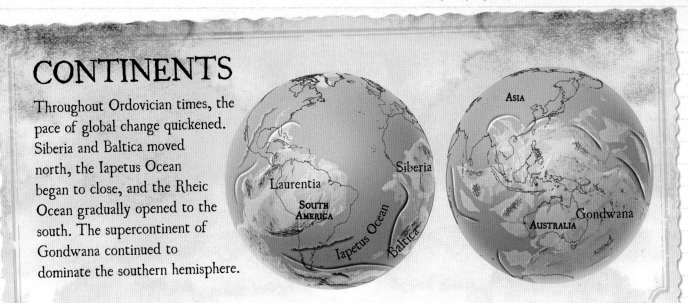

SETTING FOOT ON LAND

During this period, animals also began to move onto land, not directly from the sea, but through the "backdoor" medium of freshwater. Arthropods were ideally suited to make the transition from the supportive environment of water to dry land, with its desiccating air and primitive vegetation.

The waters of the oceans teemed with planktonic life. On the seabed, there were shellfish, corals and moss animals. Trilobites and snails searched around the seabed for food. Swimming filter feeders were the first jawless, fishlike vertebrates.

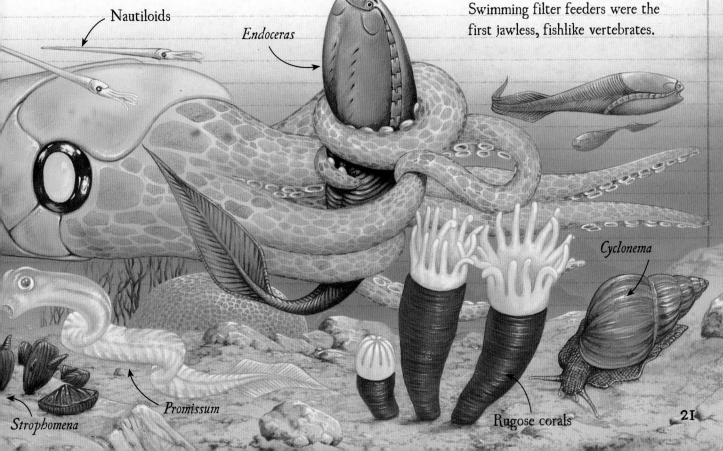

Nautiloids

Endoceras

Cyclonema

Strophomena

Promissum

Rugose corals

THE SILURIAN PERIOD

In Silurian times, life recovered after the mass extinction of the Ordovician Period and the land was colonized by new plants and arthropods. The Silurian Period began about 443 million years ago. Although it lasted a mere 26 million years, the strata and fossils from this period in Britain and North America are among the most intensely studied in the world. The Silurian Period marked a pivotal point in evolution because oceans became warmer and sea levels rose. This was the period when plants and invertebrate animals first became solidly established on land.

SEA CHANGES

The old Iapetus Ocean gradually closed, as the landmasses of Laurentia (North America), Baltica (northern Britain and Scandinavia) and Avalonia (southern Britain, Nova Scotia and Newfoundland) approached one another. Another ocean then opened up to the south.

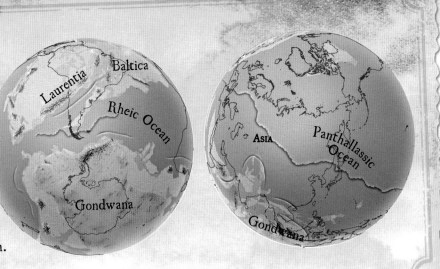

The shorelines of late Silurian times were crowded with biological innovations, as well as already familiar shellfish such as trilobites and snails. The most important developments were in the vertebrates and the land plants.

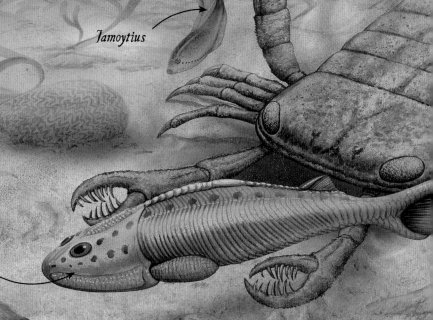

Jamoytius

Trilobite

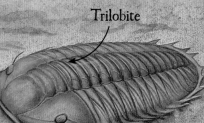

Ateleaspis

22

Silurian Coral

SEA SCORPIONS

The first giants of the Earth, living in the Silurian Period, were the eurypterids, or "sea scorpions," which evolved in Ordovician times and survived until Permian times. They were scorpion-like in shape, and some had large pincers. Their elongated, articulated bodies were covered in a tough exoskeleton, making them one of the best-armored animals of the time. However, they had to shed their exoskeleton periodically to allow for growth, a process that left them vulnerable to attack.

CORAL COMMUNITIES

Silurian corals (above), which formed the first extensive reefs, look similar to ones alive today, but belong to extinct groups.

Sea Scorpion

Large pincers

Elongated body

Tail

Pterygotus

Birkenia

Loganellia

Cooksonia

23

THE DEVONIAN PERIOD

Often called the "age of fishes," Devonian times saw many diverse life-forms in rivers, inland seas and freshwater lakes. Global climates remained warm and resulted in the formation of drier and bigger landmasses, where vast deserts formed. The period saw a remarkable expansion in vertebrate diversity. As plant species developed on land, some fish groups became almost indistinguishable from the future tetrapods (four-legged animals) that would leave the water for the land.

The oldest tetrapod fossils, of *Ichthyostega* and *Acanthostega*, have been found in late Devonian river and lake deposits from Greenland. These first four-limbed vertebrates were aquatic creatures.

MUDSKIPPER

The mudskipper is a modern bony fish that can leave the water to find food on exposed mudbanks, using its long, bony pectoral fins to prop itself up and wriggle across soft, wet mud. However, it has to remain wet and cannot stay out of the water for long.

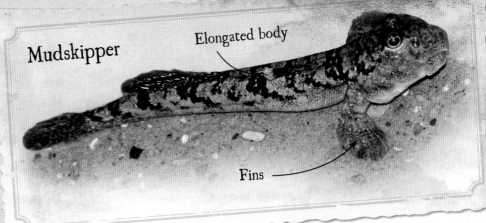

Mudskipper

Elongated body

Fins

Dipterus

Acanthostega

CONTINENTS

The Iapetus Ocean finally closed as North America and Greenland (Laurentia) collided with the British Isles (Avalonia) and Scandinavia (Baltica) to form a single continental mass. Meanwhile, the supercontinent of Gondwana moved steadily northward from its polar position.

EQUIPPING LIFE FOR LAND

The first terrestrial creatures, the centipede-like Ordovician arthropods, had inherited many pairs of jointed legs from their aquatic ancestors, but the vertebrates had to make the best of a very different evolutionary heritage. Legs evolved from the muscular fins of the lobe-finned fish but were first used for life in the water. Only later did they become adapted for life on land.

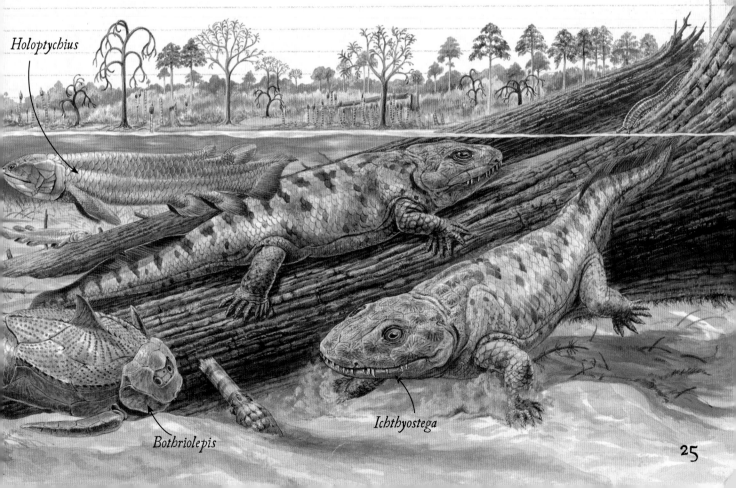

Holoptychius

Bothriolepis

Ichthyostega

THE CARBONIFEROUS PERIOD

The age of coal saw the growth of the first extensive forests on Earth. Four-legged animals emerged from the water, evolving into amphibians and reptiles. Fossils found in a limestone quarry in East Kirkton, Scotland, include the first of several different early tetrapod groups, including amphibians, an animal that combined amphibian and reptilian features, and an almost true reptile. The tetrapods of East Kirkton formed the world's oldest known vertebrate terrestrial community.

Fossilized Tree

CLUBMOSS

This closeup of a fossilized bark belongs to the *Lepidodrendon* tree, a giant clubmoss that was common during the Carboniferous Period. The tree had a thick stem and grew to be 100 feet (30 m) tall.

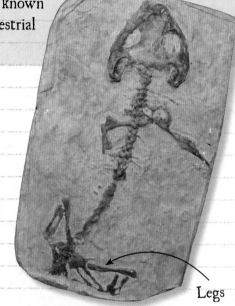

Legs

Amphibian Fossil

Gymnosperms and ferns

Balanerpeton woodi

Lungfish

CONTINENTS

During the Carboniferous (meaning "coal-bearing") Period, the great mass of the southern continents that made up Gondwana rotated clockwise. Gondwana, Laurentia and Baltica came into contact, a major step in the forming of the supercontinent of Pangea.

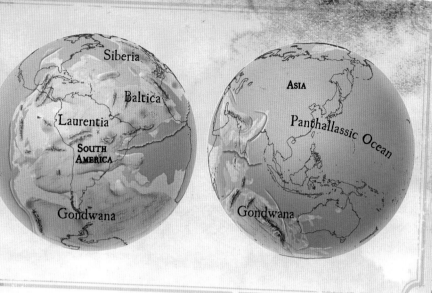

Fossils from the East Kirkton lake in Scotland offer a remarkable glimpse of the past. A dense tropical forest covered the lower slopes of volcanoes and the water was full of fish, amphibious tetrapods and eurypterids (sea scorpions).

LIFE ON LAND AND SEA

On land, true egg-laying (amniote) tetrapods evolved. Arachnids and insects, which had evolved in Silurian times, increased in size and diversified. The shallow equatorial seas produced extensive reefs occupied by a wide diversity of marine life.

Westlothiana lizziae

Millipede

Harvestman

Pulmonoscorpius

27

THE PERMIAN PERIOD

The Permian Period started when the northern continents of Eurasia and Laurentia joined the southern continent of Gondwana to form the supercontinent of Pangea. This event had a drastic effect on climates and provided an environment for the global expansion of terrestrial life. Many of the shallow seas and lakes of late Carboniferous times evaporated. Life on land evolved rapidly, giving rise to reptiles and synapsids, and then mammals. Life in the seas was decimated by another extinction event at the end of the period.

Skeleton of a *Dimetrodon*

Rib cage with 26 vertebrae

Boxlike head

Long, bony tail

Five-toed foot

Five-fingered hand

EARLY SYNAPSID

This *Dimetrodon* is a sail-backed pelycosaur from North America. It was one of the first backboned land animals that could kill other beasts of its own size.

Glossopteris

The Karroo strata show that during Permian times South Africa was home to many reptilelike forerunners of the mammals. Landscapes were dominated by plant eaters pursued by carnivores. Armored amphibians existed alongside the lizardlike *Milleretta*.

Lycaenops

Milleretta

Peltobatrachus

Lystrosaurus

PANGEA

The formation of the supercontinent of Pangea led to important changes in climate. In the northern part of Pangea, the climate generally became hot and dry within the vast continental interiors, although in the southern part they remained cooler and wetter.

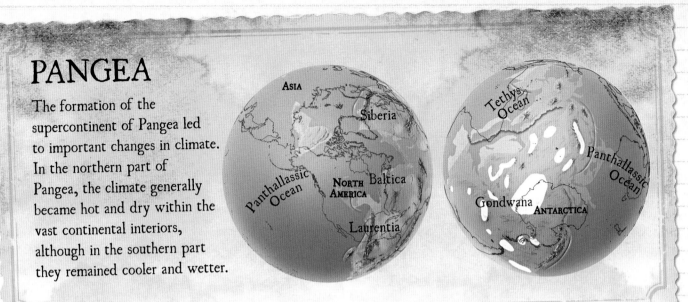

MAMMALS

A group of tetrapods called the synapsids became more diverse and widespread, moving from the northern to the southern hemisphere by the end of the Permian Period. Some species began to evolve characteristics that pointed in the direction of the future evolution of mammals.

CHANGES IN PLANT LIFE

Plant life responded to the extreme climatic changes. The humid Carboniferous forests shrank on a global scale. The lush clubmoss trees were replaced by more seed-bearing plants, and in the northern hemisphere, newly evolving conifers spread rapidly.

Dicynodon

Lycaenops

Robertia

Procynosuchus

Dicroidium

THE TRIASSIC PERIOD

As life recovered from the Permian extinction, reptiles, including the first dinosaurs, became the dominant animals. In the early Triassic, there was a recovery in the percentage of oxygen in the atmosphere, but later oxygen levels declined. In response, terrestrial ecosystems became more diverse, and plant life changed significantly. Sea levels fluctuated and marine life was transformed, with the rise of groups of bony fish that, although more modern looking, still differed greatly from sea life today.

HUNTERS

One of the richest dinosaur deposits was found in the New Mexican desert. More than a thousand skeletons of small two-footed dinosaurs were found. One, named *Coelophysis*, had all the hallmarks of a fast-moving, hunting meat eater, with its muscular body and numerous teeth. It was far from being the only predator in this environment.

PANGEA

At first, as the supercontinent of Pangea crept northward to straddle the equator, much of its vast landmass became increasingly warm and arid. By the end of the period, however, Pangea was beginning to break up and global climates had become cooler and wetter.

Siberia

Laurentia

AFRICA

SOUTH AMERICA

Pangea

Gondwana

Panthallassic Ocean

AUSTRALIA

Placerias

Cycads

Eudimorphodon

Rutiodon

Cynaphagus

Sharp teeth

A fossil of a short-tailed pterosaur, the earliest vertebrate to have evolved powered flight. Flying and gliding reptiles emerged during the Triassic Period along with the first turtles and the first frogs.

LIFE ON LAND

These environmental changes signaled major developments in the vertebrates (backboned animals). The mammalian relatives that had dominated the land in Permian times declined (although one group, the cynodonts, spread and diversified). Instead, a new wave of reptiles, the archosaurs, emerged. Later, at the end of Triassic times, some famous archosaur descendants, the dinosaurs, came to dominate life on land.

The plant-eating reptile *Desmatosuchus* was 16 feet (5 m) in length with heavy armor, including 18-inch (45 cm) shoulder spines, but it would have been no match for large carnivores, such as the crocodile-like *Rutiodon* and the land-living archosaur *Postosuchus*.

Gymnosperm forest

Coelophysis

Postosuchus

Desmatosuchus

Horsetails

THE JURASSIC PERIOD

Although popularly known as the "age of the dinosaurs," this was also a time when marine life flourished and flowering plants evolved. The Jurassic is named after rock formations found in the Jura Mountains in western Europe. Although some forms of life had suffered in the extinction event at the end of the Triassic, species of plants and animal were once again many and diverse by mid-Jurassic times. This recovery marked the start of a long period of growth, which continued through the remainder of the Mesozoic Era.

JURASSIC FISH

Like Jurassic fish, most living fish are called teleosts. In Jurassic times, the teleosts had begun to evolve, but they were still overshadowed by an older group, the holosteans, which had deep bodies and heavy, bony scales. Many holosteans became extinct in the Cretaceous age, but some, including the garpike, still thrive today. Sharks and rays, such as *Squaloraja*, also gradually increased in number and diversity.

Stegosaurus, from the late Jurassic of western North America, was the largest of the plant-eating stegosaurids. A double row of diamond-shaped plates ran along the neck and back, and the tail had two pairs of spikes.

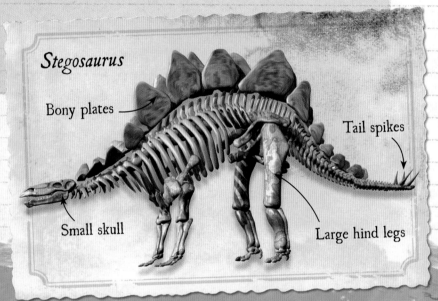

Stegosaurus

Bony plates

Tail spikes

Small skull

Large hind legs

Plesiosaurus

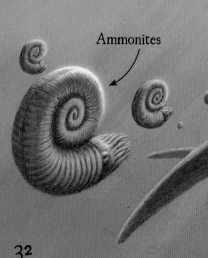

Ammonites

Rhomaleosaurus

CONTINENTS

Pangea began to break up. Gondwana moved south, and Laurasia (North America and Eurasia) separated from Gondwana. The land link between North and South America was broken. These changes had a major effect on the evolution of animals and plants.

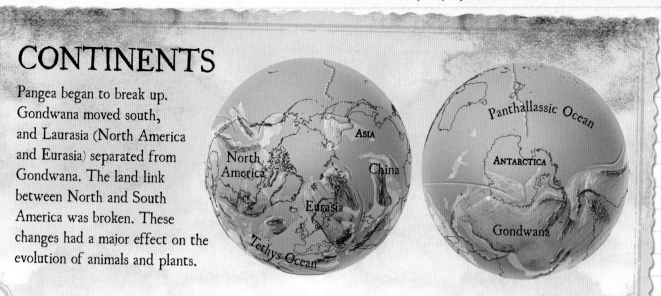

Asia

North America

China

Eurasia

Tethys Ocean

Panthallassic Ocean

Antarctica

Gondwana

In Jurassic times, life under water was just as hazardous as life on land. The seas were populated with swimming cephalopods and fish, including coelacanths, which were preyed upon by large marine reptiles. The coiled, shelled ammonites also preyed on small fish.

Pterosaur

FLORA AND FAUNA

On land, mammals thrived but some of their ancient synapsid relatives became extinct. More flying reptiles (pterosaurs) evolved, and in late Jurassic times these were joined by dinosaurs that had feathers, and some of these could fly — the birds were beginning to evolve. Landscapes were gradually transformed and colored by the evolution of new flowering plants.

Ichthyosaurus

Coelacanth

33

THE CRETACEOUS PERIOD

The breakup of the supercontinent Pangea led to divergent animal and plant development on landmasses separated by broad seas. Shallow seas abounded with marine life and vegetation changed. Dinosaurs continued to diversify and dominate the land. Theropods of the mid- and late-Cretaceous ranged from the huge tyrannosaurids, such as *T. rex*, to the ostrichlike ornithomimosaurs. Flowering plants, birds and mammals underwent explosive growth in the mid-Cretaceous hothouse. Large reptiles, such as the plesiosaurs, roamed the oceans, and the first teleost fishes appeared. At the end of the Cretaceous, about 75 percent of all animal species, including the dinosaurs, disappeared.

THE MAMMALS AND DINOSAURS OF MONGOLIA

The remote deserts of Mongolia, in the heart of central Asia, have produced fascinating fossil finds. In Cretaceous times, Mongolia was often swept by desert dust storms that buried the remains of hundreds of lizards, mammals and dinosaurs in the sandstone hills. The fossil skeletons are often complete, with even the smallest, most delicate bones preserved. During the latter part of Cretaceous times, two groups of bird-hipped (ornithischian) dinosaurs, the hadrosaurids and the ceratopsians, evolved new species and spread across the globe. Dinosaur fossils found in Mongolia also include many reptile-hipped (saurischian) dinosaurs, such as theropods, dromaeosaurs and oviraptors.

Large numbers of dinosaur predators roamed the arid deserts of Mongolia.

Tarbosaurus baatar

Mononykus

Gallimimus

Zalambdalestes

Kamptobaatar

HOTHOUSE

The opening up of the North Atlantic led to North America and Europe pulling apart, as did Africa and South America. Gondwana continued to break up, and oceanic changes during the mid- to late-Cretaceous led to a hothouse environment in which life diversified rapidly.

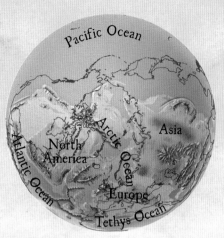
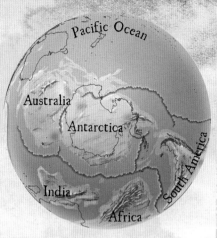

MONGOLIAN DUST STORM

Predators, such as *Velociraptor* and the large tyrannosaurid *Tarbosaurus*, would attack other dinosaurs, including plant eaters such as *Oviraptor* and *Gallimimus*. The ceratopsian *Protoceratops* laid eggs on the ground in mud-mound nests. The peculiar one-fingered dinosaur *Mononykus* had powerful, short forelimbs. At the time, small mammals, such as *Zalambdalestes*, *Kennalestes* and *Kamptobaatar*, seemed insignificant, but their descendants would take over after the dinosaurs had gone.

Iguanodon

The skull of the early Cretaceous plant eating dinosaur, *Iguanodon*.

Dust storm

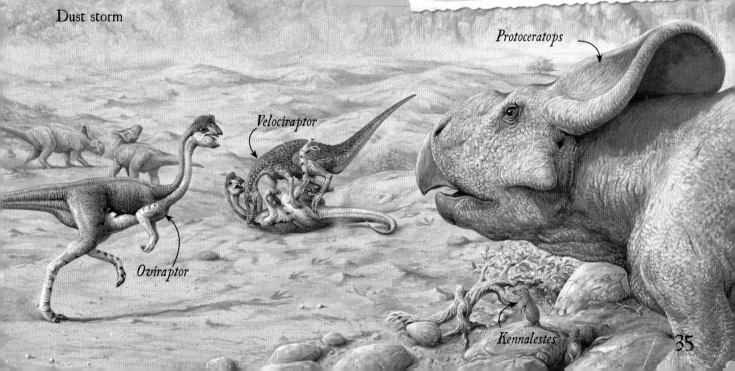

Protoceratops

Velociraptor

Oviraptor

Kennalestes

AFTER THE DINOSAURS

The period after the dinosaurs is known as the Cenozoic Era, its first 64 million years divided into two periods, the Paleogene and the Neogene. Rapid continental movement marked the time when modern animals from mammals to songbirds became dominant. Many thousands of mammal species developed, and sea creatures took on a more modern-day appearance. Between 5 and 2 million years ago, the direct ancestors of modern humans emerged. During the Quaternary Period, from 2.5 million years ago, the Earth was gripped by an ice age. Previously isolated islands and continents connected, which had a dramatic effect on the distribution of animals and plants.

COOLER

By mid-Cenozoic times, continents and oceans were close to their present global positions. About 20 million years ago, the Earth cooled, sea levels fell, and much drier conditions prevailed as the Earth headed toward the ice ages of the Quaternary Period.

North America

Pacific Ocean

South America

Asia

Africa

Indian Ocean

Woolly mammoth
(*Mammuthus primigenius*)

Woolly rhinoceros
(*Coelodonta antiquitatas*)

Horse
(*Equus*)

MODERN HUMANS EMERGE

Between 5 and 1.5 million years ago, the genus *Homo*, the direct ancestor of modern humans, evolved from an australopithecine (meaning "southern ape") ancestor in Africa. By around 2 million years ago, several species of *Homo* had evolved, including *Homo erectus* ("upright human"), the first human to migrate out of Africa. Around 200,000 years ago, modern humans, *Homo sapiens* ("wise human") appeared in Africa. A separate branch of *Homo*, *Homo neanderthalensis* (named after Neander Valley in Germany) died out around 30,000 years ago.

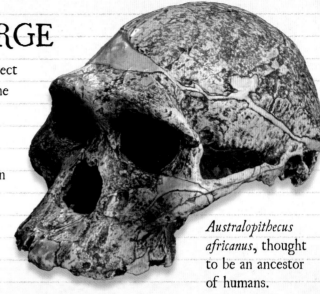

Australopithecus africanus, thought to be an ancestor of humans.

LIFE ON THE MAMMOTH STEPPE

Many animals and plants survived the last glacial period by occupying warmer, windswept lands with a summer thaw. Animals that lived in these areas included the woolly mammoth and rhinoceros. One of the richest places for fossils is on the mammoth steppe, in what is now eastern Russia. It was mostly a grassy habitat that stood between the northern ice sheet and wooded habitats farther south. It was home to many large herbivores, including woolly mammoths, horses, giant deer and the ancestors of domesticated cattle. These were prey to hunters, such as large lion-type cats and humans.

Steppe lion (*Panthera*)

Glacier

Giant deer (*Megoloceros giganteus*)

FISH

Life first appeared in the Earth's seas and oceans. At first, it was made up of simple microscopic organisms, but an explosion of life-forms during the Cambrian Period led to the development of more complex animals and, eventually, fish. The earliest fish were jawless animals, but the Silurian Period saw the evolution and dominance of jawed fish and their development into a wide range of animals, including lobe- and ray-finned fish.

THE FIRST VERTEBRATES

Animals that have a backbone are known as vertebrates. The earliest vertebrates were peculiar jawless fish, the agnathan hagfishes and lampreys. Despite their unfamiliar features, the agnathans were the ancestors of all backboned animals and possessed the fundamental characteristics of early vertebrates. These include a flexible rod running along the animal's back, known as a notochord, above which lay a dorsal nerve cord. Blocks of muscles on either side of the rod lengthen or stiffen the body so it can be flexed from side to side for swimming.

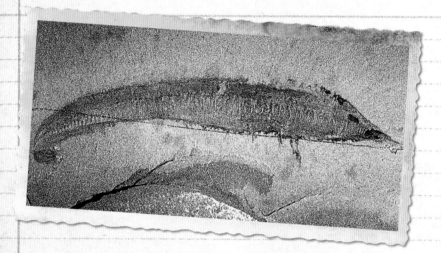

PIKAIA FOSSIL

This primitive sea creature shows the essential elements of an early vertebrate. The flattened body is divided into pairs of muscle blocks, seen as faint vertical lines. The muscles lie either side of a flexible rod, which runs from the tip of the head to the tip of the tail.

BRANCHIOSTOMA

A *Pikaia* lookalike still exists today, the lancelet *Branchiostoma*. This curious little animal was familiar to biologists long before the *Pikaia* fossil was discovered. This cutaway of *Branchiostoma* shows the lancelet's flexible stiffening rod, which runs from head to tail, and becomes the backbone in vertebrates.

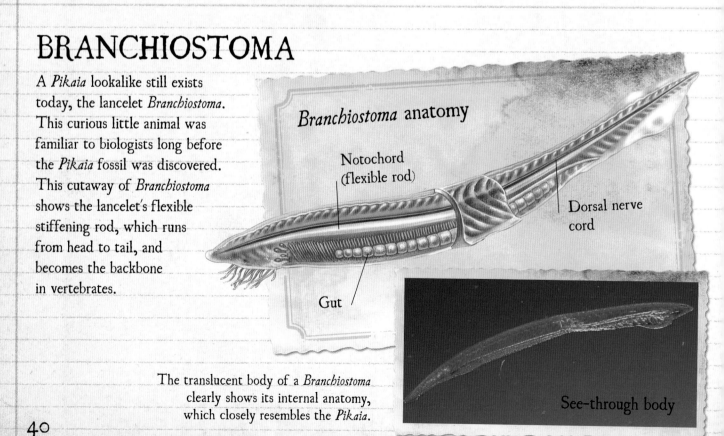

Branchiostoma anatomy

Notochord (flexible rod)

Dorsal nerve cord

Gut

The translucent body of a *Branchiostoma* clearly shows its internal anatomy, which closely resembles the *Pikaia*.

See-through body

VERTEBRATE RELATIONSHIPS

Understanding animal biology allows scientists to determine how different creatures are related. There are some surprises. For although the connection seems unlikely, starfish (echinoderms), acorn worms, and sea squirts (tunicates) are closely related to all backboned animals (vertebrates). Those closest to vertebrates are chordates with a body stiffening rod (notochord), as represented by the living lancelet.

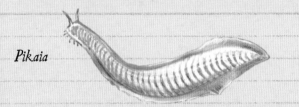

Pikaia

Vertebrate

Hemichordates

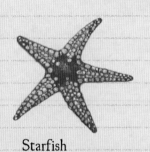

Starfish

Acorn worm

Sea squirt

Lancelet

PIKAIA

This primitive creature does not seem like a human ancestor. It looks like a worm that has been flattened sideways. But it clearly had the features of an early vertebrate, such as traces of a notochord, dorsal nerve cord, and blocks of muscles running down either side of the body.

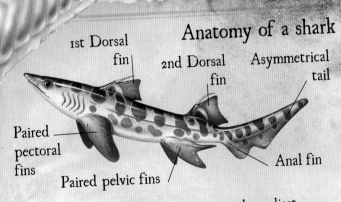

Tentacle

Paired muscle blocks

Notochord

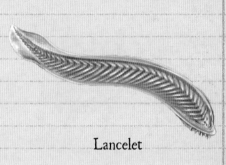

Anatomy of a shark

1st Dorsal fin

2nd Dorsal fin

Asymmetrical tail

Paired pectoral fins

Paired pelvic fins

Anal fin

Sharks and their relatives were among the earliest vertebrates to develop jaws and bony teeth. All have skeletons made entirely of gristle or cartilage.

JAWLESS FISH

The first backboned animals to evolve were agnathans, or "jawless fish." Fossil traces are found in Late Cambrian rocks more than 510 million years old. These first fish had no jaws. Nor did they have paired fins to stabilize their bodies in the water. Catching prey and eating it presented problems. Consequently,

these fish tended to be small. They were restricted to sucking up microscopic food particles from the muddy seabed or feeding on the plankton that lived in the surface waters. Despite their lack of jaws, agnathans dominated the seas and freshwaters of the northern hemisphere for about 130 million years.

Pikaia

Pikaia, at 535 million years old, is one of the earliest fossil animals to show the beginnings of vertebrate characteristics. The body of this eel-like creature was stiffened and elongated by a stiff but flexible rod called a notochord. It could be bent into sinuous waves for swimming by the contraction of muscle blocks on each side.

Size: 2 inches (5 cm) long
Subphylum: Cephalochordata
Family: Pikaiidae
Range: North America (Canada)
Pn: pik-EYE-a

Size: 6 inches (15 cm) long
Order: Pteraspidiformes
Family: Doraspididae
Range: Europe (Spitsbergen)
Pn: dor-ee-ASP-is

Doryaspis

This pteraspid (also called *Lyktaspis*) had a longer snout, or rostrum, than its relatives. There were bony spines set along the snout's length, and the mouth opened above, not below, the rostrum. This strange appendage made the creature very streamlined, and *Doryaspis'* shape suggests that it was an active swimmer.

Promissum

Promissum was an unusually large conodont, an eel-like chordate, and is found in the 500-million-year-old Late Ordovician sea deposits of South Africa. In 1994, specimens of *Promissum* were found with the conodont feeding apparatus preserved below eye capsules and in front of traces of the muscle blocks and notochord.

Size: 1 foot 4 inches (40 cm)
Order: Priodontina
Family: uncertain
Range: South Africa
Pn: PROM-i-sum

Drepanaspis

A well-adapted bottom-dweller, *Drepanaspis* lived by scavenging in the mud of the seabed for food. The front of *Drepanaspis'* body was broad and flattened, allowing it to hug the seabed as it swam, and on either side of the large, upturned mouth, its small eyes were set wide apart to give it a wide angle of vision.

Size: 1 foot (30 cm) long
Order: Pteraspidomorphes
Family: Psammosteidae
Range: Europe (Germany)
Pn: dre-pa-NAS-pis

Hemicyclaspis

This agnathan fish was a more powerful swimmer and could maneuver itself better in the water than either of its bottom-dwelling relatives, such as *Tremataspis*. It featured a dorsal fin to stabilize the body in the water, and a pair of scale-covered flaps, similar to pectoral fins, which helped the fish to steer. The tail had an enlarged upper lobe, which may have increased lift at the back of the body. This would have helped to keep the fish's head down while it sucked up food particles from the seabed.

Size: 4 inches (10 cm) long
Order: Osteostraci
Family: uncertain
Range: Europe (Estonia)
Pn: TREM-a-TASP-is

Tremataspis

This primitive agnathan had an unusual extended bony head shield, nearly circular in cross section. Its eyes and single nostril were on top of the head. The shape is thought to have made the fish good at burrowing. Its head shield was made of one piece of bone, so it is unlikely that it grew with the animal. Paleontologists think that these fish had an unarmored larva, and that the bony shield developed only when the fish was fully grown.

Size: 5 inches (13 cm) long
Order: Osteostraci
Family: uncertain
Range: Europe (England)
Pn: HEM-ee-si-CLAS-pis

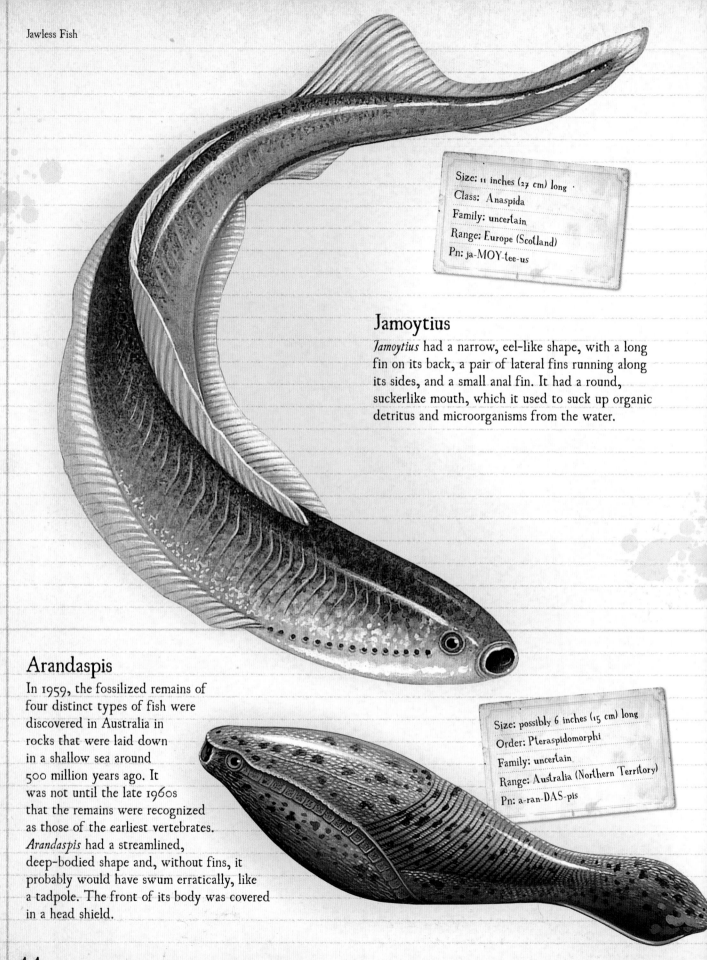

Size: 11 inches (27 cm) long
Class: Anaspida
Family: uncertain
Range: Europe (Scotland)
Pn: ja-MOY-tee-us

Jamoytius

Jamoytius had a narrow, eel-like shape, with a long fin on its back, a pair of lateral fins running along its sides, and a small anal fin. It had a round, suckerlike mouth, which it used to suck up organic detritus and microorganisms from the water.

Arandaspis

In 1959, the fossilized remains of four distinct types of fish were discovered in Australia in rocks that were laid down in a shallow sea around 500 million years ago. It was not until the late 1960s that the remains were recognized as those of the earliest vertebrates. *Arandaspis* had a streamlined, deep-bodied shape and, without fins, it probably would have swum erratically, like a tadpole. The front of its body was covered in a head shield.

Size: possibly 6 inches (15 cm) long
Order: Pteraspidomorphi
Family: uncertain
Range: Australia (Northern Territory)
Pn: a-ran-DAS-pis

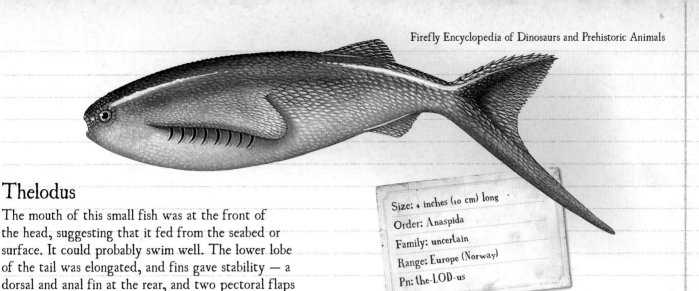

Thelodus

The mouth of this small fish was at the front of the head, suggesting that it fed from the seabed or surface. It could probably swim well. The lower lobe of the tail was elongated, and fins gave stability — a dorsal and anal fin at the rear, and two pectoral flaps at the front.

Size: 4 inches (10 cm) long

Order: Anaspida

Family: uncertain

Range: Europe (Norway)

Pn: the-LOD-us

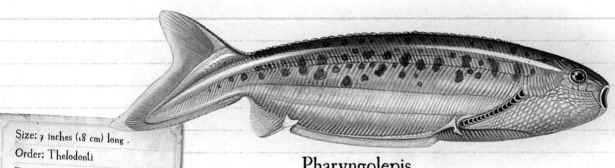

Size: 7 inches (18 cm) long

Order: Thelodonti

Family: Thelodontidae

Range: Worldwide

Pn: far-IN-gol-EP-is

Pharyngolepis

Pharyngolepis must have been a poor swimmer because it lacked basic stabilizing fins. A row of crested scales ran along its back, and bony spines stuck out from the pectoral area. There was a well-developed anal fin, and the tail was downturned. But none of these features would have stabilized its deep body. It probably fed by scooping up tiny food particles from the seabed.

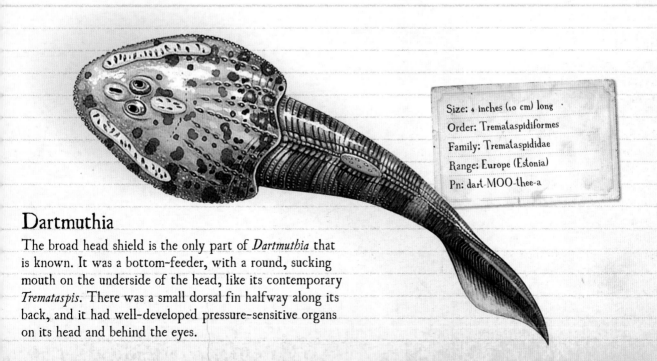

Size: 4 inches (10 cm) long

Order: Tremataspidiformes

Family: Tremataspididae

Range: Europe (Estonia)

Pn: dart-MOO-thee-a

Dartmuthia

The broad head shield is the only part of *Dartmuthia* that is known. It was a bottom-feeder, with a round, sucking mouth on the underside of the head, like its contemporary *Tremataspis*. There was a small dorsal fin halfway along its back, and it had well-developed pressure-sensitive organs on its head and behind the eyes.

CARTILAGINOUS FISH

Sharks and their relatives — the skates and rays, and the chimaeras or ratfishes — were among the earliest vertebrates to develop jaws and bony teeth. The mineralized teeth are normally the only part of these animals to be fossilized. These jawed fishes also share another feature. All of them have skeletons made entirely of gristle or cartilage, covered by a thin layer of bone. They also have paired fins, and the pelvic fins in males are modified to help hold the female during reproduction — a feature unique to these fishes. Two main groups of cartilaginous fish, elasmobranchs and holocephalians, evolved during the Early Devonian Period, about 400 million years ago.

Size: up to 6 feet (1.8 m)
Order: Cladoselachiformes
Family: Cladoselachidae
Range: North America (Ohio)
Pn: clad-OH-sel-ACK

Cladoselache

Cladoselache had a streamlined, torpedo-shaped body, with a blunt head and large eyes. Cruising the seas 370 million years ago, it looks very like a modern shark. The modern shark, however, has a pointed snout, a high first dorsal fin and an anal fin. As well as being a powerful swimmer, *Cladoselache* was a fierce carnivore.

Stethacanthus

The remarkable feature of this early shark was its T-shaped first dorsal fin, the flat surface of which was covered with teethlike denticles, as was the top of its head. Some paleontologists think these were part of a threat display, giving the impression of a large pair of jaws.

Size: 2 feet 4 inches (70 cm) long
Order: Symmoriida
Family: Stethacanthidae
Range: Europe (Scotland), North America (Illinois, Iowa, Montana, Ohio)
Pn: STETH-a-CAN-thus

Xenacanthus

Early in their evolution, a group of sharks spread into rivers and lakes all over the world. They were very successful, existing for almost 150 million years. A thick spine grew out from the back of the skull of *Xenacanthus*. Its dorsal fin ran along the length of the back, joining up with its tail.

Size: 2 feet 5 inches (75 cm) long
Order: Xenacanthida
Family: Xenacanthidae
Range: Worldwide
Pn: ZEN-a-CAN-thus

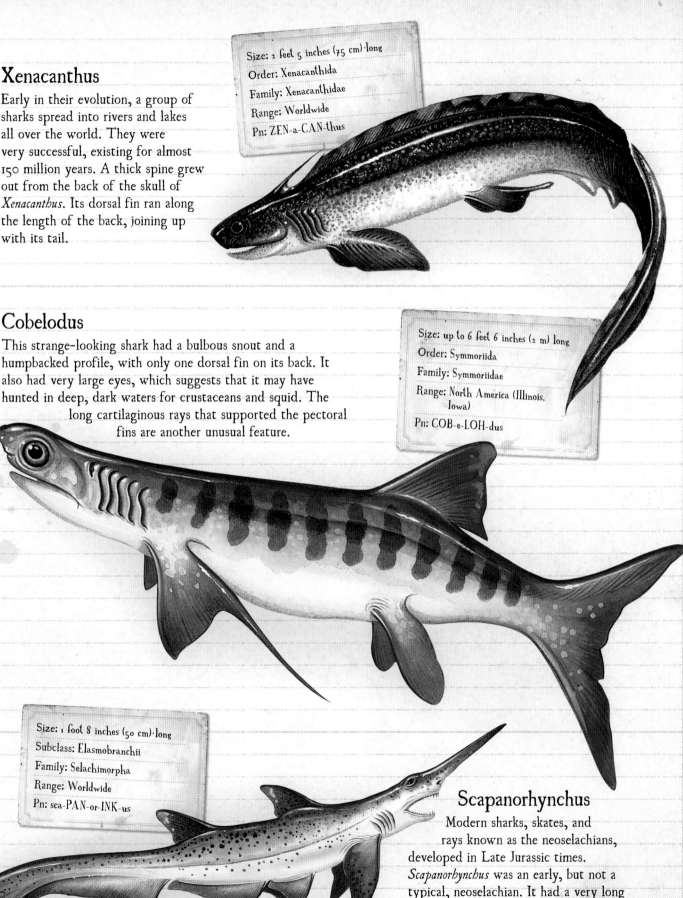

Cobelodus

This strange-looking shark had a bulbous snout and a humpbacked profile, with only one dorsal fin on its back. It also had very large eyes, which suggests that it may have hunted in deep, dark waters for crustaceans and squid. The long cartilaginous rays that supported the pectoral fins are another unusual feature.

Size: up to 6 feet 6 inches (2 m) long
Order: Symmoriida
Family: Symmoriidae
Range: North America (Illinois, Iowa)
Pn: COB-e-LOH-dus

Size: 1 foot 8 inches (50 cm) long
Subclass: Elasmobranchii
Family: Selachimorpha
Range: Worldwide
Pn: sca-PAN-or-INK-us

Scapanorhynchus

Modern sharks, skates, and rays known as the neoselachians, developed in Late Jurassic times. *Scapanorhynchus* was an early, but not a typical, neoselachian. It had a very long snout, and all of its teeth were for biting and tearing, suitable for eating fish.

Spathobatis

Spathobatis is one of the earliest known rays, and it is similar to the modern-day guitar or banjo fish that occurs in the Atlantic waters off North America. *Spathobatis'* body was like that of a shark, but it was flattened to suit a life on the seabed. The eyes and spiracles (for water intake) were repositioned on top of the ray's head, and the mouth and gill slits were on the underside of the body.

Size: 1 foot 8 inches (50 cm) long

Order: Rajiformes

Family: Rhinobatidae

Range: Europe (France, Germany)

Pn: SPA-tho-BAT-is

Size: 3 feet 3 inches (1 m) long.

Order: Batoidea

Family: Sclerorhynchidae.

Range: Africa (Morocco), Asia (Lebanon), North America (Texas)

Pn: SCLE-ro-RIN-cus

Hybodus

Hybodus was one of the most common, widespread and long-lived types of ancient shark. It looked like a modern blue shark, although it was only half the size and would have had a blunter snout. *Hybodus* had two types of teeth in its powerful jaws, suggesting a varied diet. The pointed teeth at the front seized and pierced prey, whereas the blunt teeth at the back crushed the fish bones and the hard shells of the bottom-dwelling snails, sea urchins, and crustaceans.

Sclerorhynchus

Sclerorhynchus was an early type of skate, although it looked more like a modern sawfish. Flapping its pectoral "wings," this flattened fish "flew" just above the seabed, probing and sifting the mud with its long, toothy snout for hidden shrimp, shellfish and bony flatfish as it moved.

Ischyodus

Ischyodus, which lived more than 150 million years ago, was almost identical in size and shape to the modern ratfish that is found today in the depths of the Atlantic and Mediterranean oceans. *Ischyodus* had the same large eyes, pursed lips, tall dorsal fin, and spine in front of the dorsal fin.

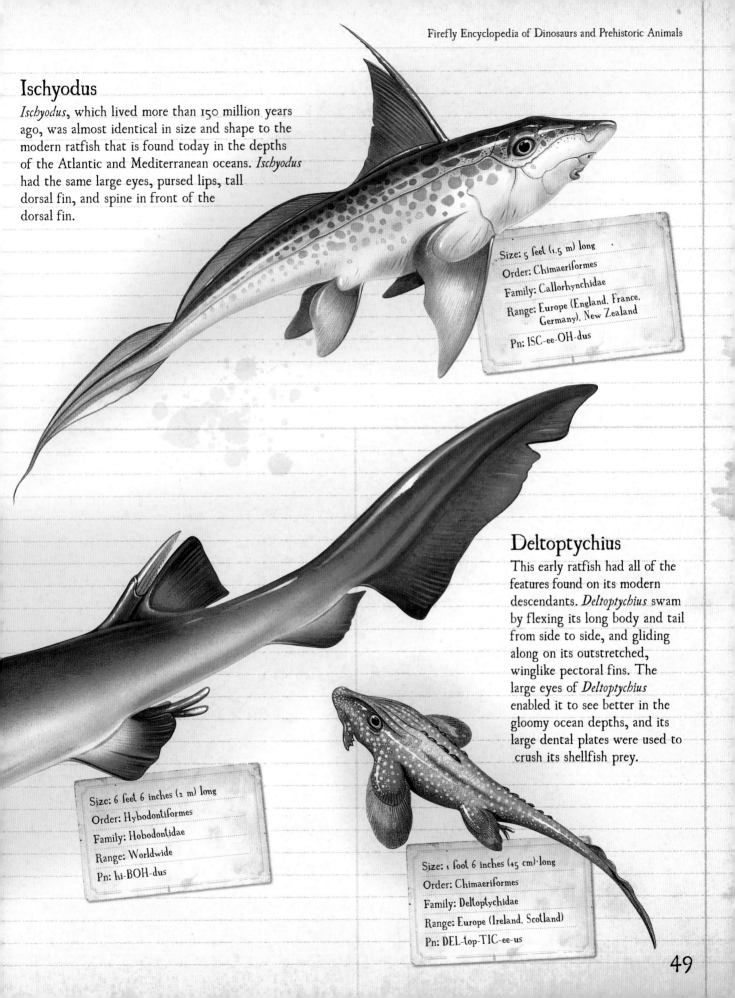

Size: 5 feet (1.5 m) long

Order: Chimaeriformes

Family: Callorhynchidae

Range: Europe (England, France, Germany), New Zealand

Pn: ISC-ee-OH-dus

Deltoptychius

This early ratfish had all of the features found on its modern descendants. *Deltoptychius* swam by flexing its long body and tail from side to side, and gliding along on its outstretched, winglike pectoral fins. The large eyes of *Deltoptychius* enabled it to see better in the gloomy ocean depths, and its large dental plates were used to crush its shellfish prey.

Size: 6 feet 6 inches (2 m) long

Order: Hybodontiformes

Family: Hobodontidae

Range: Worldwide

Pn: hi-BOH-dus

Size: 1 foot 6 inches (45 cm) long

Order: Chimaeriformes

Family: Deltoptychidae

Range: Europe (Ireland, Scotland)

Pn: DEL-top-TIC-ee-us

SPINY SHARKS AND ARMORED FISH

The acanthodians, or "spiny sharks," are among the earliest known vertebrates with jaws. These jaws are thought to have evolved from the first gill arch of some early jawless fish. Their popular name was originally used because they were generally shark shaped, with a streamlined body, paired fins, and a strongly upturned tail. Thick bony spines supported all of the fins except the tail — hence the name "spiny sharks." Fossilized spines are often all that remains of these fish in ancient sedimentary rocks.

Groenlandaspis

This fish was a better swimmer than either of its bottom-dwelling relatives, *Tremataspis* or *Dartmuthia*. It had a dorsal fin to stabilize the body in the water, and a pair of scale-covered flaps, similar to pectoral fins, to steer the fish while swimming.

Size: 3 inches (7.5 cm) long
Order: Arthrodira
Family: Groenlandaspidae
Range: Antarctica (South Victoria Land), Australia (New South Wales), Europe (England, Ireland, Turkey), North America (Greenland)
Pn: grohn-LAN-das-PIS

Size: 2 inches (6 cm) long
Order: uncertain
Family: uncertain
Range: Europe (Scotland)
Pn: pay-LEE-oh-spon-DI-lus

Palaeospondylus

This tiny creature had a long "backbone" with spines at one end, presumably supporting a tail fin, and a strangely shaped skull at the other end. It had no obvious jaws and no paired fins.

Gemuendina

The rounded and flattened body of this fish was very similar to that of a modern ray. The pectoral fins of *Gemuendina* were drawn out into wings on either side of the body, and the eyes and nostrils were located on top of the head. These features were copied about 260 million years later in an unrelated group of fishes — the rays and skates that inhabited the seabed from Jurassic times onward.

Size: 1 foot (30 cm) long
Order: Rhenanida
Family: Asterosteidae
Range: Europe (Germany)
Pn: JEM-oo-en-DEE-na

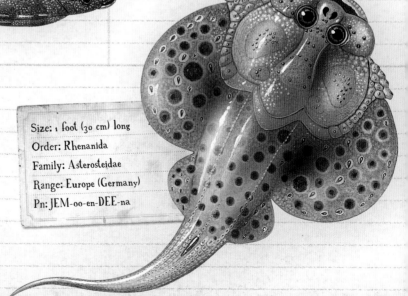

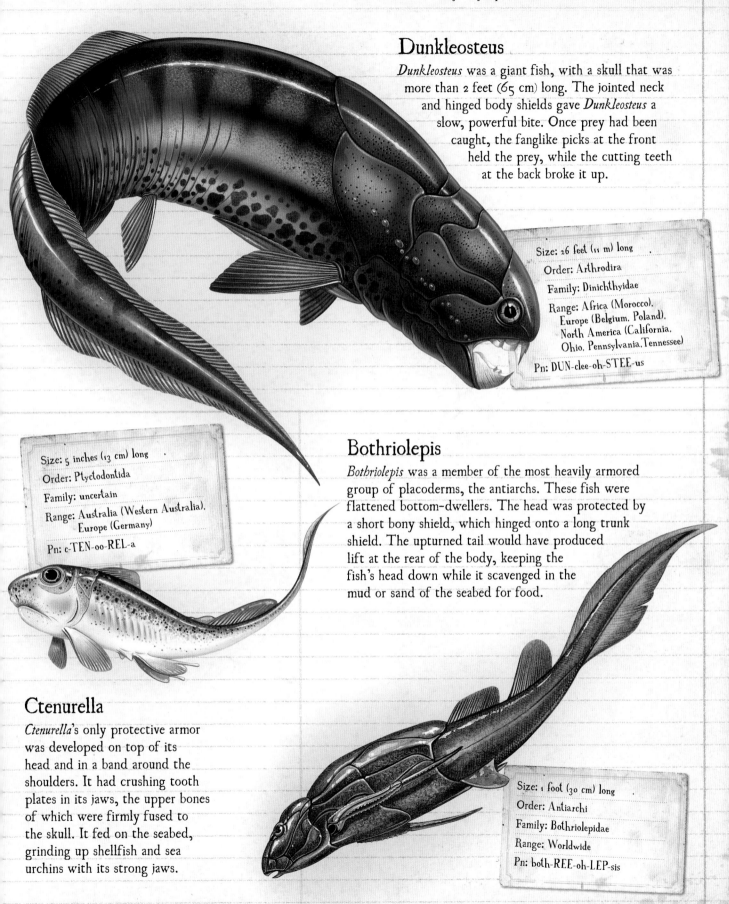

Dunkleosteus

Dunkleosteus was a giant fish, with a skull that was more than 2 feet (65 cm) long. The jointed neck and hinged body shields gave *Dunkleosteus* a slow, powerful bite. Once prey had been caught, the fanglike picks at the front held the prey, while the cutting teeth at the back broke it up.

Size: 26 feet (11 m) long

Order: Arthrodira

Family: Dinichthyidae

Range: Africa (Morocco), Europe (Belgium, Poland), North America (California, Ohio, Pennsylvania, Tennessee)

Pn: DUN-clee-oh-STEE-us

Bothriolepis

Bothriolepis was a member of the most heavily armored group of placoderms, the antiarchs. These fish were flattened bottom-dwellers. The head was protected by a short bony shield, which hinged onto a long trunk shield. The upturned tail would have produced lift at the rear of the body, keeping the fish's head down while it scavenged in the mud or sand of the seabed for food.

Size: 5 inches (13 cm) long

Order: Ptyctodontida

Family: uncertain

Range: Australia (Western Australia), Europe (Germany)

Pn: c-TEN-oo-REL-a

Ctenurella

Ctenurella's only protective armor was developed on top of its head and in a band around the shoulders. It had crushing tooth plates in its jaws, the upper bones of which were firmly fused to the skull. It fed on the seabed, grinding up shellfish and sea urchins with its strong jaws.

Size: 1 foot (30 cm) long

Order: Antiarchi

Family: Bothriolepidae

Range: Worldwide

Pn: both-REE-oh-LEP-sis

PRIMITIVE RAY-FINNED FISH

The ray-finned fish evolved some 400 million years ago. Today, this ancient group lives on in a wide range of fish, including sturgeons, paddlefishes, bowfin, garpike and birchirs. The characteristic feature of these fish, both ancient and modern, is the skeleton of parallel bony rays that supports and stiffens each fin — hence the name, "ray-finned" fish. In early species, the fins were rigid, but they later became more flexible, becoming the highly mobile fins of modern bony fish. They also developed a swim bladder, which helped the fish to control their buoyancy while swimming.

Canobius

A new development had occurred in the skull of this tiny fish. The arrangement of the skull and cheek-bones meant that *Canobius* could open its mouth wider, while at the same time the gill chambers behind the jaws were much bigger. This allowed more water to pass over the gills, allowing more oxygen to be taken out of the water.

Size: 3 inches (7 cm) long
Order: Palaeonisciformes
Family: Palaeoniscidae
Range: Europe (Scotland)
Pn: CAN-oh-BEE-us

Cheirolepis

Cheirolepis was a large, fast-moving freshwater predator. Its streamlined body was covered in a heavy coat of small, rectangular scales, arranged in diagonal rows — just like those of the spiny sharks. A row of large scales stiffened the top side of the tail, making its sweeping movements more powerful during swimming.

Size: up to 1 foot 10 inches (55 cm) long
Order: Cheirolepiformes
Family: Cheirolepidae
Range: Europe (Scotland),
       North America (Canada)
Pn: KI-roh-LEP-is

Palaeoniscum

With its torpedo-shaped body, high dorsal fin and powerful tail, *Palaeoniscum* was built for speed. It must have been a ferocious predator of other freshwater bony fish. Its jaws were filled with numerous sharp teeth, which were constantly being replaced throughout its lifetime.

Size: up to 1 foot (30 cm) long
Order: Palaeonisciformes
Family: Palaeoniscidae
Range: Europe (England, Germany), North America (United States, Greenland)
Pn: PAY-lee-oh-NIS-cum

Size: 3½ inches (9 cm) long
Order: Palaeonisciformes
Family: Stegotrachelidae
Range: Australia (Western Australia), Europe (Germany)
Pn: MOY-tho-MA-SEE-ah

Platysomus

Platysomus, which lived in both freshwater and the sea, had a deep body that had long dorsal and anal fins, while the pectoral and pelvic fins were tiny. Like Canobius, *Platysomus* had a wide gape and bulging gill chambers when the mouth was open so that it could absorb more oxygen. Platysomus probably also ate plankton.

Moythomasia

Moythomasia was covered in a new type of scale, unique to the early ray-finned fishes. A peg on the top edge of each scale fitted into a socket on the bottom edge of the scale above. As a result, all the body scales moved with each other to form a flexible and protective coat of armor.

Size: 7 inches (18 cm) long
Order: Palaeonisciformes
Family: Stegotrachelidae
Range: Worldwide
Pn: PLA-tis-OH-mus

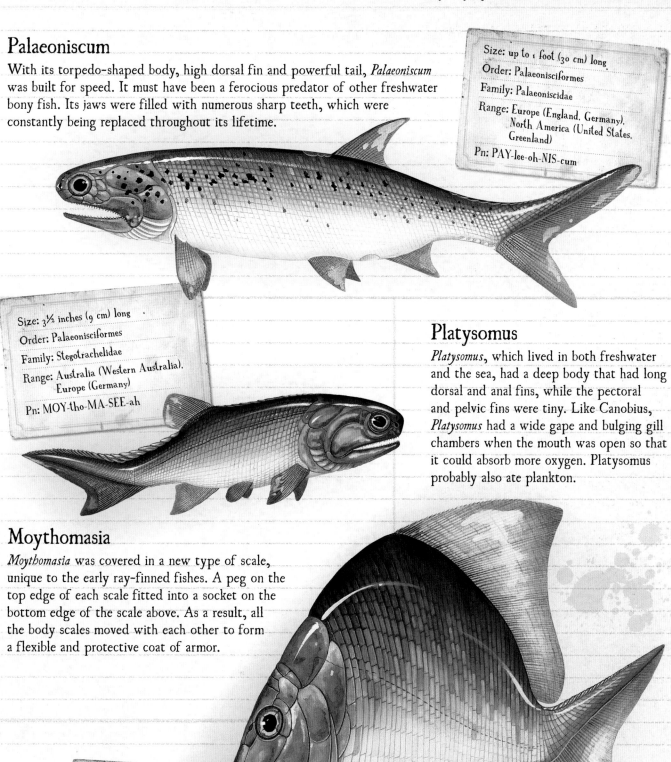

Lepidotes

Many new types of ray-finned fishes evolved toward the end of the Paleozoic Era. These fish show many features found in modern bony fishes. One of these, known as *Lepidotes*, evolved one such feature, a new jaw mechanism that allowed it to feed differently from earlier fish. Its upper jaw bones were shorter and more mobile. This allowed the mouth to be formed into a tube, so prey could be sucked in from a distance.

Size: 6 inches (15 cm) long
Order: Perleidiformes
Family: Perleididae
Range: Worldwide
Pn: PER-lay-DUS

Size: 1 foot (30 cm) long
Order: Semionotiformes
Family: Semionotidae
Range: Worldwide
Pn: LEH-pi-DOH-tees

Perleidus

Perleidus of the Triassic Period was a freshwater predator with strong, toothed jaws, which could be opened wide. It also had very flexible dorsal and anal fins, which made this fish a very agile swimmer.

Size: up to 3 feet 3 inches (1 m) long
Order: Saurichthyformes
Family: Saurichthyidae
Range: Worldwide
Pn: SAW-rick-THIS

Saurichthys

The long, narrow body of this freshwater fish is like that of the modern pike. *Saurichthys* probably also behaved like a modern pike. It may have ambushed its prey, lurking among the waterweeds or lying still on the riverbed, and seizing passing fish in its toothed jaws.

Size: 2 feet (60 cm) long

Order: Aspidorhynchiformes

Family: Aspiedorhynchidae

Range: Antarctica, Europe (England, France, Germany)

Pn: as-PI-dor-RIN-cus

Aspidorhynchus

Aspidorhynchus looked like the modern gar, or garpike, of North America. Like it, *Aspidorhynchus* must have been a ferocious predator. Its long body, protected by thick scales, was perfect for fast swimming. The jaws were studded with sharp, pointed teeth and the upper jaw was stretched into a toothless guard.

Pycnodus

Even though they weren't related, *Pycnodus* had the same deep-bodied shape and grinding teeth as *Dapedium*. This was probably in response to living in the same environment — calm reef waters —and eating similar food — hard-shelled mollusks, corals and sea urchins.

Size: 1 foot 2 inches (35 cm) long

Order: Semionotiformes

Family: Dapediidae

Range: Asia (India), Europe (England)

Pn: DAP-e-DEE-um

Dapedium

The deep, round body of *Dapedium* was covered in heavy, protective scales with a thick outer layer of tough enamel. *Dapedium* had long, peglike teeth in its jaws and crushing teeth toward the back of its mouth. These, combined with its body shape, suggest that it was a mollusk-eater, weaving slowly through the coral reefs of the Early Mesozoic seas.

Size: 5 inches (12 cm) long

Order: Pycnodontiformes

Family: Pycnodontidae

Range: Asia (India), Europe (Belgium, England, Italy)

Pn: PIC-noh-DUS

MODERN RAY-FINNED FISH

In the middle of the Cretaceous Period, fish underwent an explosive phase in their evolution, which saw the emergence of many modern species, such as the salmon and trout. The Late Cretaceous saw another burst of evolution as more highly advanced species developed. These were the spiny-rayed, perchlike fish.

Eobothus

Flatfish, such as *Eobothus*, became specialized for living and feeding on the seabed. Unlike the rays and skates, which are flattened from top to bottom, the flatfish became compressed from side to side. Young flatfish look like other fish and swim normally, but as they grow, the eye moves onto the top side.

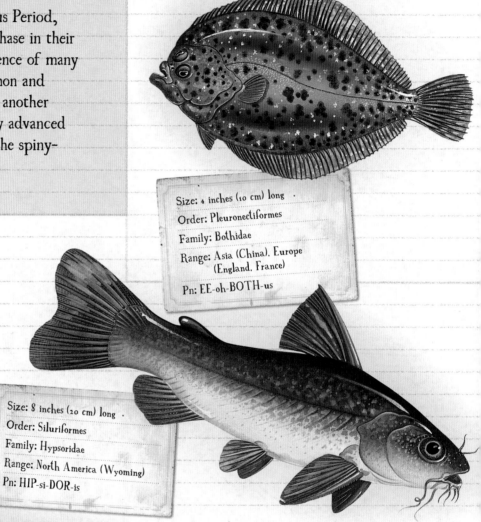

Size: 4 inches (10 cm) long

Order: Pleuronectiformes

Family: Bothidae

Range: Asia (China), Europe (England, France)

Pn: EE-oh-BOTH-us

Hypsidoris

With its whiskery feelers, *Hypsidoris* looked like a modern catfish. It lived in the subtropical rivers and lakes of western North America some 50 million years ago. The fish also had a spine in front of each pectoral fin. These spines were defensive, and they could be made to stand up when the fish was threatened.

Size: 8 inches (20 cm) long

Order: Siluriformes

Family: Hypsoridae

Range: North America (Wyoming)

Pn: HIP-si-DOR-is

Sphenocephalus

Sphenocephalus had a large head, and its pelvic fins lay beneath the pectoral fins, which were placed high on the sides of its body. The arrangement made the fish very agile. In modern cod, the pelvic fins are actually in front of the pectorals.

Size: 8 inches (20 cm) long

Order: Stephocephaliformes

Family: Stephocephalidae

Range: Europe (England, Italy)

Pn: SFEN-oh-SEF-a-LUS

Hypsocormus

Hypsocormus was a fast-swimming, fish-eating predator. It had heavy body armor made of thick, enamel-covered, rectangular scales. But the scales were comparatively smaller and allowed greater flexibility during swimming. Its jaws were flexible and mobile, and they had a powerful bite.

Size: up to 3 feet 3 inches (1 m) long
Order: Pachycormiformes
Family: Pachycormidae
Range: Europe (England, Germany)
Pn: HIP-soh-COR-mus

Size: up to 4 feet long (1.2 m) long
Order: Salmoniformes
Family: Enchodontidae
Range: Worldwide
Pn: en-KOH-dus

Protobrama

The size of *Protobrama* and its body shape suggest that it may have been a reef dweller, nipping in and out of the coral while chasing its prey.

Enchodus

Enchodus had a large head and big eyes, as well as a lightweight, streamlined body. These suggest that this fish was an agile predator of the open seas. Its mouth was filled with long pointed teeth that interlocked when the jaws were closed, trapping any prey. *Enchodus* probably preyed on plankton-eating fish in the surface waters.

Size: 6 inches (15 cm) long
Order: Crossognathiformes
Family: Tselfatiidae
Range: Asia (Lebanon)
Pn: PRO-toh-BRAH-ma

Berycopsis

Berycopsis had sharp spines that could be pulled up to protect the fish. Its pectoral fins were placed high on the side of the body for improved steering and braking. Modern relatives of this fish include the barracuda, swordfish, perch, tropical reef fish, flatfish and sea horses.

Size: 1 foot 2 inches (35 cm) long
Order: Polymixiiformes
Family: Polymixiidae
Range: Europe (England)
Pn: BER-ee-COP-sis

57

LOBE-FINNED FISH

As opposed to ray-finned fish, the pectoral and pelvic fins of lobe-finned fish consist of long, fleshy, muscular lobes (hence the name, "lobe-finned" or sarcopterygian fish). The lobed fins were very important in evolutionary terms, because a member of this group of fish was to evolve into the first tetrapod, which in turn evolved into the first amphibians and the first animals to walk onto land. Today, the coelacanths and lungfish are among the very few species of lobe-finned fish that still exist. Lobe-finned fish are separated into the coelacanths, lungfish and tetrapodomorphs, which include all four-limbed vertebrates.

Strunius

Strunius had a short body that was covered in large, rounded, bony scales. It had a jointed skull, like coelacanths, which gave the fish a more powerful bite. This was necessary, because their main prey was a type of ray-finned fish that was covered in thick bony scales.

Size: 4 inches (10 cm) long
Order: Onychodontida
Family: Onychodontidae
Range: Europe (Germany)
Pn: STROO-nee-us

Holoptychius

Holoptychius was a streamlined fish with a covering of thin, light, rounded scales, which allowed it to swim very quickly. It was a fierce predator of other bony fishes. It had fanglike teeth arranged around the edge of its mouth, as well as many smaller, pointed teeth lining the jaws. Its victims would have been held tightly between the teeth before they were swallowed whole.

Size: 1 foot 8 inches (50 cm) long
Order: Porolepiformes
Family: Holoptychiidae
Range: Worldwide
Pn: ho-LOP-ti-KEE-us

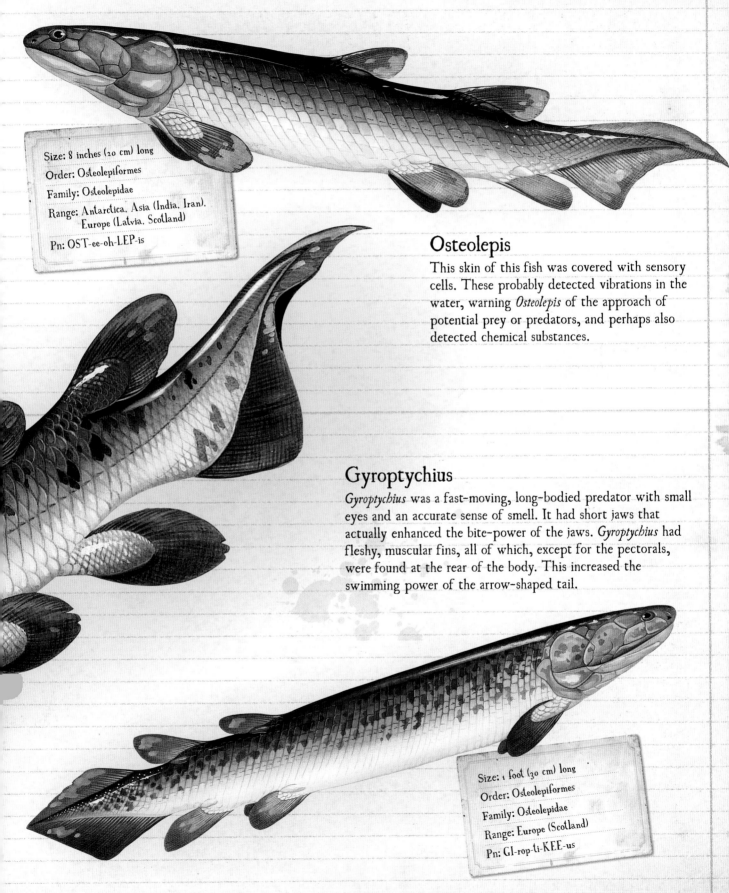

Size: 8 inches (20 cm) long

Order: Osteolepiformes

Family: Osteolepidae

Range: Antarctica, Asia (India, Iran),
Europe (Latvia, Scotland)

Pn: OST-ee-oh-LEP-is

Osteolepis

This skin of this fish was covered with sensory cells. These probably detected vibrations in the water, warning *Osteolepis* of the approach of potential prey or predators, and perhaps also detected chemical substances.

Gyroptychius

Gyroptychius was a fast-moving, long-bodied predator with small eyes and an accurate sense of smell. It had short jaws that actually enhanced the bite-power of the jaws. *Gyroptychius* had fleshy, muscular fins, all of which, except for the pectorals, were found at the rear of the body. This increased the swimming power of the arrow-shaped tail.

Size: 1 foot (30 cm) long

Order: Osteolepiformes

Family: Osteolepidae

Range: Europe (Scotland)

Pn: GI-rop-ti-KEE-us

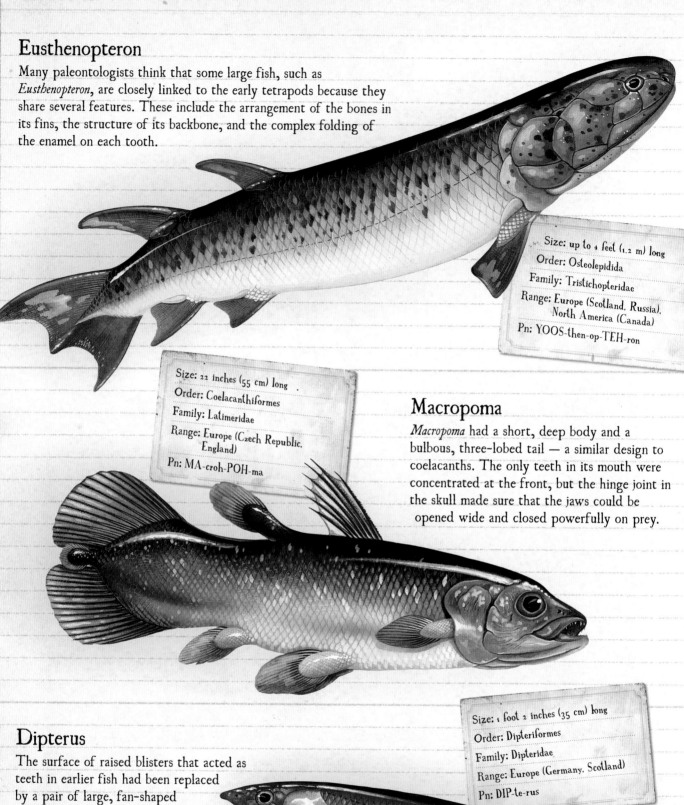

Eusthenopteron

Many paleontologists think that some large fish, such as *Eusthenopteron*, are closely linked to the early tetrapods because they share several features. These include the arrangement of the bones in its fins, the structure of its backbone, and the complex folding of the enamel on each tooth.

Size: up to 4 feet (1.2 m) long
Order: Osteolepidida
Family: Tristichopteridae
Range: Europe (Scotland, Russia),
North America (Canada)
Pn: YOOS-then-op-TEH-ron

Size: 22 inches (55 cm) long
Order: Coelacanthiformes
Family: Latimeridae
Range: Europe (Czech Republic,
England)
Pn: MA-croh-POH-ma

Macropoma

Macropoma had a short, deep body and a bulbous, three-lobed tail — a similar design to coelacanths. The only teeth in its mouth were concentrated at the front, but the hinge joint in the skull made sure that the jaws could be opened wide and closed powerfully on prey.

Size: 1 foot 2 inches (35 cm) long
Order: Dipteriformes
Family: Dipteridae
Range: Europe (Germany, Scotland)
Pn: DIP-te-rus

Dipterus

The surface of raised blisters that acted as teeth in earlier fish had been replaced by a pair of large, fan-shaped tooth plates on the palate and on the lower jaws of *Dipterus*. This type of dentition was to remain practically unchanged over the next 380 million years.

Griphognathus

Griphognathus was an early type of lungfish that had an elongated snout and small, studlike teeth that covered its palate and lower jaws. Like all the other members of the order, this lungfish was covered in large, overlapping, rounded scales, and the tail was asymmetrical.

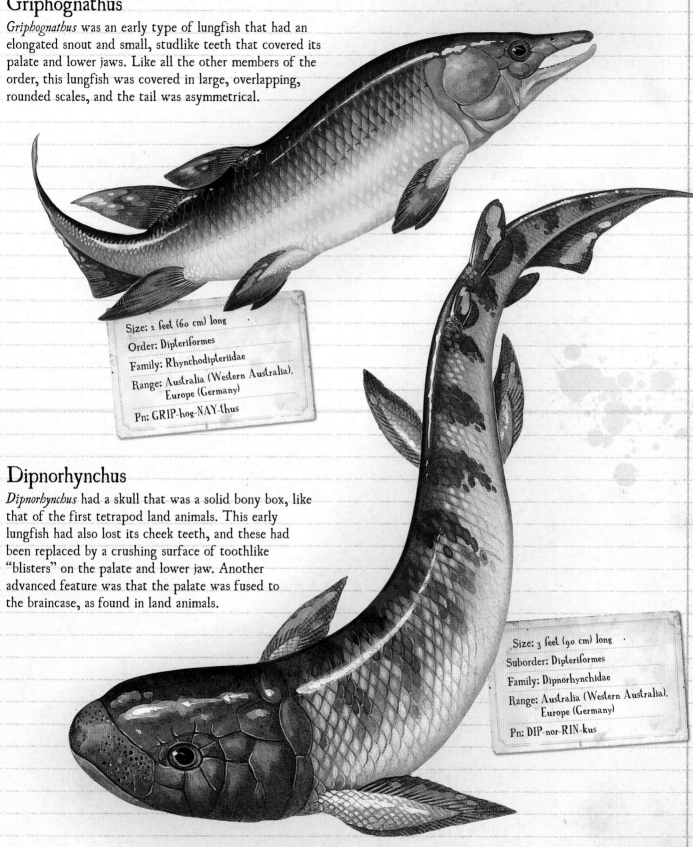

Size: 2 feet (60 cm) long

Order: Dipteriformes

Family: Rhynchodipteriidae

Range: Australia (Western Australia), Europe (Germany)

Pn: GRIP-hog-NAY-thus

Dipnorhynchus

Dipnorhynchus had a skull that was a solid bony box, like that of the first tetrapod land animals. This early lungfish had also lost its cheek teeth, and these had been replaced by a crushing surface of toothlike "blisters" on the palate and lower jaw. Another advanced feature was that the palate was fused to the braincase, as found in land animals.

Size: 3 feet (90 cm) long

Suborder: Dipteriformes

Family: Dipnorhynchidae

Range: Australia (Western Australia), Europe (Germany)

Pn: DIP-nor-RIN-kus

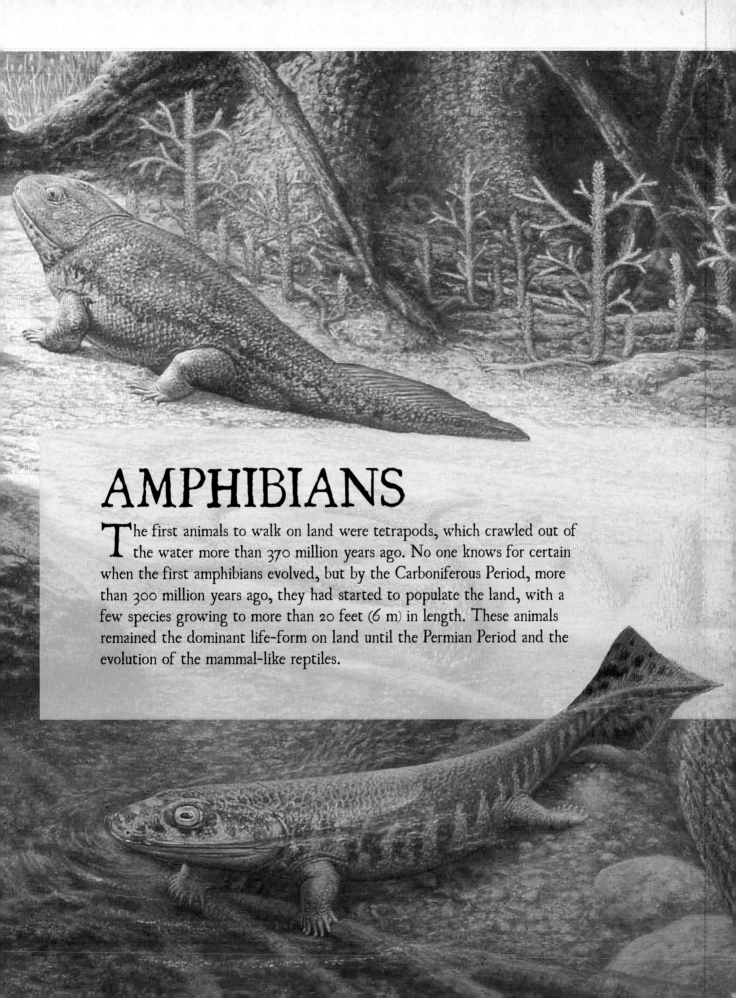

AMPHIBIANS

The first animals to walk on land were tetrapods, which crawled out of the water more than 370 million years ago. No one knows for certain when the first amphibians evolved, but by the Carboniferous Period, more than 300 million years ago, they had started to populate the land, with a few species growing to more than 20 feet (6 m) in length. These animals remained the dominant life-form on land until the Permian Period and the evolution of the mammal-like reptiles.

EARLY TETRAPODS

The tetrapods include all four-limbed vertebrates and range from early water-living animals to land-living amphibians, reptiles, mammals, birds, and their fossil ancestors. The first tetrapods evolved from lobe-finned fish into four-limbed animals that were primarily water dwelling in Late Devonian times. Environmental and climate changes in the following Carboniferous Period provided new low-lying and swampy habitats. These were home to an abundance of small animals, especially arthropods and fish, which provided food for many newly evolving early tetrapods. These early tetrapods included many now-extinct groups of amphibians, which reproduced in water, and reptiles, which laid eggs on land.

Crassigyrinus

Crassigyrinus had a fishlike body with a long tail and tiny finlike limbs. Its teeth are those of a fish eater, and the streamlined body indicates a fast-moving predator. The large eyes may suggest that it hunted in the dark, murky Carboniferous swamps.

Size: 6 feet 6 inches (2 m) long
Order: "Stem tetrapod"
Family: Whatcheeridae
Range: Europe (Scotland)
Pn: KRA-sig-i-RIN-us

Δ

Cacops was well adapted to life on land. Bony plates covered its body, and a row of thick armor ran down the backbone. Its legs were well suited for walking, and were almost reptilelike in structure. A broad opening called the otic notch, behind each eye, was covered by a taut membrane that acted as an eardrum.

Size: 1 foot 4 inches (40 cm) long
Order: Temnospondyli
Family: Dissorophidae
Range: North America (Texas)
Pn: KAY-kops

Size: 3 feet 3 inches (1 m) long
Order: "Stem tetrapod"
Family: Ichthyostegidae
Range: North America (Greenland)
Pn: ick-THEE-oh-STAY-ga

Ichthyostega

Ichthyostega had a long, deep body and a heavy skull of solid bone. Its four limbs were well developed, but not suitable for movement on land. The hind limbs were directed backward, like those of a seal, and were better adapted for a paddling mode of swimming than for walking.

Size: 5 feet (1.5 m) long
Order: Colosteoidea
Family: Colosteidae
Range: North America (West Virginia)
Pn: GREE-rer-PEH-ton

Greererpeton

Greererpeton lived in the water. Its slim body shape would have been ideal for moving through water with a snakelike movement. The low flat head was about 7 inches (18 cm) long. The elongated body, which had 40 vertebrae, about twice the usual number, ended in a long tail. The legs were short, and they each had five toes for steering and braking.

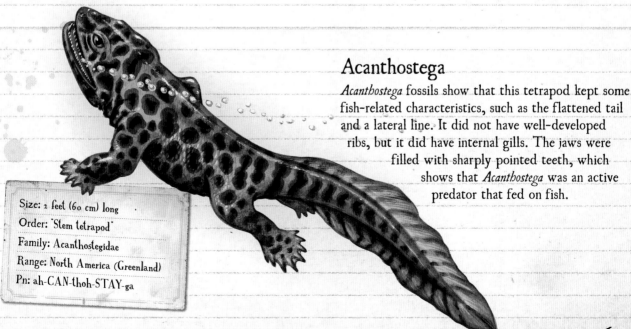

Acanthostega

Acanthostega fossils show that this tetrapod kept some fish-related characteristics, such as the flattened tail and a lateral line. It did not have well-developed ribs, but it did have internal gills. The jaws were filled with sharply pointed teeth, which shows that *Acanthostega* was an active predator that fed on fish.

Size: 2 feet (60 cm) long
Order: "Stem tetrapod"
Family: Acanthostegidae
Range: North America (Greenland)
Pn: ah-CAN-thoh-STAY-ga

Platyhystrix

Platyhystrix's most noticeable feature was the spectacular "sail" on its back, made of tall spines that grew up from the vertebrae. Blood-rich skin may have covered the whole structure. It is thought that the sails helped these cold-blooded reptiles regulate their body temperature.

Size: 2 feet 3 inches (70 cm) long
Order: Temnospondyli
Family: Peltobatrachidae
Range: Africa (Tanzania)
Pn: pel-TOH-ba-TRAK-us

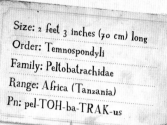

Size: 3 feet 3 inches (1 m) long
Order: Temnospondyli
Family: Dissorophidae
Range: North America (Texas)
Pn: PLAT-i-HISS-trix

Peltobatrachus

Peltobatrachus was a slow-moving, fully terrestrial amphibian. Its body was enclosed in heavy armor, like that of an armadillo, which served as protection against the dominant carnivores of the day. *Peltobatrachus'* bony armor plating was arranged in broad shields over the shoulders and behind the hips, and in close-fitting bands across the body. The teeth of this amphibian have not been found, but it probably ate insects, worms, and snails.

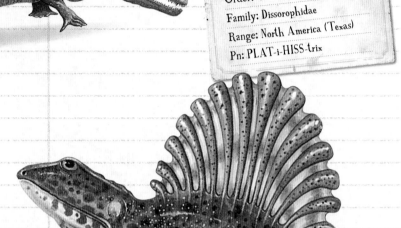

Paracyclotosaurus

By Triassic times, two groups of mammal-like reptiles, the dicynodonts and cynodonts, dominated the land. *Paracyclotosaurus*, and other related amphibians, had been forced to return to the water. The head of the bulky *Paracyclotosaurus* had a flat top and was almost 2 feet (60 cm) long.

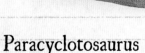

Size: 7 feet 5 inches (2.3 m) long
Order: Temnospondyli
Family: Capitosauridae
Range: Australia (Queensland)
Pn: pa-ra-si-CLO-toh-SAW-rus

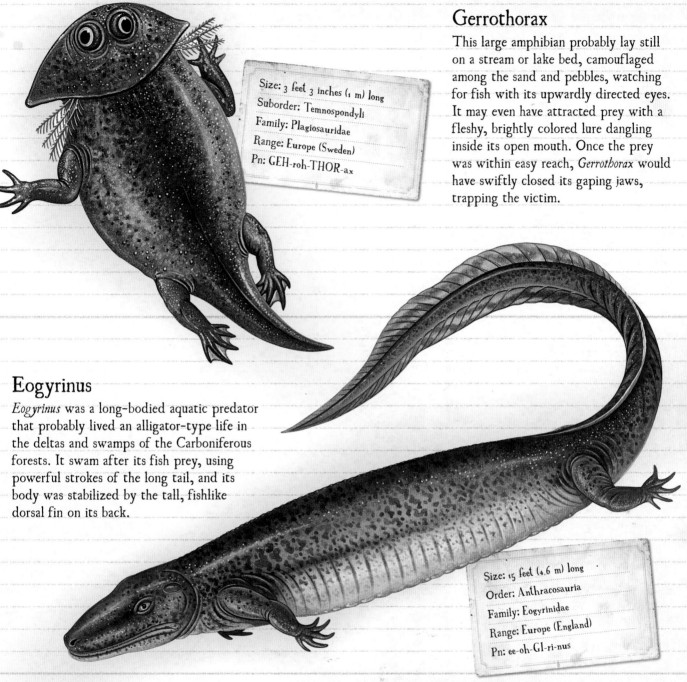

Gerrothorax

This large amphibian probably lay still on a stream or lake bed, camouflaged among the sand and pebbles, watching for fish with its upwardly directed eyes. It may even have attracted prey with a fleshy, brightly colored lure dangling inside its open mouth. Once the prey was within easy reach, *Gerrothorax* would have swiftly closed its gaping jaws, trapping the victim.

Size: 3 feet 3 inches (1 m) long
Suborder: Temnospondyli
Family: Plagiosauridae
Range: Europe (Sweden)
Pn: GEH-roh-THOR-ax

Eogyrinus

Eogyrinus was a long-bodied aquatic predator that probably lived an alligator-type life in the deltas and swamps of the Carboniferous forests. It swam after its fish prey, using powerful strokes of the long tail, and its body was stabilized by the tall, fishlike dorsal fin on its back.

Size: 15 feet (4.6 m) long
Order: Anthracosauria
Family: Eogyrinidae
Range: Europe (England)
Pn: ee-oh-GI-ri-nus

Seymouria

Seymouria was a well-adapted land dweller, with many reptilian features. In fact, *Seymouria* was originally thought to be an early reptile, until fossilized juveniles were found. Their skulls showed the marks of fishlike, lateral line canals, whose function is to detect vibrations in the water.

Size: 2 feet (60 cm) long
Order: Seymouriamorpha
Family: Seymouriidae
Range: North America (Texas)
Pn: say-MOR-ee-ah

67

LEPOSPONDYLS

Lepospondyls were a group of small specialized tetrapods that evolved in early Carboniferous times and died out in early Permian times. None of them grew to much more than 3 feet (1 m) in size but they developed a wide range of body shapes and habits, ranging from eel-shaped to lizard-shaped forms, some of which were terrestrial, others amphibious, and others water dwelling. Some five major groups have been recognized including the aistopods, nectrideans and microsaurs. Their evolutionary relationships to living amphibians (Lissamphibia) and the egg-laying amniotes such as the reptiles are unclear and they may not form a single natural (monophyletic) group.

Ophiderpeton

About 230 vertebrae made up the body of this snakelike creature. There is no trace of limbs within the skeleton, and the eyes were large and placed forward on the skull, which was about 6 inches (15 cm) long. *Ophiderpeton* must have led the life of a burrower, feeding on insects, worms, centipedes, snails and other invertebrates.

Size: 2 feet 4 inches (70 cm) long
Order: Aistopoda
Family: Ophiderpetontidae
Range: Europe (Czech Republic),
       North America (Ohio)
Pn: oh-fi-DERP-pe-ton

Keraterpeton

The tail of *Keraterpeton* was more than twice the length of the animal's body and head combined. It was flattened sideways, and would have pushed the animal through the murky waters of the coal swamps in which it lived. The five-toed hind legs were longer than the four-toed forelegs and the short and rounded skull had eyes set far forward.

Size: 1 foot (30 cm) long
Order: Nectridea
Family: Keraterpetontidae
Range: Europe (Czech Republic),
       North America (Ohio)
Pn: KE-ra-TER-peh-ton

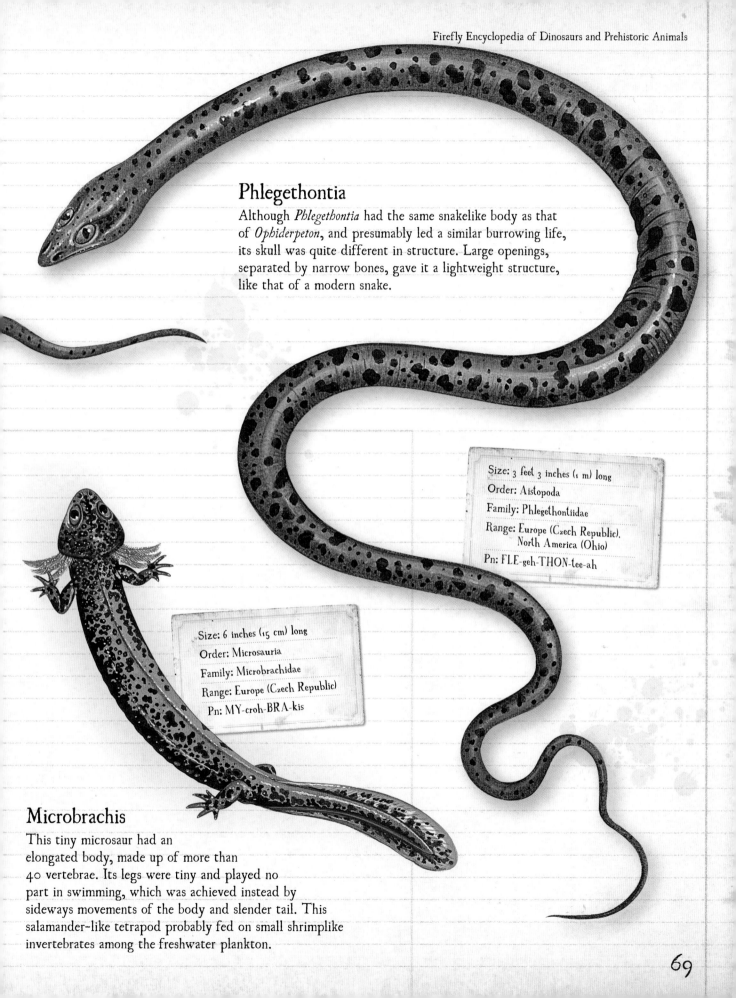

Phlegethontia

Although *Phlegethontia* had the same snakelike body as that of *Ophiderpeton*, and presumably led a similar burrowing life, its skull was quite different in structure. Large openings, separated by narrow bones, gave it a lightweight structure, like that of a modern snake.

Size: 3 feet 3 inches (1 m) long
Order: Aistopoda
Family: Phlegethontiidae
Range: Europe (Czech Republic), North America (Ohio)
Pn: FLE-geh-THON-tee-ah

Size: 6 inches (15 cm) long
Order: Microsauria
Family: Microbrachidae
Range: Europe (Czech Republic)
Pn: MY-croh-BRA-kis

Microbrachis

This tiny microsaur had an elongated body, made up of more than 40 vertebrae. Its legs were tiny and played no part in swimming, which was achieved instead by sideways movements of the body and slender tail. This salamander-like tetrapod probably fed on small shrimplike invertebrates among the freshwater plankton.

Size: Just over 1 inch (3 cm) long
Order: Anura
Family: uncertain
Range: South America (Argentina)
Pn: VI-er-RAY-la

Triadobatrachus

This tiny creature lived about 240 million years ago. Its hip structure suggests that it swam by kicking out with its short hind legs. This motion may have evolved over millions of years into the jumping action of modern frogs. It would have been able to hear well on land, because the bony parts of the ear were well developed, and there was a broad eardrum on either side to pick up sounds.

Size: 4 inches (10 cm) long .
Order: Anura
Family: Triadobatradidae
Range: Africa (Madagascar)
Pn: TRY-ad-oh-ba-TRA-kus

Vieraella

The first true frogs appeared in the Early Jurassic. *Vieraella* is the oldest known frog. In all respects, its anatomy is essentially the same as that of a modern frog, with the characteristic latticework skull, long hip girdle, which is shaped like a three-pronged fork, and long jumping legs.

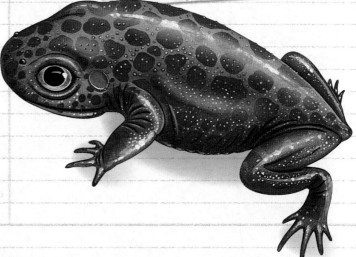

Pantylus

A great head on a small, scaly body characterized this microsaur. It was a well-adapted land animal, moving around on short, sturdy limbs. It probably lived like a modern lizard, scuttling around after insects and other small invertebrates, which were crushed by the numerous large, blunt teeth.

Size: 10 inches (25 cm) long .
Order: Microsauria
Family: Pantylidae
Range: North America (Texas)
Pn: pan-TEYE-lus

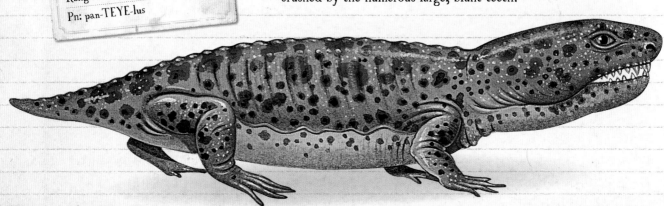

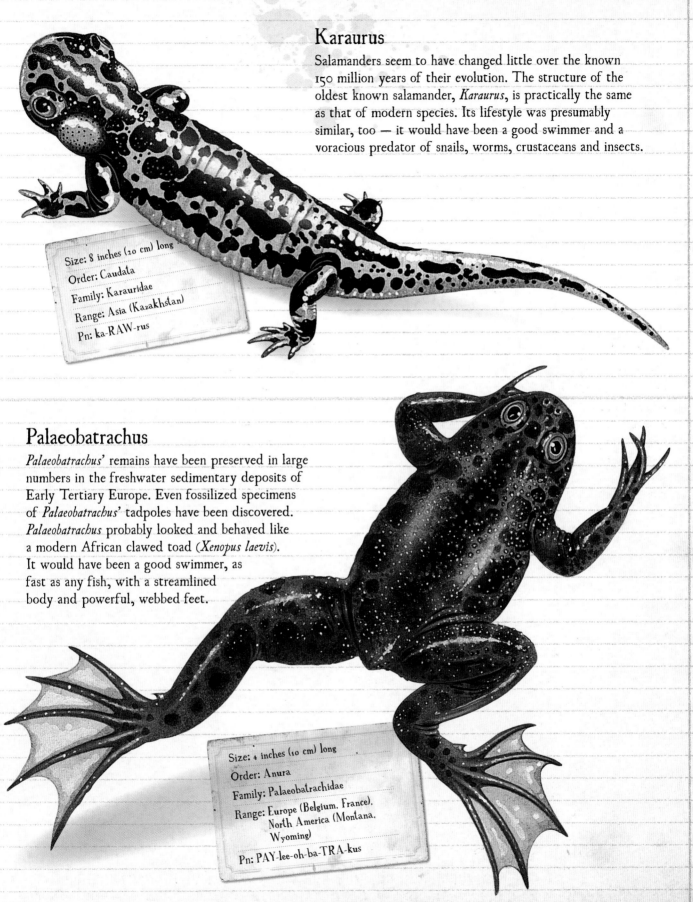

Karaurus

Salamanders seem to have changed little over the known 150 million years of their evolution. The structure of the oldest known salamander, *Karaurus*, is practically the same as that of modern species. Its lifestyle was presumably similar, too — it would have been a good swimmer and a voracious predator of snails, worms, crustaceans and insects.

Size: 8 inches (20 cm) long

Order: Caudata

Family: Karauridae

Range: Asia (Kazakhstan)

Pn: ka-RAW-rus

Palaeobatrachus

Palaeobatrachus' remains have been preserved in large numbers in the freshwater sedimentary deposits of Early Tertiary Europe. Even fossilized specimens of *Palaeobatrachus'* tadpoles have been discovered. *Palaeobatrachus* probably looked and behaved like a modern African clawed toad (*Xenopus laevis*). It would have been a good swimmer, as fast as any fish, with a streamlined body and powerful, webbed feet.

Size: 4 inches (10 cm) long

Order: Anura

Family: Palaeobatrachidae

Range: Europe (Belgium, France), North America (Montana, Wyoming)

Pn: PAY-lee-oh-ba-TRA-kus

EARLY REPTILES

Reptiles evolved from early tetrapods during the Carboniferous Period more than 300 million years ago. They rapidly evolved into a diverse range of groups, including flying reptiles, such as pterosaurs, swimming reptiles, such as ichthyosaurs, and the dinosaurs, which dominated the land during the Triassic, Jurassic and Cretaceous periods.

WHAT WERE THE EARLY REPTILES?

Reptiles are a group of tetrapods, known as amniotes, whose ability to lay eggs allowed them to become independent of water for reproduction and take up life on land. Internal fertilization allows the fertilized egg to be covered in a membrane within the mother's body before it is laid. The egg contains enough nutrient to support the development of the embryo and helps protect it from the elements. After the appearance of the first reptiles in the Late Carboniferous, different types of reptile began to spread all over the world. At the same time, marine forms, such as plesiosaurs and ichthyosaurs, were beginning to thrive in the sea. Crocodiles and flying reptiles belonged to the archosaur, or "ruling reptile," group, as did the dinosaurs. Of these, only crocodiles remain today.

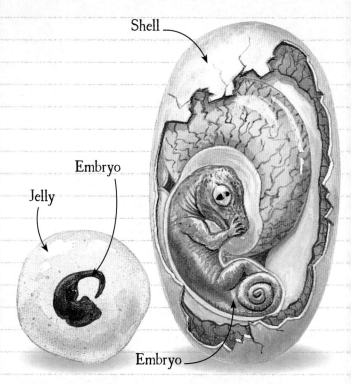

Amphibian egg   Reptile egg

A SHELLED EGG

An amphibian egg is protected only by a jelly coating. The egg of a reptile is protected by a tough membrane or shell, which keeps the embryo from drying out. It also protects it from predators.

AN EARLY REPTILE

One of the first reptiles and earliest of all land vertebrates, *Hylonomus* was a lightly built, lizardlike creature. Its jaws were more powerful than those of its tetrapod ancestors and its hips and shoulders were stronger to help support it on land.

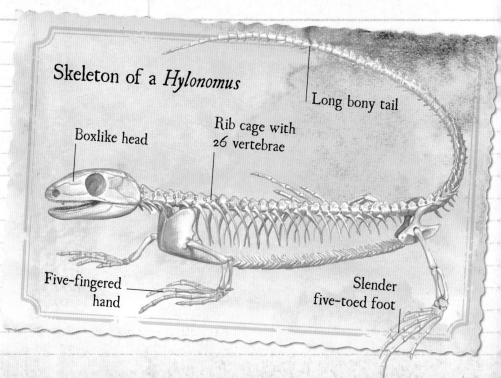

Skeleton of a *Hylonomus*

Boxlike head

Rib cage with 26 vertebrae

Long bony tail

Five-fingered hand

Slender five-toed foot

TYPES OF REPTILE

Early reptile
Hylonomus

Early anapsid reptiles (see below), such as *Hylonomus*, developed in the Late Carboniferous. The only anapsids today are turtles and tortoises.

Therapsid synapsid
Dicynodon

Synapsids, such as the extinct pelycosaurs and therapsids, evolved from reptilian tetrapods and gave rise to the mammals.

Ichthyosaurs were well adapted to life at sea and gave birth to live young.

Ichthyosaur
Stenopterygius

Crocodiles lived alongside the dinosaurs and thrive today. Their well-armored bodies have changed little.

Crocodile
Teleosaurus

Lizard
Ardeosaurus

The first lizards lived in the middle of the Jurassic. Today, lizards are a successful group with thousands of species.

Flying reptiles, called pterosaurs, first appeared in the Late Triassic. They were the first vertebrate animals to take to life in the air.

The first turtles lived in the Late Triassic. Like turtles and tortoises today, they had a hard shell that enclosed and protected the body.

Turtle
Archelon

Flying reptile
Pteranodon

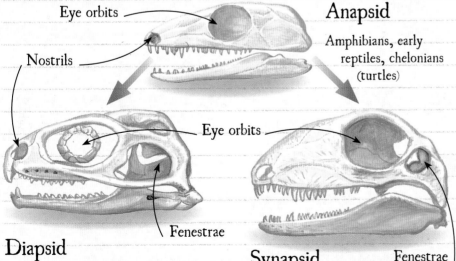

Eye orbits

Nostrils

Anapsid

Amphibians, early reptiles, chelonians (turtles)

Eye orbits

TYPES OF SKULL

The earliest reptiles, called anapsids, had boxlike skulls with openings for only the eyes and nostrils. Later reptiles, the diapsids and synapsids, developed skulls with extra openings called fenestrae. These made the skulls much lighter.

Diapsid

Crocodiles, dinosaurs, sphenodonts (tuatara)

Fenestrae

Synapsid

Mammals and extinct early relatives

Fenestrae

A REPTILE FAMILY TREE

The first reptiles, which appeared in the Late Carboniferous about 300 million years ago, were the primitive anapsids. These reptiles are still represented today by tortoises and turtles (Chelonia). The anapsid reptiles gave rise to the diapsid reptiles, which later included dinosaurs as well as modern lizards and snakes. Many of these groups of reptiles are now extinct.

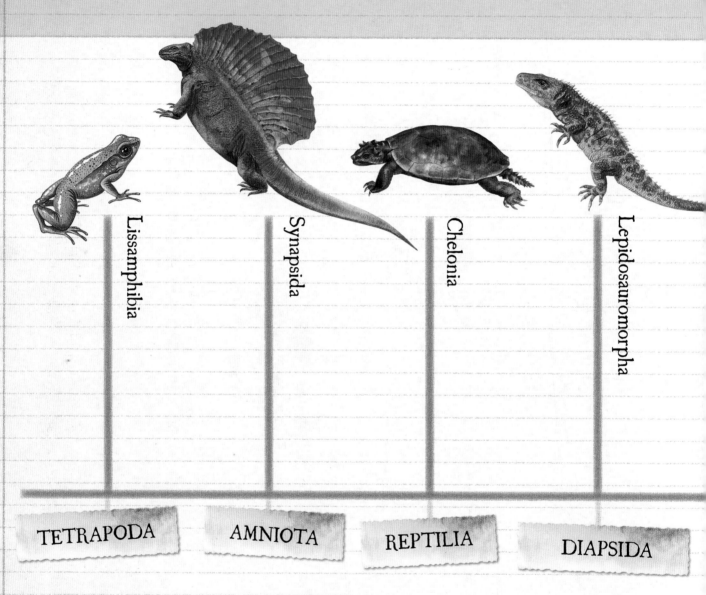

Lissamphibia

Synapsida

Chelonia

Lepidosauromorpha

TETRAPODA

AMNIOTA

REPTILIA

DIAPSIDA

THE CHART

Modern classification groups together organisms that share one or more unique characters and are descended from a common ancestor. For instance, all living birds are descended from a group of saurischian reptiles, which along with the ornithischian reptiles are grouped as the Dinosauria. Mammals are not descended from the reptiles but from a separate group of amniotes known as the synapsids.

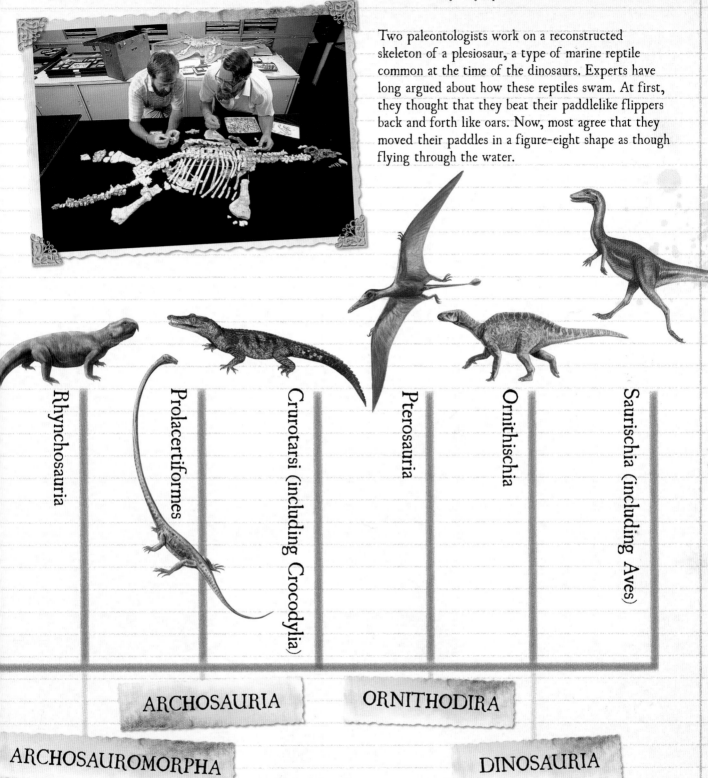

Two paleontologists work on a reconstructed skeleton of a plesiosaur, a type of marine reptile common at the time of the dinosaurs. Experts have long argued about how these reptiles swam. At first, they thought that they beat their paddlelike flippers back and forth like oars. Now, most agree that they moved their paddles in a figure-eight shape as though flying through the water.

Rhynchosauria

Prolacertiformes

Crurotarsi (including Crocodylia)

Pterosauria

Ornithischia

Saurischia (including Aves)

ARCHOSAURIA

ORNITHODIRA

ARCHOSAUROMORPHA

DINOSAURIA

REPTILE GROUPS

Traditionally, animals have been classified into groups of different sizes. The smallest is the species, and every species is contained in a genus (plural, genera). So for *Pterodactylus kochi*, *kochi* is the species name and *Pterodactylus* the genus. Genera have been classified into a hierarchy of larger groups, namely families, orders, classes and phyla.

THE FIRST REPTILES

Reptiles evolved during the Late Carboniferous Period about 300 million years ago. Many groups thrived before the archosaurs, or ruling reptiles — which included dinosaurs — began to dominate. The earliest, most primitive reptiles, called anapsids, had one feature in common: the skull was a heavy box of bone with no openings other than for the eyes and nostrils. Because the jaw muscles were inside the skull, they were not very big and this meant that the mouth could not be opened wide. Later reptiles, or diapsids, had a pair of openings, called fenestrae, on each side of the skull behind the eye. The jaw muscles stretched across these holes, allowing the jaws to be opened wider.

Size: 2 feet 5 inches (75 cm) long
Order: Captorhinida
Family: Captorhinidae
Range: North America (Texas)
Pn: LAB-id-o-SAW-rus

Labidosaurus

This primitive, heavily built reptile was squat with a large head and a short tail. Its shape suggests that it was at home on land. A typical captorhinid, *Labidosaurus* had several rows of teeth in its jaws, which were capable of crushing hard-shelled animals, such as insects and snails, or grinding down tough plant material.

Milleretta

This small lizardlike creature could move quickly and probably fed on insects. So far, millerettids have only been found from the Late Permian Period in South Africa. Although its skull did have openings on either side, *Milleretta* was a primitive anapsid reptile.

Size: 2 feet (60 cm) long
Order: Millerosauria
Family: Millerettidae
Range: Africa (South Africa)
Pn: MILL-er-ETT-ah

78

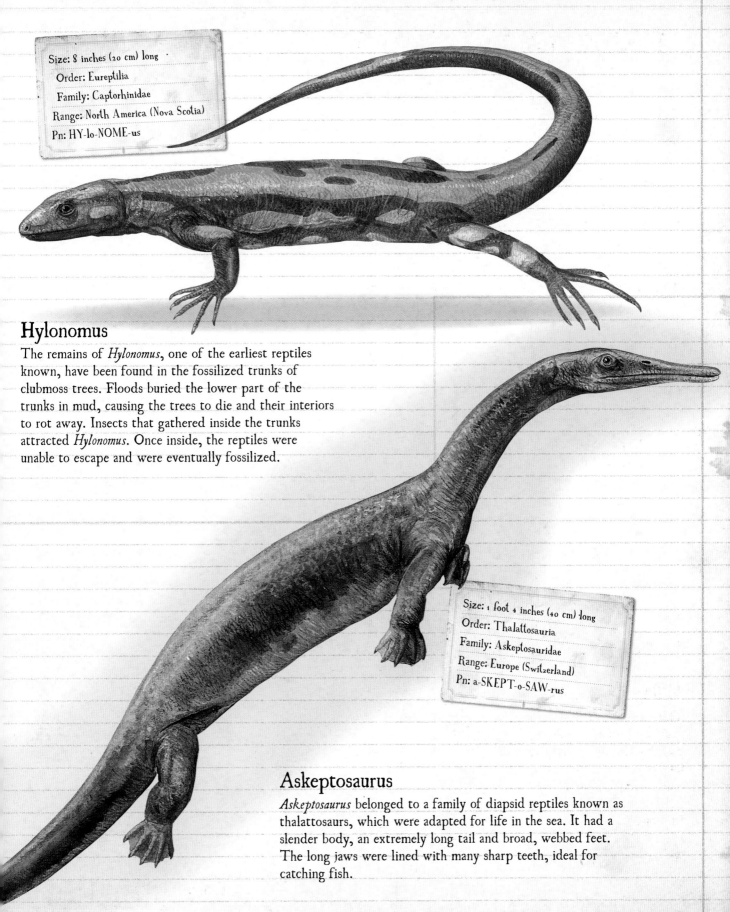

Size: 8 inches (20 cm) long
Order: Eureptilia
Family: Captorhinidae
Range: North America (Nova Scotia)
Pn: HY-lo-NOME-us

Hylonomus

The remains of *Hylonomus*, one of the earliest reptiles known, have been found in the fossilized trunks of clubmoss trees. Floods buried the lower part of the trunks in mud, causing the trees to die and their interiors to rot away. Insects that gathered inside the trunks attracted *Hylonomus*. Once inside, the reptiles were unable to escape and were eventually fossilized.

Size: 1 foot 4 inches (40 cm) long
Order: Thalattosauria
Family: Askeptosauridae
Range: Europe (Switzerland)
Pn: a-SKEPT-o-SAW-rus

Askeptosaurus

Askeptosaurus belonged to a family of diapsid reptiles known as thalattosaurs, which were adapted for life in the sea. It had a slender body, an extremely long tail and broad, webbed feet. The long jaws were lined with many sharp teeth, ideal for catching fish.

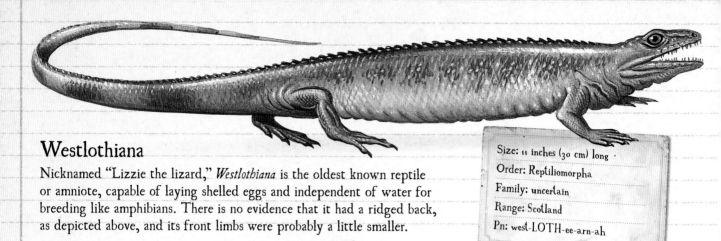

Westlothiana

Nicknamed "Lizzie the lizard," *Westlothiana* is the oldest known reptile or amniote, capable of laying shelled eggs and independent of water for breeding like amphibians. There is no evidence that it had a ridged back, as depicted above, and its front limbs were probably a little smaller.

Size: 11 inches (30 cm) long
Order: Reptiliomorpha
Family: uncertain
Range: Scotland
Pn: west-LOTH-ee-arn-ah

Hypsognathus

Among the earliest reptiles were the procolophonids, which lived until the Late Triassic. *Hypsognathus* was one of the later members of the family. It had a wide squat body and was probably not a fast runner. The spikes around its head would have helped protect it from any enemies.

Size: 1 foot 1 inch (33 cm) long
Order: Procolophonomorpha
Family: Procolophonidae
Range: North America (New Jersey)
Pn: HIP-sog-NAY-thus

Size: 2 feet (60 cm) long
Order: Procolophonomorpha
Family: Pareiasauridae
Range: Europe (Scotland)
Pn: eli-GIN-ee-ah

Eliginia

One of the smallest in the pareiasaur family, *Elginia* had a little skull decorated with an incredible array of bony head spikes. Their purpose was probably more for display than for defense — it perhaps shook its elaborately decorated head back and forth to threaten a rival male, or to attract the attention of a female.

Size: 1 foot 4 inches (40 cm) long

Order: Araeosclelidia

Family: Petrolacosauridae

Range: North America (Kansas)

Pn: pe-trol-ak-oh-SAW-rus

Petrolacosaurus

One of the first diapsid reptiles, *Petrolacosaurus* had a slender lizardlike body. It had longer legs than a typical lizard and its tail was as long as its head and body combined. It probably chased insects to eat, snapping them up in its small sharp teeth.

Size: 3 feet 3 inches (1 m) long

Order: Mesosauria

Family: Mesosauridae

Range: Southern Africa, South America (Brazil)

Pn: MES-oh-SAW-rus

Mesosaurus

This creature was one of the first reptiles to revert to a water-dwelling existence. Its long tail was flattened from side to side, possibly with a fin running along its length. Its hind legs were long, and the elongated foot bones were splayed and probably webbed, as were its shorter forelegs.

TRIASSIC TIMES

When the Triassic Period began about 250 million years ago, life on the Earth was dominated by archosaur reptiles and the therapsid ancestors of the mammals. Frogs, turtles and fish swam in rivers, and in the seas were marine reptiles, such as ichthyosaurs and nothosaurs. Toward the end of the Triassic, the first dinosaurs appeared and quickly spread across Pangea. Many of the earlier reptiles had died out by the time the dinosaurs became the dominant large animals.

TRIASSIC GERMANY

This scene in what is now southern Germany shows a group of plant-eating dinosaurs browsing on conifer branches. They are disturbed by the arrival of a predatory ceratosaur, *Liliensternus*. Small crocodiles, *Terrestrisuchus*, and shrewlike mammals feed on insects in the tangled undergrowth of cycads and horsetails, while pterosaurs soar overhead.

Liliensternus

Terrestrisuchus

Dragonfly

Fern

THE TRIASSIC WORLD

In the Triassic Period, the continents were all joined in one supercontinent, known as Pangea, which lay across the equator. The animals and plants were able to spread across the world with ease. The climate was warm and there were no polar ice caps.

Asia

Germany —— Europe

Central Asia   China

North America

PANTHALASSIC OCEAN

PALEO-TETHYS OCEAN

EQUATOR   PANGEA   *TETHYS OCEAN*

Africa

India

Australia

Antarctica

KEY TO MAP

Landmass

Ocean

Sea-covered continent

Plateosaurus, a prosauropod

Peteinosaurus, a flying reptile (pterosaur)

Thecodontosaurus, a prosauropod

Conifer

Shrewlike mammal

Moss

TURTLES, TORTOISES AND TERRAPINS

Turtles and their relatives first appeared in the Late Triassic more than 200 million years ago. Even then, a typical turtle had a hard shell enclosing its body and probably looked remarkably like the turtles and tortoises of today. Like their modern relatives, many prehistoric turtles could pull their heads and legs into their shells for protection from enemies. The shell over the back was made of bony plates, covered with a layer of smooth horn — like the "tortoise shell" from which combs and other accessories used to be made. Bony plates protected the underside. Like turtles and tortoises today, most early forms of turtles and tortoises had toothless jaws and a hard beak made of horn for cropping plants.

Archelon

This giant turtle did not have the heavy shell typical of most of its land and freshwater relatives. Instead, its body was protected by a framework of bony struts, which were probably covered by a thick layer of rubbery skin. Its limbs were massive paddles, which it used to propel itself through water. Like modern leatherback turtles, *Archelon* may have fed on jellyfish.

Proganochelys

This is one of the earliest known turtles. A broad, domed shell covered its back, and bony plates protected its soft underside. It also had a number of extra plates around the edges of its shell, which gave the legs some protection. *Proganochelys* did have some teeth in its mouth, but it also had a toothless, horn-covered beak similar to that of today's turtles.

Size: 3 feet (1 m) long
Order: Testudines
Family: Proganochelyidae
Range: Europe (Germany)
Pn: pro-gan-oh-KEEL-is

Size: 12 feet (4 m) long
Order: Testudines
Family: Protostegidae
Range: North America (Kansas, South Dakota)
Pn: ar-KEE-lon

Meiolania

This large turtle had large bony spikes on its head. Two of these stuck out on either side, giving the head a width of about 2 feet (60 cm), and they would have made it impossible for *Meiolania* to withdraw its head into its shell. The tail was encased in bony armor and ended in a spiked club.

Size: 8 feet (2.5 m) long
Order: Testudines
Family: Meiolaniidae
Range: Australia
Pn: MY-oh-LAN-ee-ah

Size: 6 feet 6 inches (2 m) long
Order: Testudines
Family: Podocnemididae
Range: South America (Venezuela)
Pn: stup-END-em-is

Stupendemys

The largest freshwater turtle ever, *Stupendemys* has been extinct for about 3 million years. In comparison, the largest freshwater turtle today is only 2 feet 6 inches (75 cm) long. This giant lived in water, where it probably fed on weeds, like aquatic turtles today.

Palaeotrionyx

Palaeotrionyx was a soft-shelled turtle. Its low, rounded shell did not have a covering of horn protecting the bony plates. Instead, a layer of leathery skin covered the shell. It had a long, mobile neck and a sharp beak, which it probably used to crop aquatic weeds and snap up insects and small fishes.

Size: 8 feet (2.5 m) long
Order: Testudines
Family: Testudinidae
Range: Asia (India)
Pn: TEST-oo-doh-AT-las

Size: 1 foot 6 inches (45 cm) long
Order: Testudines
Family: Trionychidae
Range: North America
Pn: PAY-lee-oh-TRY-on-ix

Testudo atlas

This was the largest land tortoise ever known and may have weighed as much as 4 tons (4 tonnes). It was more than twice the length of the giant tortoises of today. *Testudo* probably fed on plants. If attacked, it would have pulled its head and legs into its heavy, bony shell for protection.

LIZARDS AND SNAKES

Today, lizards and snakes are a highly successful group of reptiles, with more than 7,000 species. They live on every continent except Antarctica. The first known lizards were small, insect-eating creatures that lived in England during the mid-Jurassic. By the Late Jurassic, many different types of lizard had developed. Earlier groups of lizardlike reptiles include the sphenodonts, such as *Planocephalosaurus*, and aquatic reptiles, such as *Hovasaurus*. Snakes may have evolved from slender, water-living reptiles, such as *Pachyrhachis*.

Size: 30 feet (10 m) long
Order: Squamata
Family: Mosasauridae
Range: North America (Kansas)
Pn: PLOT-oh-SAW-rus

Plotosaurus

Mosasaurs, such as *Plotosaurus*, were sea-living lizards. The limbs were adapted into short flippers and at the end of the long tail was a vertical fin. The fin would have helped this marine lizard move its large body through the water.

Planocephalosaurus

The sphenodont group, to which this lizardlike creature belonged, first appeared in the Late Triassic. Today, the only remaining sphenodont is the tuatara, found in New Zealand. A "living fossil," the tuatara has remained unchanged for 220 million years.

Size: 8 inches (20 cm) long
Order: Sphenodontida
Family: Sphenodontidae
Range: Europe (England)
Pn: PLAN-oh-KEF-al-oh-SAW-rus

Size: 5½ inches (14 cm) long
Order: Squamata
Family: Ardeosauridae
Range: Europe (Germany)
Pn: AR-dee-oh-SAW-rus

Ardeosaurus

An early type of gecko, *Ardeosaurus* had the flattened head and large eyes typical of its modern relatives. Like them, it may have hunted insects and spiders at night, snapping them up in powerful jaws. With its slender body, long tail, and legs sprawled out sideways, *Ardeosaurus* looked very like the lizards of today.

Hovasaurus

This lizardlike, aquatic reptile had a tail that was twice the length of its body. The tail, which was deep and flattened from side to side, made an excellent paddle. *Hovasaurus* probably swallowed stones to help it sink in the water when diving for prey.

Size: 1 foot 8 inches (50 cm) long
Order: Eosuchia
Family: Tangasauridae
Range: Africa (Madagascar)
Pn: HOVE-a-SAW-rus

Megalania

Monitor lizards first appeared in the Late Cretaceous and have changed little since. *Megalania* may have weighed four times as much as the Komodo dragon — the largest lizard alive today. It probably hunted large marsupials on the plains of Australia, where it lived.

Size: 26 feet (8 m) long
Order: Squamata
Family: Varanidae
Range: Australia
Pn: MEG-ah-LAN-ee-ah

Size: 2 feet (60 cm) long
Order: Sphenodontia
Family: Pleurosauridae
Range: Europe (Germany)
Pn: PLOO-roh-SAW-rus

Pachyrhachis

A water-living lizard, *Pachyrhachis* had the long body of a snake and the large head of a monitor lizard. It had tiny back legs and swam by snakelike movements of its long body. This reptile may be one of the ancestors of today's snakes.

Size: 3 feet (1 m) long
Order: Squamata
Family: Pachyrhachidae
Range: Asia (Israel)
Pn: PAK-ee-RAK-iss

Pleurosaurus

Pleurosaurus belonged to a group of slender, snakelike sphenodonts that lived in water. The limbs were tiny, probably of little use on land, and the long tail could have been used to move the reptile through water. *Pleurosaurus* had an extremely long body and some species may have had as many as 57 vertebrae.

PLACODONTS AND NOTHOSAURS

During the time of the dinosaurs, there were several groups of marine reptiles living in the seas and oceans of the ancient world. Some, however, such as the Triassic Period placodonts, were equally at home on the shore or in shallow water, searching for shellfish to eat. Nothosaurs were better suited to life in the sea. They were fish eaters and typically had a streamlined body, long tail and webbed feet. Both placodonts and nothosaurs died out at the end of the Triassic. Claudiosaurs were an earlier group of semiaquatic reptiles that lived in the Late Permian. They may have been a link between land-living reptiles and later marine reptiles, including nothosaurs and plesiosaurs.

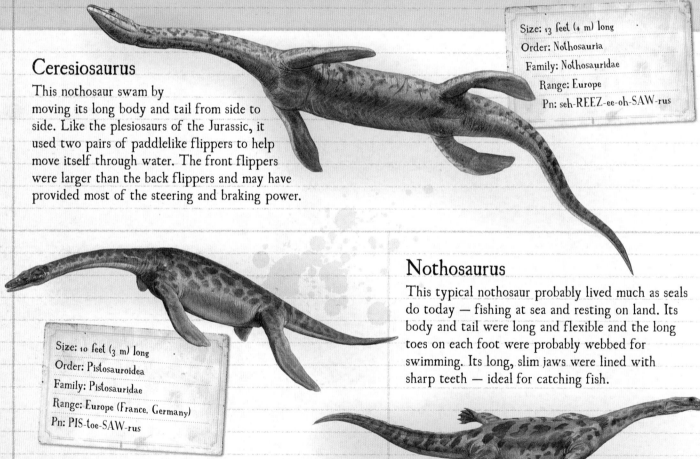

Ceresiosaurus

This nothosaur swam by moving its long body and tail from side to side. Like the plesiosaurs of the Jurassic, it used two pairs of paddlelike flippers to help move itself through water. The front flippers were larger than the back flippers and may have provided most of the steering and braking power.

Size: 13 feet (4 m) long
Order: Nothosauria
Family: Nothosauridae
Range: Europe
Pn: seh-REEZ-ee-oh-SAW-rus

Nothosaurus

This typical nothosaur probably lived much as seals do today — fishing at sea and resting on land. Its body and tail were long and flexible and the long toes on each foot were probably webbed for swimming. Its long, slim jaws were lined with sharp teeth — ideal for catching fish.

Size: 10 feet (3 m) long
Order: Pistosauroidea
Family: Pistosauridae
Range: Europe (France, Germany)
Pn: PIS-toe-SAW-rus

Pistosaurus

This marine reptile had features of both the nothosaurs and the plesiosaurs. Its body was similar to that of other nothosaurs, but it had a stiff backbone like the plesiosaurs. This meant that it used its paddlelike limbs to push itself through water instead of moving its body and tail.

Size: 10 feet (3 m) long
Order: Nothosauria
Family: Nothosauridae
Range: Asia (China, Israel, Russia), Europe, North Africa
Pn: NOTH-oh-SAW-rus

Henodus

This placodont had a square-shaped body covered with bony plates. These made a strong shell to protect it from attack by other marine reptiles, such as ichthyosaurs. Although toothless, *Henodus* probably had a horn-covered beak like that of a turtle, which it could use to crush prey such as shellfish.

Size: 3 feet (1 m) long
Order: Placodontia
Family: Henodontidae
Range: Europe (Germany)
Pn: HEN-oh-dus

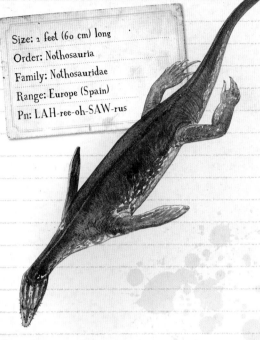

Size: 2 feet (60 cm) long
Order: Nothosauria
Family: Nothosauridae
Range: Europe (Spain)
Pn: LAH-ree-oh-SAW-rus

Lariosaurus

One of the smaller nothosaurs, *Lariosaurus* probably spent much of its time walking on the shore and paddling in shallow coastal water, feeding on small fishes and shrimp. It had a shorter neck than most nothosaurs and small toes that would not have been much use for swimming.

Claudiosaurus

This lizardlike creature probably lived much like modern marine iguanas. Like them, it may have spent a good deal of its time resting on rocky beaches, warming its body before going hunting. In water, it held its legs against its body to give a more streamlined shape as it searched for food among seaweeds and rocks.

Size: 2 feet (60 cm) long
Order: Neodiapsida
Family: Claudiosauridae
Range: Africa (Madagascar)
Pn: CLAWED-ee-oh-SAW-rus

Placodus

Placodus had a stocky body, and its only aquatic features were its webbed feet and long tail. Its teeth suggest that it fed mostly on shellfish. *Placodus* may have plucked shellfish from the rocks with the blunt teeth sticking out at the front of its jaws and then crushed them with the broad, flat back teeth.

Size: 6 feet 6 inches (2 m) long
Order: Placodontia
Family: Placodontidae
Range: Europe (the Alps)
Pn: PLAK-oh-dus

PLESIOSAURS AND ICHTHYOSAURS

Plesiosaurs and ichthyosaurs were the most successful of all the marine reptiles. They dominated the world's seas throughout the Jurassic and Cretaceous periods. There were two groups of plesiosaurs — pliosaurs and the plesiosaurs themselves. Plesiosaurs had long necks and short heads and fed on smaller sea creatures. Pliosaurs were fierce hunters. With their powerful jaws, they could catch sharks and large squid. The ichthyosaurs were best adapted of all to marine life. Typically, they had a streamlined, fishlike body and a tail that could beat from side to side to power their high-speed swimming.

Size: 12 feet (3.5 m) long
Order: Ichthyosauria
Family: Ichthyosauridae
Range: Europe (England, France), western North America, South America (Argentina)
Pn: OFF-thal-moh-SAW-rus

Ophthalmosaurus

This ichthyosaur had huge eyes, measuring up to 4 inches (10 cm) across. A ring of bony plates surrounded each eyeball to keep the soft eye from collapsing under the pressure of the water. The large eyes of the *Ophthalmosaurus* suggest that it hunted at night.

Size: 6 feet 6 inches (2 m) long
Order: Ichthyopterygia
Family: Ichthyosauridae
Range: Europe (England, Germany), North America (Alberta, Greenland)
Pn: IK-thee-oh-SAW-rus

Ichthyosaurus

So many fossils of *Ichthyosaurus* have been found that it is one of the best known of all prehistoric animals. In some of these fossils, the tiny bones of young were inside the adult bodies, showing that ichthyosaurs, like dolphins today, gave birth to live young at sea.

Size: 49 feet (15 m) long
Order: Ichthyosauria
Family: Shastasauridae
Range: North America (Nevada)
Pn: SHOWN-ih-SAW-rus

Shonisaurus

The biggest of the ichthyosaurs, *Shonisaurus* had extremely long jaws, with teeth only at the front. All of its paddlelike flippers were about the same length — in most ichthyosaurs the front flippers were longer than the back pair.

Kronosaurus

The largest known pliosaur, *Kronosaurus* had a huge, flat-topped skull, measuring almost a quarter of its total body length. A fierce predator, it moved at high speed, flapping its strong flippers up and down as though flying through the water.

Size: 42 feet (13 m) long
Order: Plesiosauria
Family: Pliosauridae
Range: Australia (Queensland)
Pn: KRONE-oh-SAW-rus

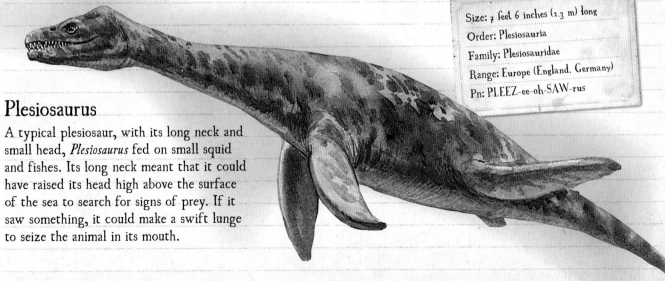

Size: 7 feet 6 inches (2.3 m) long
Order: Plesiosauria
Family: Plesiosauridae
Range: Europe (England, Germany)
Pn: PLEEZ-ee-oh-SAW-rus

Plesiosaurus

A typical plesiosaur, with its long neck and small head, *Plesiosaurus* fed on small squid and fishes. Its long neck meant that it could have raised its head high above the surface of the sea to search for signs of prey. If it saw something, it could make a swift lunge to seize the animal in its mouth.

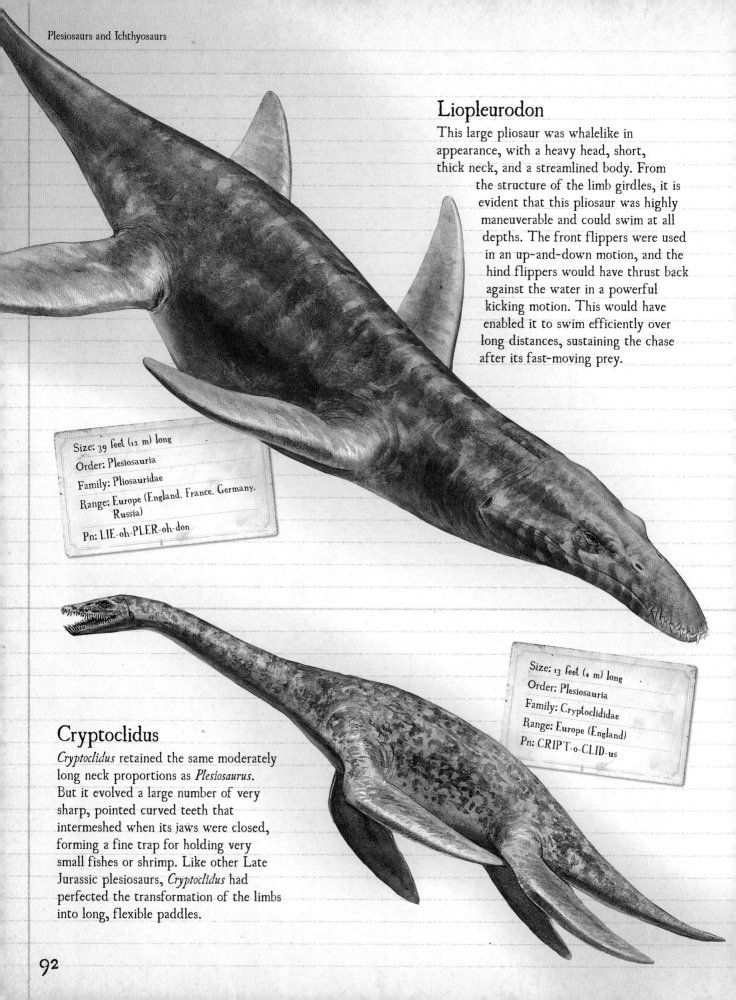

Liopleurodon

This large pliosaur was whalelike in appearance, with a heavy head, short, thick neck, and a streamlined body. From the structure of the limb girdles, it is evident that this pliosaur was highly maneuverable and could swim at all depths. The front flippers were used in an up-and-down motion, and the hind flippers would have thrust back against the water in a powerful kicking motion. This would have enabled it to swim efficiently over long distances, sustaining the chase after its fast-moving prey.

Size: 39 feet (12 m) long
Order: Plesiosauria
Family: Pliosauridae
Range: Europe (England, France, Germany, Russia)
Pn: LIE-oh-PLER-oh-don

Size: 13 feet (4 m) long
Order: Plesiosauria
Family: Cryptoclididae
Range: Europe (England)
Pn: CRIPT-o-CLID-us

Cryptoclidus

Cryptoclidus retained the same moderately long neck proportions as *Plesiosaurus*. But it evolved a large number of very sharp, pointed curved teeth that intermeshed when its jaws were closed, forming a fine trap for holding very small fishes or shrimp. Like other Late Jurassic plesiosaurs, *Cryptoclidus* had perfected the transformation of the limbs into long, flexible paddles.

Peloneustes

Although smaller than *Macroplata*, this pliosaur had a head and neck of almost equal length. *Peloneustes'* more streamlined shape enabled it to swim rapidly after its fast-moving prey. Its teeth were adapted to its diet, being fewer and less sharp than those of the fish-eating plesiosaurs, and better for catching soft-bodied squid and crushing the hard shells of ammonites.

Size: 10 feet (3 m) long
Order: Plesiosauria
Family: Pliosauridae
Range: Europe (England, Russia)
Pn: PEL-on-OO-stes

Macroplata

This early pliosaur had a slender crocodile-like skull, which was only a little larger proportionally than that of early plesiosaurs. It still had a long neck, with 29 slightly shortened vertebrae, which was twice the length of its head. The pliosaurs progressively improved the limbs into powerful paddles.

Size: 20 feet (6 m) long
Order: Plesiosauria
Family: Cryptocleididae
Range: Europe (England, France)
Pn: moo-RAYN-oh-SAW-rus

Muraenosaurus

The neck of *Muraenosaurus* was as long as its body and tail combined and was supported by 44 vertebrae. The head, perched at the end of this cranelike neck, was tiny — only about $1/16$ of the total body length. Its stout, rigid body would have helped to make the flippers more effective propulsion organs.

Size: 15 feet (4.5 m) long
Order: Plesiosauria
Family: Rhomaleosauridae
Range: Europe (England)
Pn: MAC-ro-PLAR-ta

93

Eurhinosaurus

This extraordinary-looking ichthyosaur had an upper jaw that was twice the length of its lower jaw, giving it the appearance of a modern sawfish. Teeth stuck out sideways along the bladelike projection, but the function of this strange structure is not known for sure.

Size: 6 feet 6 inches (2 m) long
Order: Ichthyosauria
Family: Leptonectidae
Range: Europe (Germany)
Pn: yur-RIN-oh-SAW-rus

Stenopterygius

A find of ichthyosaur skeletons near Holzmaden in Germany includes well-preserved specimens of *Stenopterygius*. *Stenopterygius* was similar in build to *Ichthyosaurus*, but it had a smaller head and the narrow paddles characteristic of its family.

Size: 10 feet (3 m) long
Order: Ichthyosauria
Family: Stenopterygiidae
Range: Europe (England, Germany)
Pn: sten-OP-terr-idge-EE-us

Size: 33 feet (10 m) long
Order: Ichthyosauria
Family: Cymbospondylidae
Range: North America (Nevada)
Pn: sim-BOS-pon-DIL-us

Cymbospondylus

This large ichthyosaur was one of the least fishlike of the group. With a long body and tail, there was no fin on its back nor on its tail, features that were to develop in later ichthyosaurs. It did have the typical long, beaklike jaws and pointed teeth — the sign of a fish eater.

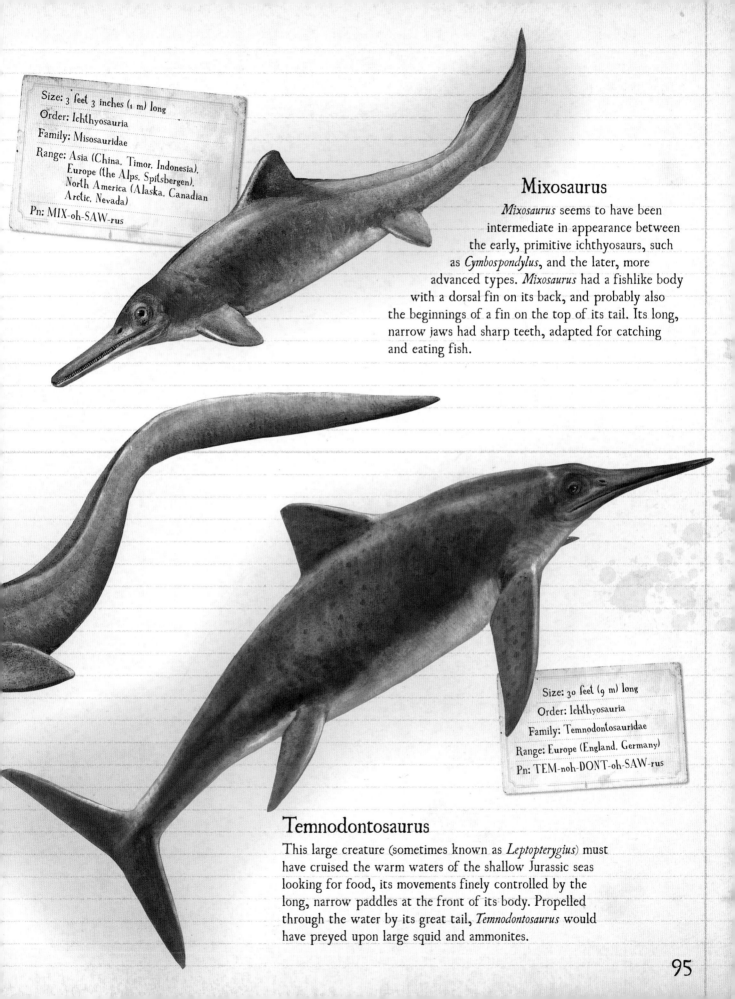

Size: 3 feet 3 inches (1 m) long
Order: Ichthyosauria
Family: Misosauridae
Range: Asia (China, Timor, Indonesia),
Europe (the Alps, Spitsbergen),
North America (Alaska, Canadian
Arctic, Nevada)
Pn: MIX-oh-SAW-rus

Mixosaurus

Mixosaurus seems to have been intermediate in appearance between the early, primitive ichthyosaurs, such as *Cymbospondylus*, and the later, more advanced types. *Mixosaurus* had a fishlike body with a dorsal fin on its back, and probably also the beginnings of a fin on the top of its tail. Its long, narrow jaws had sharp teeth, adapted for catching and eating fish.

Size: 30 feet (9 m) long
Order: Ichthyosauria
Family: Temnodontosauridae
Range: Europe (England, Germany)
Pn: TEM-noh-DONT-oh-SAW-rus

Temnodontosaurus

This large creature (sometimes known as *Leptopterygius*) must have cruised the warm waters of the shallow Jurassic seas looking for food, its movements finely controlled by the long, narrow paddles at the front of its body. Propelled through the water by its great tail, *Temnodontosaurus* would have preyed upon large squid and ammonites.

SEA CREATURES

In the time of the dinosaurs, the seas were packed with life. Fishes with bodies protected by thick bony scales, such as *Lepidotes*, hunted worms, mollusks and other small creatures. Crinoids, animals related to starfish, lived on the seabed, catching tiny prey in their feathery, multibranched arms. Also common were belemnites and ammonites, extinct relatives of octopus and squid. Ammonites had a soft body coiled inside a shell with many chambers, whereas belemnites had a straight body and long tentacles, similar to today's squid. Among the biggest creatures were the many types of marine reptiles, such as ichthyosaurs and plesiosaurs, which cruised the oceans preying on fishes, squid and belemnites.

UNDERWATER BIRTH

Ichthyosaurs are thought to have given birth underwater. The young came out tail first, like those of dolphins and whales. This fossil shows a female ichthyosaur with her young just emerging from her body.

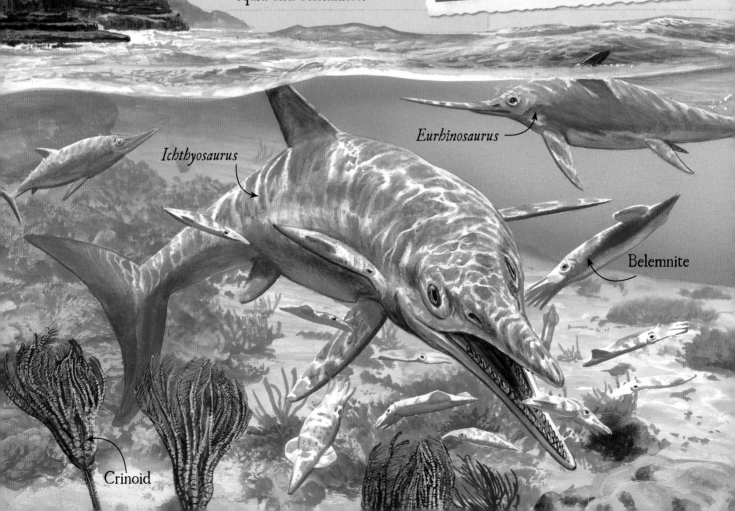

Dimorphodon

Ichthyosaurus

Eurhinosaurus

Belemnite

Crinoid

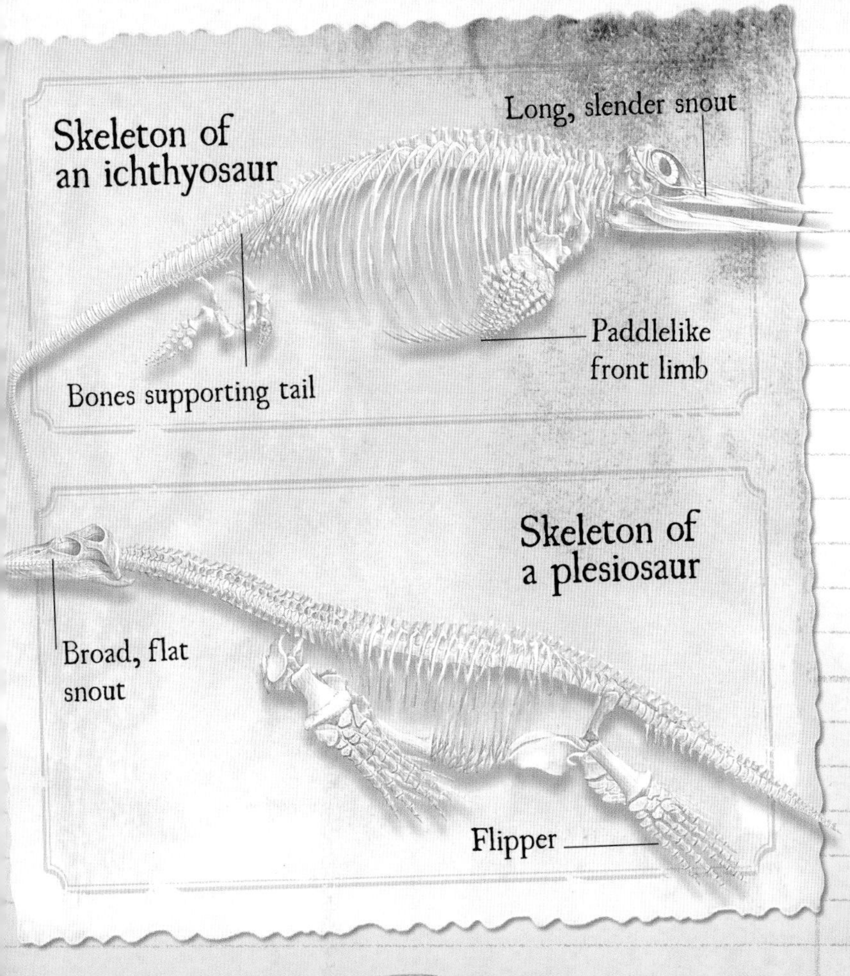

MARINE REPTILES

Skeleton of
an ichthyosaur

Long, slender snout

Paddlelike
front limb

Bones supporting tail

Skeleton of
a plesiosaur

Broad, flat
snout

Flipper

A typical ichthyosaur had a streamlined body, similar to that of a dolphin today. The main swimming power was provided by the large tail, which beat back and forth as the reptile sped through the water. The paddlelike front limbs were used for steering. A plesiosaur swam more slowly, beating its large flippers to move itself along. In contrast to an ichthyosaur, a plesiosaur had a short tail, long neck, and relatively small head.

In this Jurassic ocean, a school of belemnites scatters as an *Ichthyosaurus* swims into them, grasping prey in its long jaws. Meanwhile another ichthyosaur, an *Eurhinosaurus*, rises to the surface to take a breath.

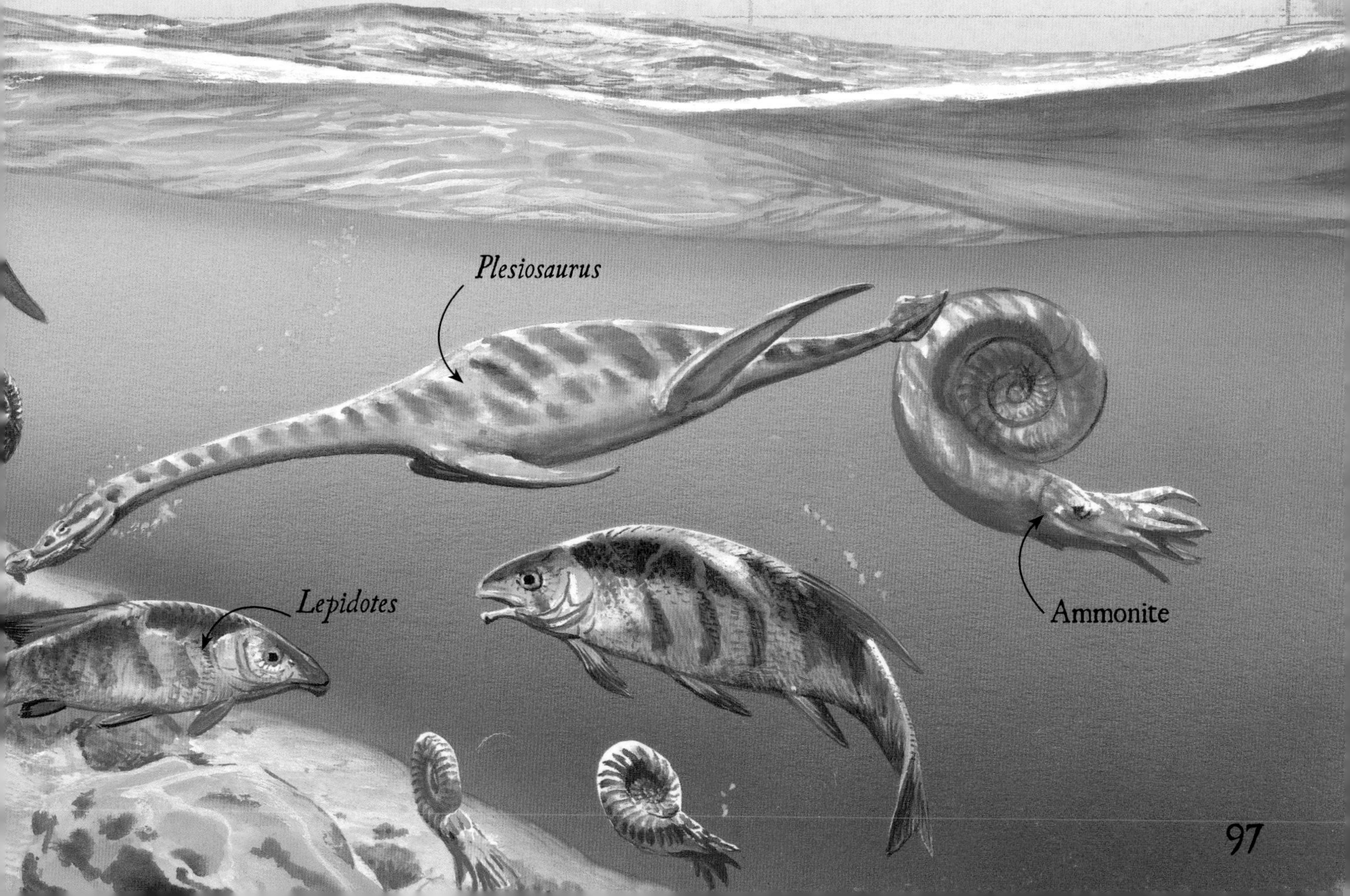

Plesiosaurus

Ammonite

Lepidotes

EARLY RULING REPTILES

Archosaurs, or ruling reptiles, were the group to which dinosaurs belonged. There were several different groups of archosaurs, but the only ones that survive today are the crocodiles. Among the earliest were the proterosuchids, some of which were hunters that resembled crocodiles.

Others lived on land. Later came the crurotarsans, such as *Ornithosuchus*, and the aquatic phytosaurs. Aetosaurs, such as *Desmatosuchus*, were the first plant-eating archosaurs, and they spread throughout much of the world.

Size: 16 feet (5 m) long
Order: Aetosauria
Family: Stagenolepididae
Range: North America (Texas)
Pn: DEZ-mat-oh-SOOK-us

Desmatosuchus

Despite its fierce appearance, *Desmatosuchus* was a plant eater with small, leaf-shaped teeth. The bulky body was encased in heavy plates of bone. A pair of spines, up to 1 foot 6 inches (45 cm) long, projected sideways from its shoulders. The body armor defended bulky, slow-moving *Desmatosuchus* from predators.

Euparkeria

This little archosaur was a slimly built creature with a light armor of bony plates running down its back and tail. It could probably rear up on its back legs to run away from danger, and its long tail would have helped balance its body as it ran. A carnivore, it had sharp teeth.

Size: 10 feet (3 m) long
Order: Pseudosuchia
Family: Ornithosuchidae
Range: Europe (Scotland)
Pn: OR-nith-oh-SOOK-us

Size: 20 inches (50 cm) long
Order: Archosauriformes
Family: Euparkeriidae
Range: Africa (South Africa)
Pn: YOO-park-EE-ree-a

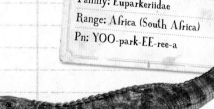

Ornithosuchus

Ornithosuchus looked remarkably like a dinosaur. Its back legs were held vertically beneath its body and it could probably move upright on two legs. The structure of its ankle joints, however, was different from that of true dinosaurs.

Hyperodapedon

Hyperodapedon were heavy, barrel-shaped plant eaters, and the most abundant reptiles of the day. The success, though short-lived, of *Hyperodapedon* and its rhynchosaur relatives can be attributed to their teeth. In its upper jaw, there were several rows of teeth and a groove running down the middle, into which the lower jaw teeth fitted when closed. This gave a strong chopping action, which was well suited to the animal's vegetarian diet.

Size: 4 feet 3 inches (1.3 m) long
Order: Rhynchosauria
Family: Hyperodapedontidae
Range: Asia, Europe
Pn: HI-per-o-dap-EE-don

Size: 4 feet 3 inches (1.3 m) long
Order: Dinosauriformes
Family: uncertain
Range: South America (Argentina)
Pn: MAH-rah-SOOK-us

Marasuchus

This reptile shared many skeletal features with dinosaurs, such as front legs that were less than half the length of the back legs. Lightly built and a fast mover, it may have run upright on its back legs as well as on all fours. *Marasuchus* would have fed on small reptiles and insects.

Erythrosuchus

This early archosaur was one of the biggest land predators of its time. It had a large head and strong jaws lined with sharp teeth. Its legs were held more directly under the body than those of the sprawling *Proterosuchus*, allowing it to move well on land.

Size: 15 feet (4.5 m) long
Order: Archosauriformes
Family: Erythrosuchidae
Range: Africa (South Africa)
Pn: er-ITH-ro-SOOK-us

99

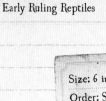

Size: 6 inches (15 cm) long

Order: Sauropsida

Family: Longisquamidae

Range: Central Asia

Pn: LONG-ih-SQUAM-a

Longisquama

A curious, lizardlike creature, *Longisquama* was a tiny ornithosuchid. A remarkable row of tall scales, stiff and V-shaped, rose from its back. Their function is unknown. They could have been used for attracting a mate or warning away rivals, for gliding through the air, or as heat-exchange devices; they may even have been an early stage in the evolution of feathers.

Stagonolepis

The deep body of *Stagonolepis* is typical of the herbivorous aetosaurs and was developed to accommodate the longer intestines needed to digest plant food. A slow-moving browser, *Stagonolepis* also needed its heavy body armor to protect itself from attack by its agile, carnivorous relatives. *Stagonolepis* had a small head for its size and a flattened snout, a good shape for rooting in the undergrowth.

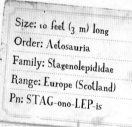

Size: 10 feet (3 m) long

Order: Aetosauria

Family: Stagenolepididae

Range: Europe (Scotland)

Pn: STAG-ono-LEP-is

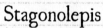

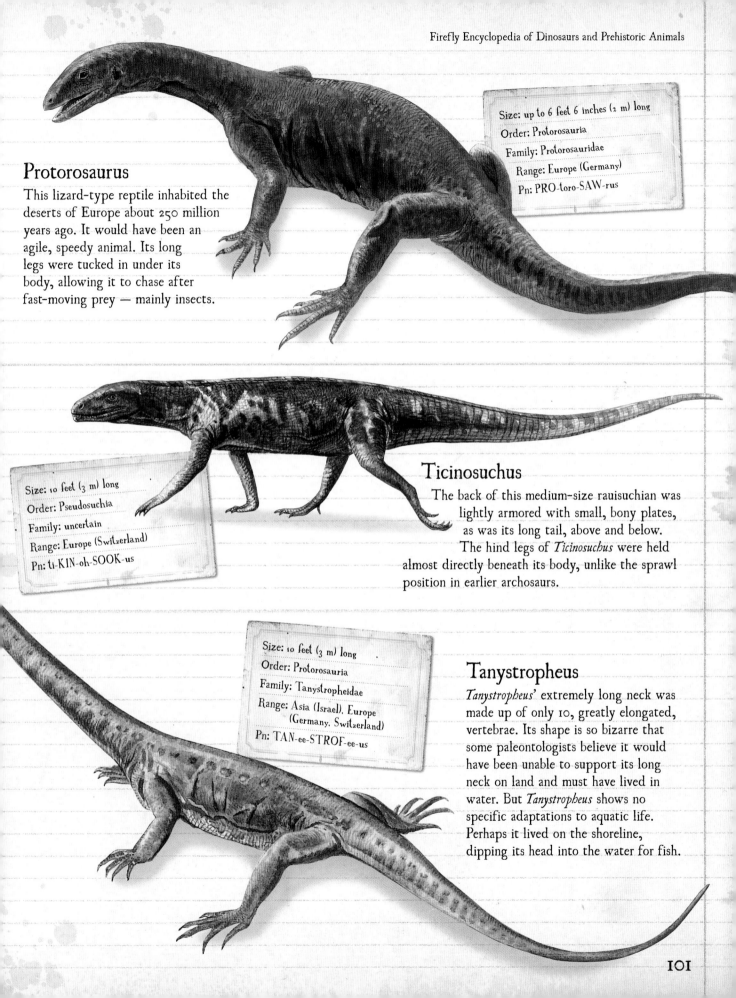

Protorosaurus

This lizard-type reptile inhabited the deserts of Europe about 250 million years ago. It would have been an agile, speedy animal. Its long legs were tucked in under its body, allowing it to chase after fast-moving prey — mainly insects.

Size: up to 6 feet 6 inches (2 m) long
Order: Protorosauria
Family: Protorosauridae
Range: Europe (Germany)
Pn: PRO-toro-SAW-rus

Size: 10 feet (3 m) long
Order: Pseudosuchia
Family: uncertain
Range: Europe (Switzerland)
Pn: ti-KIN-oh-SOOK-us

Ticinosuchus

The back of this medium-size rauisuchian was lightly armored with small, bony plates, as was its long tail, above and below. The hind legs of *Ticinosuchus* were held almost directly beneath its body, unlike the sprawl position in earlier archosaurs.

Size: 10 feet (3 m) long
Order: Protorosauria
Family: Tanystropheidae
Range: Asia (Israel), Europe (Germany, Switzerland)
Pn: TAN-ee-STROF-ee-us

Tanystropheus

Tanystropheus' extremely long neck was made up of only 10, greatly elongated, vertebrae. Its shape is so bizarre that some paleontologists believe it would have been unable to support its long neck on land and must have lived in water. But *Tanystropheus* shows no specific adaptations to aquatic life. Perhaps it lived on the shoreline, dipping its head into the water for fish.

CROCODILES

The first crocodiles appeared in the Triassic, some 220 million years ago. They are the only members of the archosaur, or ruling reptile, group alive today. The earliest examples of the order Crocodylia, such as *Terrestrisuchus*, were lightly built long-legged creatures that probably fed on insects. True crocodiles evolved in the Jurassic and look remarkably similar to modern crocodiles. Some lived on land, whereas others were semiaquatic as crocodiles are today. A few families, such as the metriorhynchs, were adapted to life in the sea. All crocodiles, even the early ones, have long narrow skulls with muscles set far back to allow the jaws to open wide for grasping large prey.

Size: 50 feet (15 m) long
Order: Crocodylia
Superfamily: Alligatoroidea
Range: North America (Texas)
Pn: DINE-oh-SOOK-us

Deinosuchus

Only a skull, measuring more than 6 feet 6 inches (2 m), has been found of *Deinosuchus*, showing that it was probably the biggest crocodile of all time. It may have lived like the crocodiles of today, but some scientists believe that *Deinosuchus* had longer legs than modern crocodiles and lived on land, preying on dinosaurs.

Size: 10 feet (3 m) long
Order: Mesoeucrocodylia
Family: Metriorhynchidae
Range: Europe (England, France),
South America (Chile)
Pn: MET-ree-oh-RINK-us

Metriorhynchus

This crocodile and other members of its family were well adapted for life in the sea. Its limbs were paddlelike flippers and its tail had a large fishlike fin for swimming. It did not have bony protective plates on its body like crocodiles today — these would have made its body too heavy in the water.

Terrestrisuchus

An early member of the crocodile group, this lightly built reptile had long back legs and may have moved upright. It probably fed on insects and other small creatures. Although *Terrestrisuchus* does not look like a crocodile, there are many typical features of the group in the bone structure of its skull and front limbs.

Size: 1 foot 8 inches (50 cm) long
Order: Crocodylomorpha
Family: Saltoposuchidae
Range: Europe (Wales)
Pn: ter-EST-ri-SOOK-us

Size: 2 feet (60 cm) long
Order: Crocodylomorpha
Family: Bernissartiidae
Range: Europe (Belgium, England)
Pn: BER-nih-SART-ee-ah

Bernissartia

This little crocodile probably lived in water and on land. It had two types of teeth in its jaws. At the front were long, pointed teeth, suitable for catching fishes. At the back were broader, flatter teeth, which could have been used to crush shellfish or the bones of dead animals.

Protosuchus

Fossils of *Protosuchus* have been found in the same rocks as the remains of dinosaurs. This suggests that this land-living crocodile preyed on other land creatures. Like today's crocodiles, *Protosuchus* had a pair of long teeth at the front of the lower jaw that fitted into notches on the upper jaw when the mouth was closed.

Size: 3 feet (1 m) long
Order: Crocodylomorpha
Family: Protosuchidae
Range: North America (Arizona)
Pn: PROE-toh-SOOK-us

Size: 10 feet (3 m) long
Order: Mesoeucrocodylia
Family: Teleosauridae
Range: Europe (France)
Pn: TELL-ee-oh-SAW-rus

Teleosaurus

A sea-living crocodile, *Teleosaurus* had extremely long, narrow jaws lined with many sharp teeth. These teeth interlocked when the mouth was closed, forming a trap ideal for catching slippery fishes or squid. It probably swam by moving its long slender body and tail, with its short front legs held against its body.

PREHISTORIC FLIGHT

Pterosaurs lived at the same time as dinosaurs and may share the same ancestor. Scientists now believe that these flying reptiles were good, if slow, fliers, able to flap their wings as birds do, instead of gliding through the air. It was thought that they could not take off from the ground but required an elevated perch. It is now known that many could take off from the ground. Pterosaurs ate a range of foods. Those with long skulls and sharp teeth probably fed on fish. Others ate insects or even plants. *Tapejara's* long beak, for example, may have been used to pick fruit.

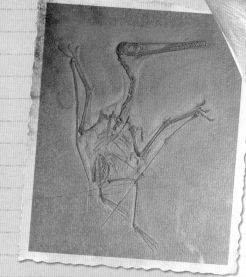

This pterosaur, named *Pterodactylus*, lived in Europe in Jurassic times. The well-preserved fossil clearly shows the body structure, including the long slender jaws.

Santanadactylus

Cearadactylus

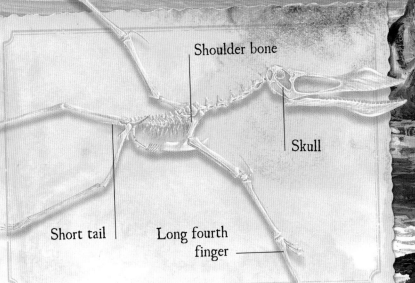

PTEROSAUR SKELETON

A pterosaur had an extremely light skeleton that allowed it to fly. Its bones were slender and many were also hollow to make them lighter still. Its first three fingers were short and tipped with sharp claws, but the fourth finger was very long and helped to support the wing. The wing was also attached to the side of the body. On each foot were five toes. Four were long and tipped with claws. The fifth toe was short and did not have a claw.

Shoulder bone

Skull

Short tail

Long fourth finger

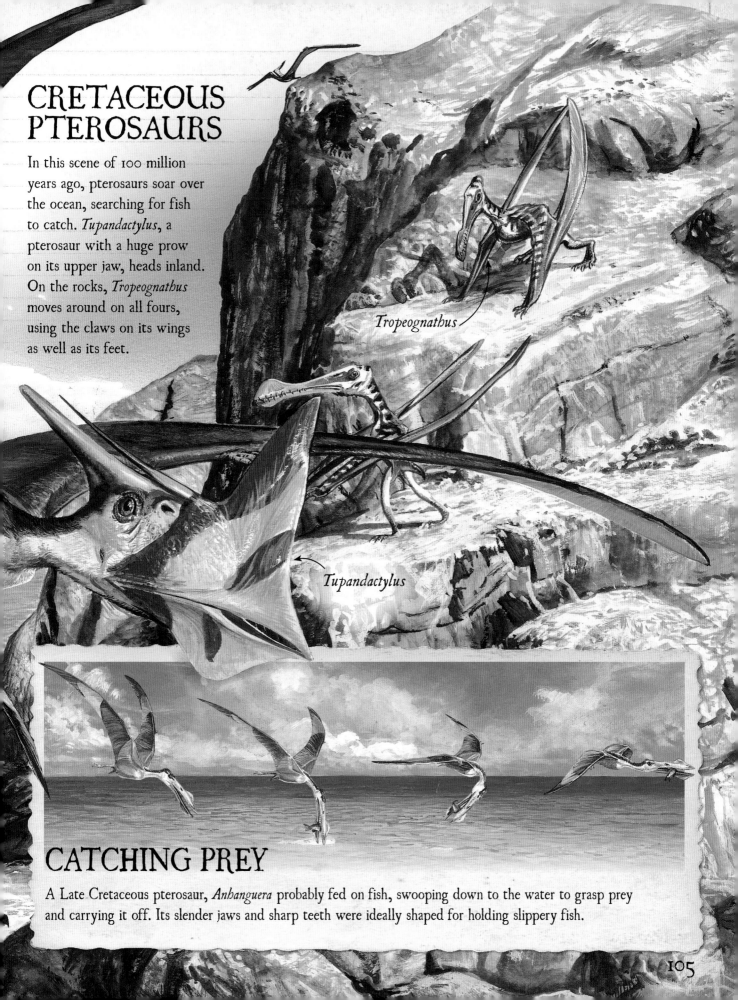

CRETACEOUS PTEROSAURS

In this scene of 100 million years ago, pterosaurs soar over the ocean, searching for fish to catch. *Tupandactylus*, a pterosaur with a huge prow on its upper jaw, heads inland. On the rocks, *Tropeognathus* moves around on all fours, using the claws on its wings as well as its feet.

Tropeognathus

Tupandactylus

CATCHING PREY

A Late Cretaceous pterosaur, *Anhanguera* probably fed on fish, swooping down to the water to grasp prey and carrying it off. Its slender jaws and sharp teeth were ideally shaped for holding slippery fish.

FLYING REPTILES

Pterosaurs were the first vertebrates (animals with backbones) to take to life in the air. They first evolved in the Late Triassic and became extinct at the end of the Cretaceous at the same time as the dinosaurs. More than 120 different species of pterosaur have been discovered so far. The earliest were the rhamphorhynchoids, which had a long tail and short neck. Later came the pterodactyloids, which grew much larger and typically had short tail and long neck and skull.

Size: 2 feet 6 inches (75 cm) wingspan
Order: Eudimorphodontidae
Family: Dimorphodontidae
Range: Europe (Italy)
Pn: yoo-dee-MORF-oh-don

Eudimorphodon

This rhamphorhynchoid is one of the earliest pterosaurs known. It had a long bony tail, which made up about half its total length. Like many other pterosaurs, it had a small diamond-shaped flap at the tip of the tail that may have acted like a rudder to help the pterosaur change direction in the air.

Size: 3 feet (1 m) wingspan
Order: Pterosauria
Family: Dimorphodontidae
Range: Europe (Germany),
    Africa (Tanzania)
Pn: dy-MORF-oh-don

Dimorphodon

This pterosaur had an unusually large head, similar in shape to a puffin's. Inside the mouth were two types of teeth — spiky ones at the front and much smaller teeth farther back. These may have helped the pterosaur to catch insects in the air or on the ground.

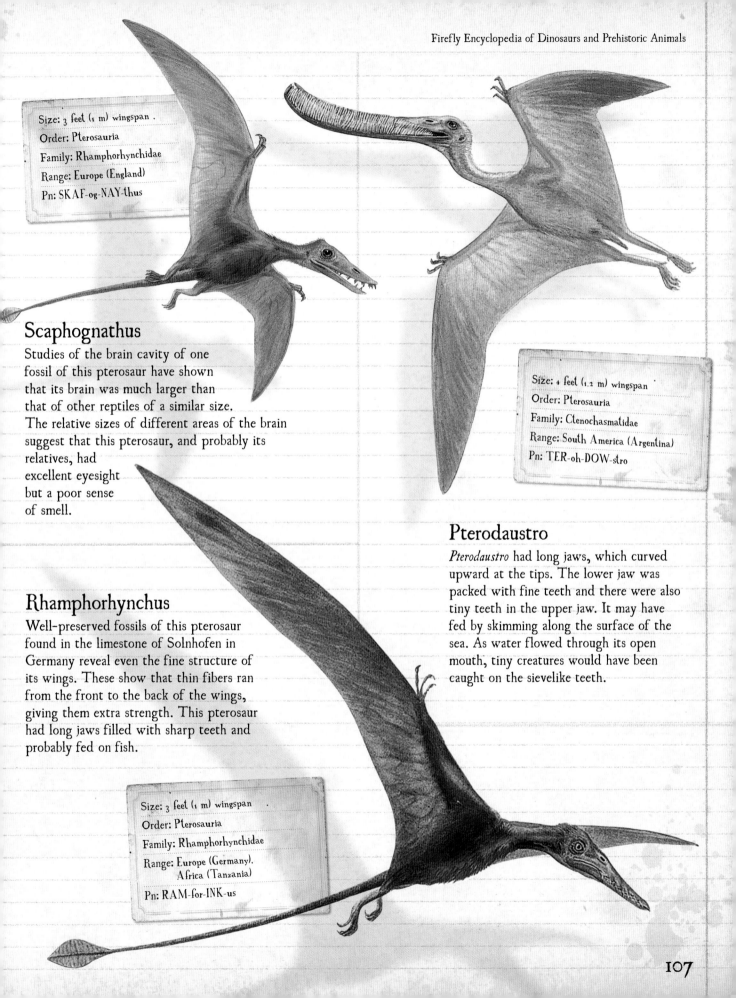

Size: 3 feet (1 m) wingspan.
Order: Pterosauria
Family: Rhamphorhynchidae
Range: Europe (England)
Pn: SKAF-og-NAY-thus

Scaphognathus

Studies of the brain cavity of one fossil of this pterosaur have shown that its brain was much larger than that of other reptiles of a similar size. The relative sizes of different areas of the brain suggest that this pterosaur, and probably its relatives, had excellent eyesight but a poor sense of smell.

Size: 4 feet (1.2 m) wingspan
Order: Pterosauria
Family: Ctenochasmatidae
Range: South America (Argentina)
Pn: TER-oh-DOW-stro

Pterodaustro

Pterodaustro had long jaws, which curved upward at the tips. The lower jaw was packed with fine teeth and there were also tiny teeth in the upper jaw. It may have fed by skimming along the surface of the sea. As water flowed through its open mouth, tiny creatures would have been caught on the sievelike teeth.

Rhamphorhynchus

Well-preserved fossils of this pterosaur found in the limestone of Solnhofen in Germany reveal even the fine structure of its wings. These show that thin fibers ran from the front to the back of the wings, giving them extra strength. This pterosaur had long jaws filled with sharp teeth and probably fed on fish.

Size: 3 feet (1 m) wingspan.
Order: Pterosauria
Family: Rhamphorhynchidae
Range: Europe (Germany),
       Africa (Tanzania)
Pn: RAM-for-INK-us

Dsungaripterus

Dsungaripterus had a peculiar bony crest running along its snout, and long, narrow jaws that curved upward to a fine point at the tip. These forcepslike jaws could have been used to pry shellfish off rocks or out of crannies on the seashore. The flattened teeth at the back of the jaws crushed the shells.

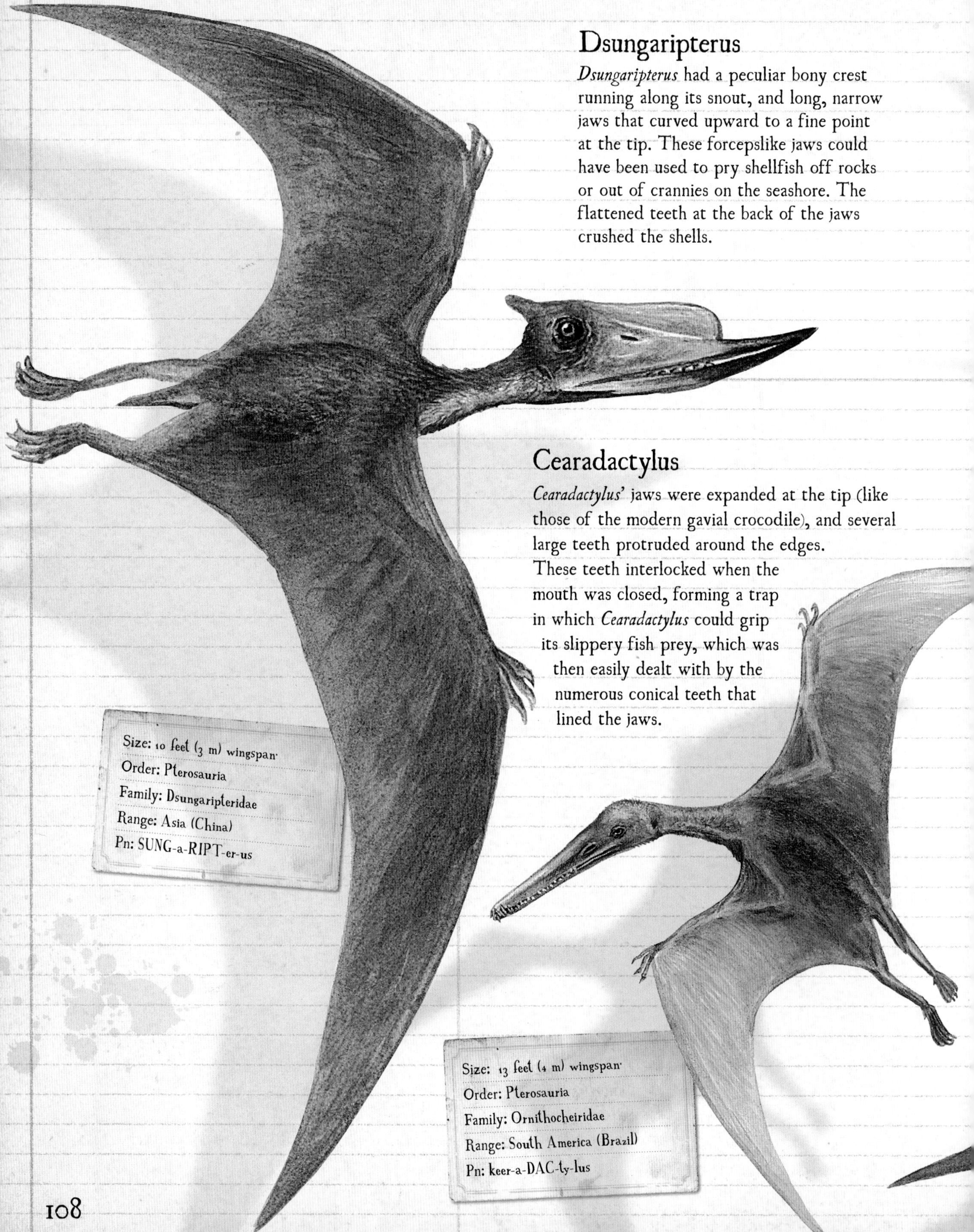

Cearadactylus

Cearadactylus' jaws were expanded at the tip (like those of the modern gavial crocodile), and several large teeth protruded around the edges. These teeth interlocked when the mouth was closed, forming a trap in which *Cearadactylus* could grip its slippery fish prey, which was then easily dealt with by the numerous conical teeth that lined the jaws.

Size: 10 feet (3 m) wingspan
Order: Pterosauria
Family: Dsungaripteridae
Range: Asia (China)
Pn: SUNG-a-RIPT-er-us

Size: 13 feet (4 m) wingspan
Order: Pterosauria
Family: Ornithocheiridae
Range: South America (Brazil)
Pn: keer-a-DAC-ty-lus

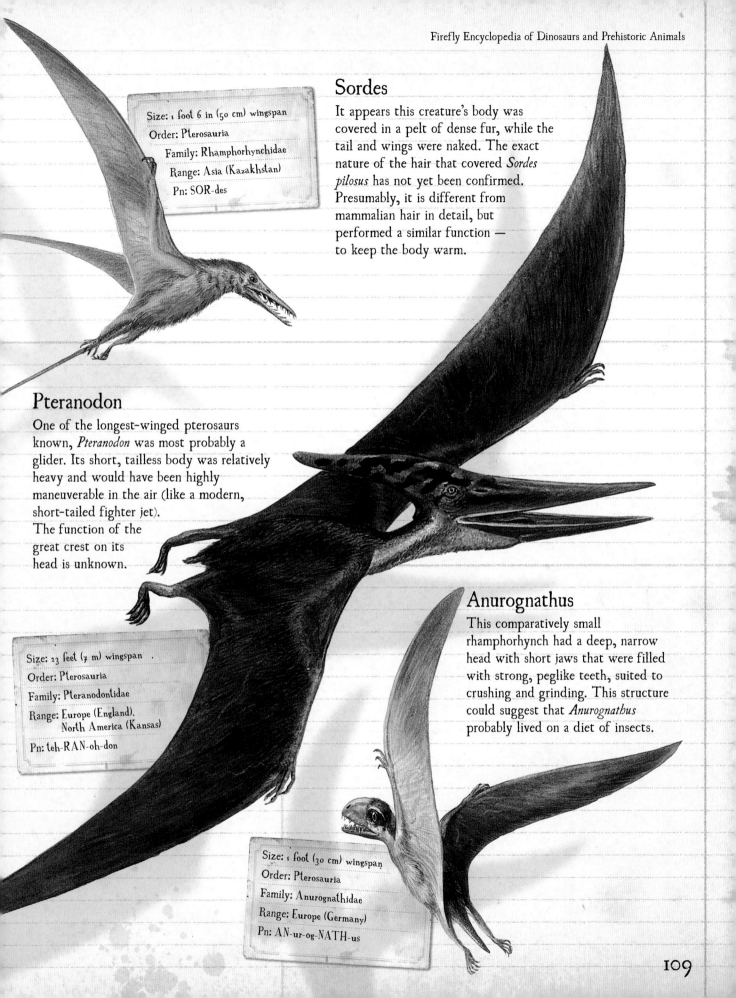

Sordes

It appears this creature's body was covered in a pelt of dense fur, while the tail and wings were naked. The exact nature of the hair that covered *Sordes pilosus* has not yet been confirmed. Presumably, it is different from mammalian hair in detail, but performed a similar function — to keep the body warm.

Size: 1 foot 6 in (50 cm) wingspan

Order: Pterosauria

Family: Rhamphorhynchidae

Range: Asia (Kazakhstan)

Pn: SOR-des

Pteranodon

One of the longest-winged pterosaurs known, *Pteranodon* was most probably a glider. Its short, tailless body was relatively heavy and would have been highly maneuverable in the air (like a modern, short-tailed fighter jet). The function of the great crest on its head is unknown.

Size: 23 feet (7 m) wingspan .

Order: Pterosauria

Family: Pteranodontidae

Range: Europe (England), North America (Kansas)

Pn: teh-RAN-oh-don

Anurognathus

This comparatively small rhamphorhynch had a deep, narrow head with short jaws that were filled with strong, peglike teeth, suited to crushing and grinding. This structure could suggest that *Anurognathus* probably lived on a diet of insects.

Size: 1 foot (30 cm) wingspan

Order: Pterosauria

Family: Anurognathidae

Range: Europe (Germany)

Pn: AN-ur-og-NATH-us

DINOSAURS

These amazing reptiles were probably the most successful large land animals that have ever lived. The first dinosaurs lived about 225 million years ago, during the Triassic Period, and more and more species developed during the Jurassic and Cretaceous periods. Dinosaurs became large and widespread until the non-avian dinosaurs mysteriously disappeared at the end of the Cretaceous about 65 million years ago.

WHAT WAS A DINOSAUR?

A dinosaur was a type of reptile and had a bony skeleton and thick, leathery skin. Around 800 species of dinosaur have been named so far, and there may be many more yet to be found. They ranged in size from creatures of 3 feet 3 inches (1 m) long to giants of 100 feet (30 m) or more. Dinosaurs all lived on land and laid eggs. There were two groups of dinosaurs: saurischians (lizard-hipped) and ornithischians (bird-hipped), which differed in the structure of their hip bones. Most ornithischians fed on plants, but the saurischian group included several species of fierce, meat-eating hunters as well as plant eaters.

WAYS OF MOVING

Most early reptiles moved like lizards today, with their legs sprawled out to the sides. Dinosaurs had a much better way of moving. Their legs were held straight down beneath the body, which meant they could carry more weight and take longer, faster strides.

Lizard

Dinosaur

A dramatic encounter between the meat-eating tyrannosaur *Albertosaurus* and the plant-eating horned dinosaur *Centrosaurus* is reconstructed in this display at the Royal Tyrrell Museum in Drumheller, Canada.

THE TWO GROUPS OF DINOSAURS

Dinosaurs are divided into two main groups: saurischian, or "lizard-hipped" dinosaurs, and ornithischians, or "bird-hipped" dinosaurs. One of the main differences is the orientation of the pelvic bones, especially the pubis. In saurischians, the pubis points forward and down, whereas in ornithischians it supports the intestines and helps the dinosaur to breathe.

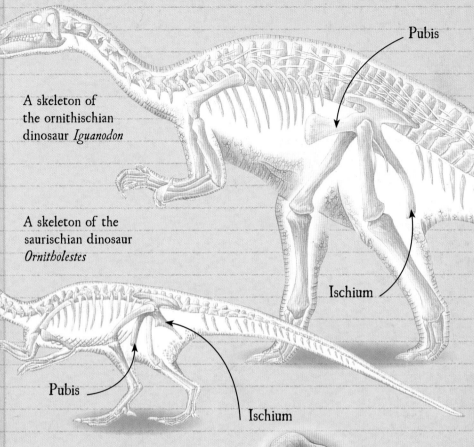

A skeleton of the ornithischian dinosaur *Iguanodon*

Pubis

Ischium

A skeleton of the saurischian dinosaur *Ornitholestes*

Pubis

Ischium

DINOSAUR LEGS

Slender, birdlike dinosaurs, such as *Gallimimus*, had long thighbones and shinbones with big muscles in the thigh to power the leg. The ankle- and foot bones were also long and slim. Such dinosaurs could probably run at up to 40 mph (65 km/h). The legs of sauropods, such as *Camarasaurus*, were very different. The bones were large and bulky and the foot spread out to form a large pad to support the dinosaur's massive weight. Sauropods plodded along on all four legs, whereas *Gallimimus* ran on its two slender back legs.

Thighbone

Shinbone

Back leg of *Gallimimus*

Long slender anklebones

Slim three-toed foot

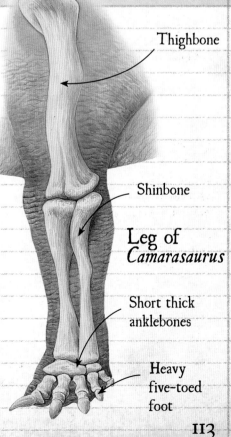

Thighbone

Shinbone

Leg of *Camarasaurus*

Short thick anklebones

Heavy five-toed foot

113

A DINOSAUR FAMILY TREE

The word "dinosaur," meaning "terrible lizard," was first used in 1842 by Richard Owen, one of the first experts on this huge group of reptiles. Since the 19th century, views on the relationships between the different groups of dinosaur have changed dramatically, because more species have been found and new discoveries made. The chart here shows a dinosaur family tree that is accepted by most experts and includes all known types of dinosaur. It also shows the close relationship of birds (Aves) to dinosaurs.

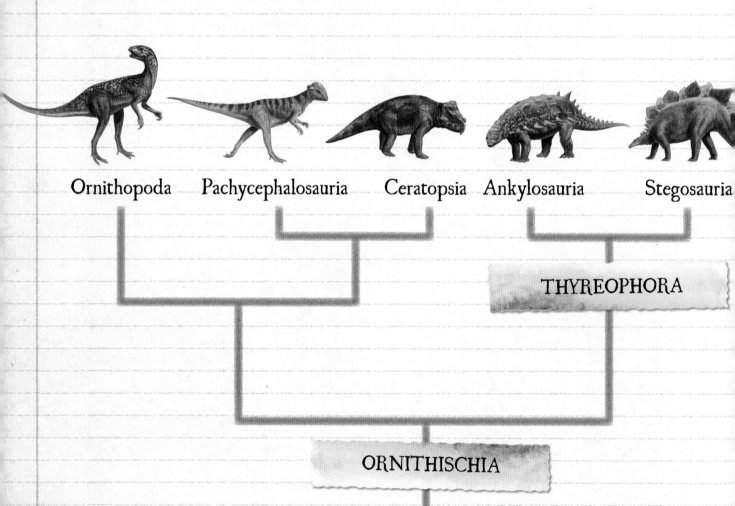

Ornithopoda   Pachycephalosauria   Ceratopsia   Ankylosauria   Stegosauria

THYREOPHORA

ORNITHISCHIA

DINOSAUR GROUPS

All dinosaurs fall into one of two groups: Saurischia and Ornithischia. These in turn are subdivided into smaller groups, each of which is united by at least one unique character and shares a common ancestor. As a result, the birds are classified as avian theropod dinosaurs and, consequently, it is no longer true to say that all the dinosaurs became extinct — the birds are a group of living dinosaurs.

A 19th-century British paleontologist, Richard Owen, worked on a number of life-size models of dinosaurs for an exhibition in London. In 1853, a special dinner held in his honor took place in the half-completed model of an *Iguanodon*.

Prosauropods   Sauropoda   Non-Avian Theropods   Birds

SAUROPODOMORPHA   THEROPODA

SAURISCHIA

DINOSAURIA

CERATOSAURS

Ceratosaurs were meat-eating theropod dinosaurs, ranging from tiny *Compsognathus* to large predators, such as *Carnotaurus*. The composition of the group is not agreed upon by all experts, some of whom exclude early forms, such as *Eoraptor* and *Coelophysis*, from the group.

All walked upright on their back legs and had short arms. Several ceratosaurs had strangely shaped crests or horns on their heads. These were probably not used in battle but in visual displays for attracting mates in the breeding season.

Eoraptor

One of the earliest known dinosaurs, *Eoraptor* was a carnivore. It was smaller and more lightly built than its relative *Herrerasaurus*. Its teeth were sharp and slightly serrated for cutting through meat, but it did not have the flexible jaw joint of *Herrerasaurus*.

Size: 10 feet (3 m) long
Order: Theropoda
Family: uncertain
Range: South America (Argentina)
Pn: he-rer-ah-SORE-us

Size: 11 feet 6 inches (1 m) long
Order: Theropoda
Family: uncertain
Range: South America (Argentina)
Pn: ee-oh-RAP-tor

Herrerasaurus

Like *Eoraptor*, *Herrerasaurus* was one of the earliest known dinosaurs. It would have moved upright on its legs, which were more than twice the length of its arms. Its fingers were strong and had large curved claws for grasping prey. Sliding joints in the lower jaws allowed for more flexibility when biting.

Size: 11 feet 6 in (3.5 m) long
Order: Neoceratosauria
Family: uncertain
Range: Africa (Tanzania)
Pn: e-LAF-roh-SORE-us

Elaphrosaurus

Only one skeleton of *Elaphrosaurus* has been found and, unfortunately, the skull was missing. Since the characteristic feature of the ornithomimids was that they had no teeth, it is impossible to say whether *Elaphrosaurus* belonged to this family. It may be that *Elaphrosaurus*, or a close relative, was the ancestor of the ostrich dinosaurs.

Dilophosaurus

This dinosaur had a pair of semicircular bony crests, one on each side of its skull. Some experts believe that only the males had these crests and that they were used to attract females. Its teeth were sharp but slender, suggesting that this dinosaur may have killed its prey with its clawed feet and hands instead of with its jaws.

Size: 20 feet (6 m) long
Order: Coelophysioidea
Family: uncertain
Range: North America (Arizona)
Pn: die-LOAF-oh-SAW-rus

Size: up to 10 feet (3 m)
Order: Coelophysioidea
Family: Coelophysidae
Range: North America (Connecticut, New Mexico)
Pn: seel-oh-FY-sis

Coelophysis

Built for speed, *Coelophysis* had a light, slender body and long, slim legs and tail. The narrow jaws were lined with sharp, serrated teeth for attacking prey. Remains of more than 1,000 skeletons were found in the same location in New Mexico, suggesting that this dinosaur lived in herds.

Size: 25 feet (8 m) long
Order: Neoceratosauria
Family: Abelisauridae
Range: South America (Argentina)
Pn: kar-noh-TORE-us

Carnotaurus

Discovered in 1985, this dinosaur had a deep, bull-like head with big horns above the eyes — its name means "meat-eating bull." Its arms were extremely small and probably almost useless. Well-preserved skin impressions found near the bones show that small cone-shaped spines covered the sides of its body.

TETANURANS

The tetanurans were a group of large predatory theropod dinosaurs, most of which were large and lived in the Jurassic and Cretaceous periods. Despite their appearance, these dinosaurs were closely related to birds. They included groups such as the allosaurs and megalosaurs, as well as more recently discovered dinosaurs, such as *Giganotosaurus*. All the tetanurans had a large opening in each upper jaw bone that made the skull much lighter than it looks. The rear part of the tail was stiffened by special interlocking bony structures on the vertebrae — the name tetanuran means "stiff tail."

Size: up to 39 feet (12 m) long

Order: Allosauroidea

Family: Allosauridae

Range: North America (Colorado, Utah, Wyoming), Africa (Tanzania), Australia

Pn: AL-oh-SAW-rus

Allosaurus

Mighty *Allosaurus* probably weighed between 1 and 2 tons (1–2 tonnes) and stood about 15 feet (4.5 m) tall. Packs of these fierce dinosaurs may have hunted together so they could bring down even larger creatures, such as sauropods and stegosaurs.

Yangchuanosaurus

This dinosaur was first discovered in China in 1978. A typical allosaur, it had a huge head, powerful jaws and jagged-edged teeth. Its long tail made up about half of its body length and helped to balance the heavy body as the dinosaur strode along on its sturdy legs.

Size: up to 33 feet (10 m) long

Order: Allosauroidea

Family: Sinraptoridae

Range: Asia (China)

Pn: yang-choo-AN-oh-saw-rus

Giganotosaurus

First discovered in South America in 1993, *Giganotosaurus* was one of the largest of all meat-eating dinosaurs. It may have weighed as much as 8 tons (7.2 tonnes). As well as hunting its own prey, it may have scared other predators away and stolen their catches.

Size: 43 feet (13 m) long

Order: Saurischia

Family: Abelisauridae

Range: South America (Patagonia)

Pn: jig-a-NOT-o-SAW-rus

Megalosaurus

This was the first dinosaur to be scientifically named, in 1824. A typical meat eater, it had a large head, powerful jaws and curved, saw-edged teeth. With its strong, clawed fingers and toes, it was well equipped to attack large plant-eating dinosaurs.

Size: 30 feet (9 m) long
Order: Spinosauroidea
Family: Megalosauridae
Range: Europe (England, France),
Africa (Morocco)
Pn: MEG-ah-loh-SAW-rus

Suchomimus

Fossils of this dinosaur were discovered in 1998 in the Sahara desert. A member of a group of fish-eating dinosaurs called spinosaurs, it had a long narrow snout like a crocodile and thumb claws measuring 12 inches (30 cm).

Size: 33 feet (10 m) long
Order: Spinosauroidea
Family: Spinosauridae
Range: Africa (Niger)
Pn: SOOK-o-MEEM-us

Cryolophosaurus

This large meat eater was discovered in Antarctica in 1994. It had a unique crest that ran across its skull, with two small horns on each side. The crest was too thin to have been a weapon, so experts think that it was probably used for display during the mating season.

Size: 26 feet (8 m) long
Order: Allosauroidea
Family: Carcharodontosauridae
Range: Africa (Egypt, Morocco, Tunisia)
Pn: kar-kar-o-don-toh-SAW-rus

Size: 23–26 feet (7–8 m) long
Order: Carnosauria
Family: uncertain
Range: Antarctica
Pn: cry-oh-LOF-oh-SAW-rus

Carcharodontosaurus

In 1996, scientists discovered fossils of a giant meat-eating dinosaur in the Moroccan desert. Its skull alone measured more than 5 feet (1.5 m) and was longer than that of *Tyrannosaurus*. Its teeth were 5 inches (12 cm) long, giving this dinosaur its name, which means "shark-toothed reptile."

JURASSIC TIMES

During the Jurassic Period, which began 208 million years ago, the climate became wetter, with a thick covering of plants, such as ferns, conifers and ginkgos, over much of the land. New kinds of dinosaurs developed, feeding on the lush plant life. These included sauropods, which were the biggest creatures ever to live on land. They ate more than 1 ton (1 tonne) of plant food a day. Plentiful prey allowed more types of meat-eating dinosaur to thrive. In the air were flying insects and pterosaurs, as well as the first species of birds.

MID-JURASSIC CHINA

In this mid-Jurassic scene in what is now southwest China, a stegosaur, *Huayangosaurus*, rears back in fear as fast-moving meat eaters, *Gasosaurus*, approach. Sauropods, *Shunosaurus*, look up from feeding on tree ferns — despite their great bulk, even they could fall prey to a group of these sharp-toothed predators.

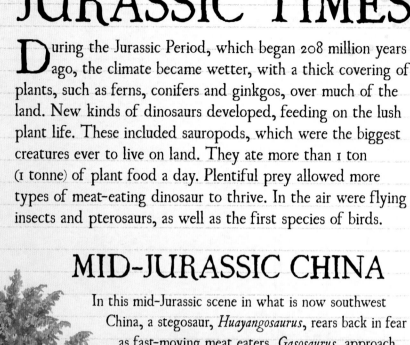

Shunosaurus, a sauropod

Tree fern

Frog

THE JURASSIC WORLD

During the Jurassic Period, the supercontinent of Pangea split into two, creating the land areas of Laurasia in the north and Gondwana in the south. The climate was still warm all over the world but rainfall increased.

Map labels:

Siberia
LAURASIA
China
North America
Iran
Tibet
PACIFIC OCEAN
TETHYS OCEAN
EQUATOR
South America
Africa
southwest China
GONDWANA
India
Australia
Antarctica

KEY TO MAP

- Landmass
- Ocean
- Sea-covered continent

Angustinaripterus, a flying reptile (pterosaur)

Gasosaurus, a tetanuran

Ginkgo

Conifer

Huayangosaurus, a stegosaur

Horsetails

Cycad

Fern

Salamander

BIRD RELATIVES

This group of theropods, known as the Maniraptora, includes several types of birdlike dinosaurs, such as dromaeosaurs and troodontids, as well as birds themselves. A feature shared by all of these creatures was a special flexible wrist joint that allowed the front limb to be folded against the body. The dinosaurs in this group were probably all fast-moving hunters that ran on two legs. *Archaeopteryx*, one of the earliest known birds, lived about 150 million years ago and had features of both birds and reptiles. Like birds today, it had wings and feathers. But like reptiles, it had toothed jaws and a long bony tail.

Size: 1 foot 1 inch (34 cm) long

Order: Eumaniraptora

Family: uncertain

Range: Western China

Pn: an-kee-OR-nis

Size: 10–13 feet (3–4 m) long

Order: Eumaniraptora

Family: Dromaeosauridae

Range: North America (Montana)

Pn: die-NON-i-kus

Anchiornis

Pigeon-sized *Anchiornis* is the smallest known prehistoric dinosaur. It was feathered and had relatively long legs, indicating that it was a strong runner. Its fossil was so well preserved that scientists were able to determine its gray-and-black feather pigment coloration accurately. *Anchiornis* could probably glide short distances, but it was a poor flier.

Deinonychus

A fast, agile predator, *Deinonychus* had a special weapon. The second toe on each foot bore a large, curved claw, 5 inches (12 cm) long. The dinosaur could have stood on one leg and used the claw of the other foot to slash into its victim's flesh.

Dromaeosaurus

Like *Deinonychus*, this dinosaur had large, curved claws on its feet that it used as weapons to kill prey. These fierce, fast-moving creatures probably hunted in packs that could have brought down animals much larger than themselves.

Size: 6 feet (1.8 m) long
Order: Eumaniraptora
Family: Dromaeosauridae
Range: North America (Alberta)
Pn: DROH-may-oh-SORE-us

Archaeopteryx

Unlike birds today, *Archaeopteryx* did not have a large breastbone to support powerful flying muscles. It probably could not fly far and may have had to climb up trees in order to launch itself into the air and then flap and glide short distances in search of insect prey.

Size: 1 foot 2 inches (35 cm) long
Order: Eumaniraptora
Family: Archaeopterygidae
Range: Europe (Germany)
Pn: ark-ee-OP-ter-iks

Velociraptor

A fast-moving hunter, *Velociraptor* had a long, flat-snouted head. Two fossilized skeletons found in Mongolia revealed *Velociraptor* locked in battle with a horned dinosaur, *Protoceratops*. Scientists think that they died in a sandstorm that developed during the fight.

Size: 6 feet (1.8 m) long
Order: Eumaniraptora
Family: Dromaeosauridae
Range: North America (Alberta)
Pn: vel-O-si-RAP-tor

OSTRICH DINOSAURS

With their slender legs, long necks and small heads, the ostrich dinosaurs looked similar to the ostriches of today. Like ostriches, these theropod dinosaurs were fast runners and may have been able to sprint at up to 40 mph (65 km/h) as they searched for food, such as lizards and frogs. They may also have eaten leaves and fruit, which they could have pulled from the trees with the slender clawed fingers on their hands. Possible relatives of the ornithomimids are the therizinosaurids (also known as segnosaurids). Complete skeletons of these creatures have only recently been discovered. Unlike other theropods, they probably fed on plants.

Size: 13 feet (4 m) long
Order: Ornithomimosauria
Family: Ornithomimidae
Range: Asia (Mongolia)
Pn: gal-lee-MEEM-us

Gallimimus

One of the largest of the ostrich dinosaurs, *Gallimimus* was twice the size of a modern ostrich. Like the rest of its group, it did not have strong teeth or sharp claws to defend itself from attackers. Instead it relied on speed — few other dinosaurs could catch it when it ran.

Caudipteryx

Despite the long feathers on its arms, it is unlikely that *Caudipteryx* was able to fly. It had a mixture of reptile and bird features, such as long legs and hollow bones that made this creature a light, agile runner. As such, it could run down any prey or escape from a predator.

Size: 12 feet (3.5 m) long
Order: Oviraptosauria
Family: Caudipterygidae
Range: North America (Colorado), Asia (China)
Pn: caw-DIP-ter-ix

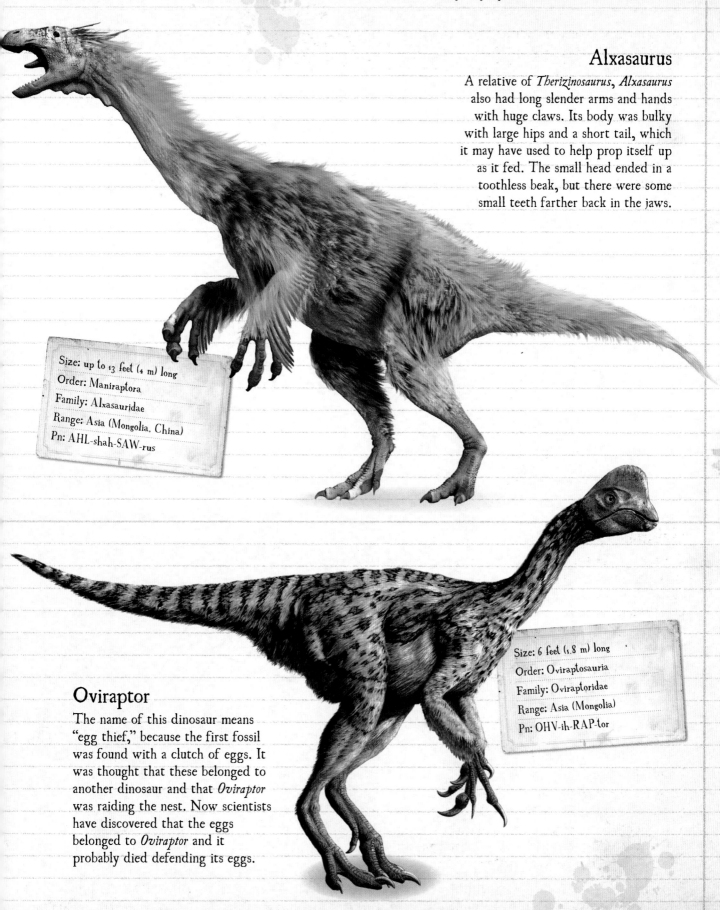

Alxasaurus

A relative of *Therizinosaurus*, *Alxasaurus* also had long slender arms and hands with huge claws. Its body was bulky with large hips and a short tail, which it may have used to help prop itself up as it fed. The small head ended in a toothless beak, but there were some small teeth farther back in the jaws.

Size: up to 13 feet (4 m) long
Order: Maniraptora
Family: Alxasauridae
Range: Asia (Mongolia, China)
Pn: AHL-shah-SAW-rus

Size: 6 feet (1.8 m) long
Order: Oviraptosauria
Family: Oviraptoridae
Range: Asia (Mongolia)
Pn: OHV-ih-RAP-tor

Oviraptor

The name of this dinosaur means "egg thief," because the first fossil was found with a clutch of eggs. It was thought that these belonged to another dinosaur and that *Oviraptor* was raiding the nest. Now scientists have discovered that the eggs belonged to *Oviraptor* and it probably died defending its eggs.

TYRANNOSAURS

Huge, flesh-eating dinosaurs, tyrannosaurs lived in Asia and North America during the Late Cretaceous. These theropods were among the largest land carnivores that have ever lived. All tyrannosaurs had massive heads and strong jaws lined with sharp teeth, some of which were up to 6 inches (15 cm) long. They walked upright on their two back legs and could probably move at 20 mph (30 km/h) or more. Their front limbs were so small they did not even reach the mouth. Some experts think that a tyrannosaur may have used its tiny arms to lift itself off the ground after sleeping or feeding.

Alioramus

Although most tyrannosaurs had deep skulls and short snouts, *Alioramus* had a long, narrow skull. There were also a number of bony knobs on the snout and near the eyes. Like other tyrannosaurs, it may have lain in wait for prey, ready to pounce when the victim came near.

Size: 20 feet (6 m) long
Order: Coelurosauria
Family: Tyrannosauridae
Range: Asia (Mongolia)
Pn: ay-lee-oh-RAY-mus

Siamotyrannus

First discovered in Thailand in 1996, this creature may be the oldest known tyrannosaur. It lived some 50 million years before *Tyrannosaurus*. Like its relative, *Siamotyrannus* had jagged, curved teeth and probably fed on plant-eating dinosaurs much larger than itself.

Size: 16-23 feet (5-7 m) long
Order: Tyrannoraptora
Family: Tyrannosauridae
Range: Asia (Thailand)
Pn: sigh-AM-oh-tie-ran-us

Gorgosaurus

This large predator was closely related to *Albertosaurus*, although its forelimbs were smaller. Its long, heavy tail acted as a counterweight to the massive head. *Gorgosaurus* was an apex predator, roaming the lush floodplains of an inland sea, where it preyed on large herds of ceratopsids and hadrosaurs.

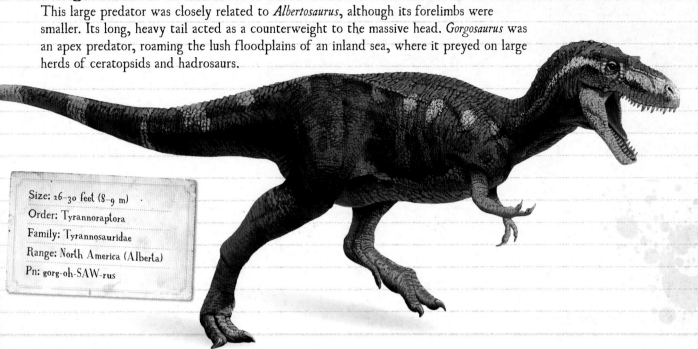

Size: 26–30 feet (8–9 m)

Order: Tyrannoraptora

Family: Tyrannosauridae

Range: North America (Alberta)

Pn: gorg-oh-SAW-rus

Tyrannosaurus

Up to 20 feet (6 m) tall and weighing more than an African elephant, *Tyrannosaurus* was one of the most fearsome creatures of the Cretaceous. Some scientists think that its bulk may have made it hard for it to chase prey and believe that it scavenged for food, eating animals that were already dead. However, like lions today, *Tyrannosaurus* probably both hunted and scavenged.

Size: up to 50 feet (15 m) long

Order: Tyrannoraptora

Family: Tyrannosauridae

Range: North America (Alberta, Montana, Saskatchewan, Texas, Wyoming), Asia (Mongolia)

Pn: ti-RAN-oh-SAW-rus

FEEDING

What did dinosaurs eat? Like large animals today, many dinosaurs were plant eaters, although some would have hunted and killed other creatures. The largest hunters, such as *Tyrannosaurus*, could have hunted on their own. Some smaller carnivores possibly hunted in packs, attacking dinosaurs much larger than themselves. There were many more plant-eating dinosaurs than flesh eaters, but they could have avoided competition by feeding at different levels. Small dinosaurs, such as *Protoceratops*, would have grazed at ground level. Larger horned dinosaurs could have fed on low bushes, but had short necks and could not stretch up far. Hadrosaurs could have reared up on their hind legs to reach leaves higher in the trees. Biggest of all were the mighty sauropods, which could stretch up to eat leaves at the tops of trees, where no other creatures could reach.

The fossilized droppings of dinosaurs are known as coprolites and provide valuable clues about what dinosaurs ate. Coprolites that have been studied show the remains of conifer stems, cycad leaves and flesh, for example. But although experts can tell what a dropping contains, it is hard to know to which species it belonged.

Fossilized droppings

SKULL STRUCTURE

A plant eater, such as a duck-billed dinosaur, had a toothless beak that was used to chop mouthfuls of leaves. The food was then ground down on the packed teeth farther back in the jaws. A meat eater, such as an allosaur, had powerful jaws lined with sharp teeth.

Plant eater's skull

Meat eater's skull

MIGHTY HUNTERS

The largest hunters, such as the tyrannosaurs, were built for power and strength. They had massive, daggerlike teeth, which they could use to rip apart prey in seconds. Hunters may have had to spend time tracking down and catching prey, but one good meal could have satisfied them for several days.

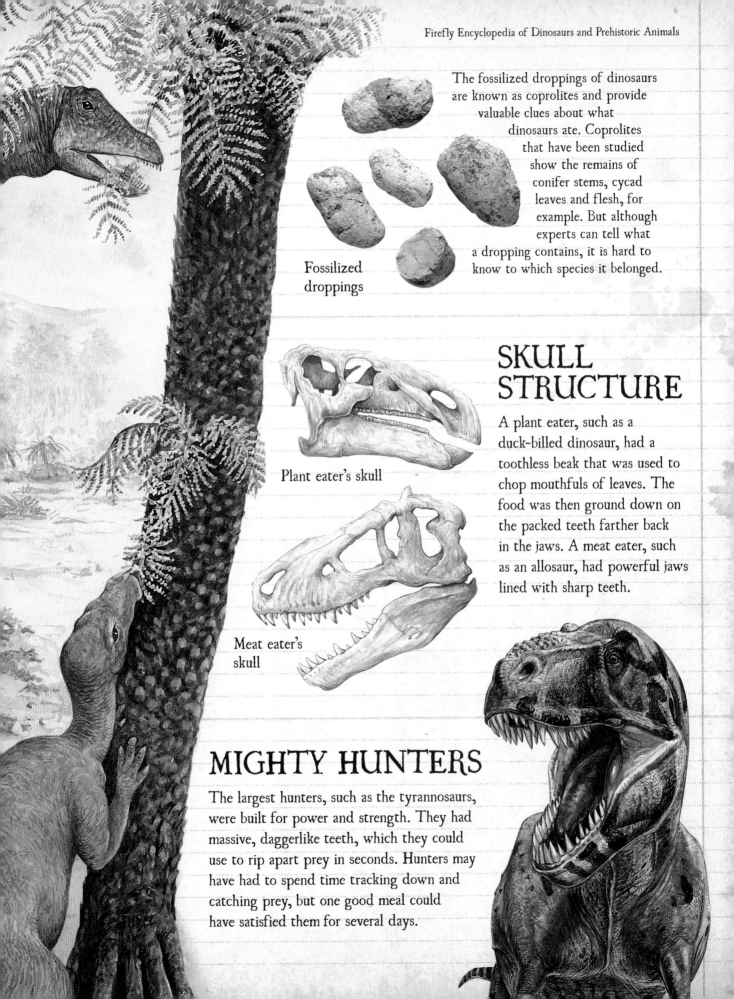

PROSAUROPODS

This group of long-necked dinosaurs first appeared in the Late Triassic. There were two main groups: the plateosaurids, which had large, heavy bodies, and the anchisaurids, which were smaller and more lightly built. Like the later sauropods, prosauropods are thought to have been plant eaters. Although these dinosaurs have some similarities to sauropods, they are not an early form of sauropod as their name suggests. They are probably a side branch of the group, and they had died out by the end of the Early Jurassic.

Size: 10 feet (3 m) long

Order: Plateosauria

Family: Plateosauridae

Range: South America (Argentina)

Pn: moo-SAW-rus

Mussaurus

In 1979, a group of tiny *Mussaurus* hatchlings was found in a nest in Argentina. Two small eggs lay nearby, each measuring only 1 inch (2.5 cm) long. Other skeletons found were about 1 foot (30 cm) long and probably belonged to young animals.

Massospondylus

Massospondylus had a small head on a very long, flexible neck. Its large, five-fingered hands could have been used for collecting food or for walking when on all fours. Stones have been found with some skeletons — the dinosaur probably swallowed these to help it grind down tough plants in the stomach.

Size: 13 feet (4 m) long

Order: Plateosauria

Family: Plateosauridae

Range: North America (Arizona), Africa (South Africa, Zimbabwe)

Pn: MASS-oh-SPOND-i-lus

Thecodontosaurus

Like Anchisaurus, this dinosaur was lightly built, but it had a shorter neck and more teeth than its relative. It was first named in 1842 after its fossilized bones were found in southwest England.

Size: 7 feet (2.1 m) long

Order: Sauropodomorpha

Family: Thecodontosauridae

Range: Europe (England), southern Africa

Pn: THEK-oh-DON-toh-SAW-rus

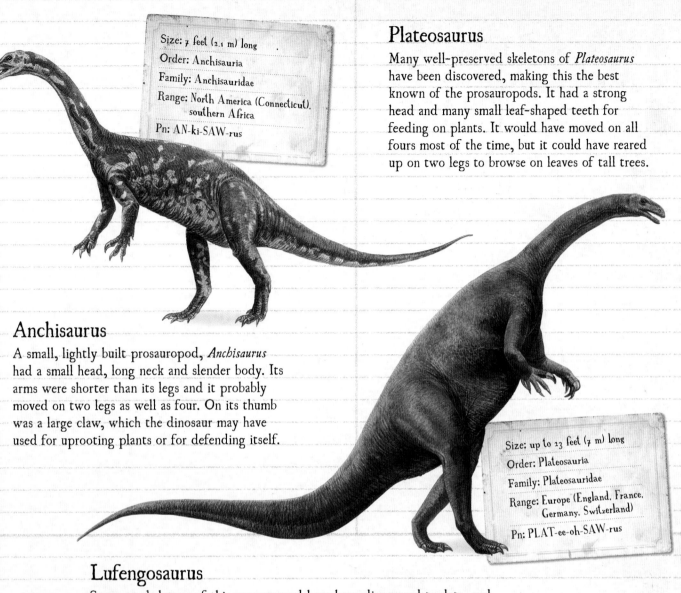

Size: 7 feet (2.1 m) long

Order: Anchisauria

Family: Anchisauridae

Range: North America (Connecticut), southern Africa

Pn: AN-ki-SAW-rus

Plateosaurus

Many well-preserved skeletons of *Plateosaurus* have been discovered, making this the best known of the prosauropods. It had a strong head and many small leaf-shaped teeth for feeding on plants. It would have moved on all fours most of the time, but it could have reared up on two legs to browse on leaves of tall trees.

Anchisaurus

A small, lightly built prosauropod, *Anchisaurus* had a small head, long neck and slender body. Its arms were shorter than its legs and it probably moved on two legs as well as four. On its thumb was a large claw, which the dinosaur may have used for uprooting plants or for defending itself.

Size: up to 23 feet (7 m) long

Order: Plateosauria

Family: Plateosauridae

Range: Europe (England, France, Germany, Switzerland)

Pn: PLAT-ee-oh-SAW-rus

Lufengosaurus

Some 30 skeletons of this prosauropod have been discovered to date, and *Lufengosaurus* was the first complete dinosaur to be mounted and displayed in China. It also appeared on the first ever dinosaur postage stamp, issued in China in 1958. A large, heavily built animal, *Lufengosaurus* had large hands, broad feet, and widely spaced teeth.

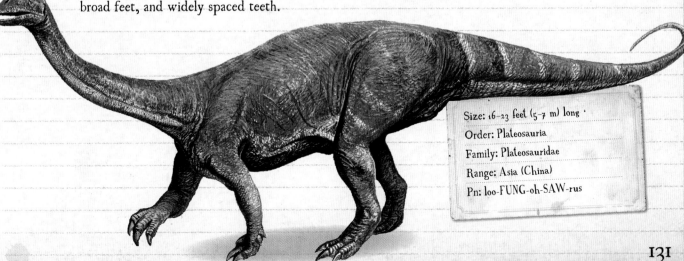

Size: 16-23 feet (5-7 m) long

Order: Plateosauria

Family: Plateosauridae

Range: Asia (China)

Pn: loo-FUNG-oh-SAW-rus

FOSSILS

Fossils are the remains of once-living organisms — plant or animal — preserved in rock. Hard parts of the body, such as teeth, bones and scales, are most likely to form fossils, but fossilized eggs and droppings have also been found. A fossil may also be formed of an imprint in the ground, such as a giant dinosaur footprint. Fossils only develop in certain conditions. Imagine, for example, that a dinosaur has died on a bank of a river. The flesh is eaten by scavengers and insects, leaving only the bones, which slowly sink into the mud. Over the years, more mud piles up over the bones. Water filters down through the ground, carrying natural substances called minerals. These turn the mud and bones into rock. The skeleton may keep its shape or be flattened, as soft sediment is squeezed into rock.

Teeth fossilize well and can reveal much about the lifestyle of the owner. This long, sharp tooth would have belonged to a meat-eating dinosaur.

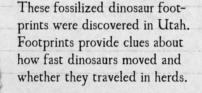

These fossilized dinosaur footprints were discovered in Utah. Footprints provide clues about how fast dinosaurs moved and whether they traveled in herds.

HOW A FOSSIL IS FORMED

1. Most of the dead dinosaur's flesh is eaten by carnivores or other scavenging reptiles, and the rest soon decays.

2. The dinosaur's skeleton lies on the bed of the lake and sinks into the mud.

3. Over millions of years, more layers of lake sediment are deposited above the dinosaur skeleton.

4. The land has risen and erosion has started to remove some of the rock above the skeleton.

5. Finally, the last layers of rock are eroded to reveal the fossil bones.

EUDIMORPHODON

The teeth in this fossil of *Eudimorphodon*, one of the oldest flying reptiles, are particularly well preserved. Their shape would have been ideally suited to grasping slippery fish.

133

SAUROPODS

These long-necked, plant-eating dinosaurs include the largest land animals ever known. The smallest were at least 33 feet (10 m) long and the largest may have measured as much as 125 feet (38 m). All were similar in appearance, with a small head on a long neck, a deep body, thick pillarlike legs and a long tapering tail. They walked on all fours and probably moved slowly. There were several different families of sauropods. Brachiosaurs were some of the biggest and heaviest, whereas diplodocids, such as *Seismosaurus*, were even longer but had lighter bones.

Brachiosaurus

This giant may have weighed 88 tons (80 tonnes), more than 12 African elephants. Like a giraffe, it had a very long neck and front legs that were longer than its back legs so that the body sloped down from the shoulders. It probably fed like a giraffe, too, reaching up to eat leaves on the highest trees.

Size: 75 feet (23 m) long

Order: Macronaria

Family: Brachiosauridae

Range: North America (Colorado), Africa (Tanzania, Algeria)

Pn: BRACK-ee-oh-SAW-rus

Size: 125 feet (38 m) long

Order: Neosauropoda

Family: Diplodocidae

Range: North America (New Mexico)

Pn: SIZE-moh-SAW-rus

Seismosaurus

The remains of this sauropod, possibly the longest land animal ever, were first found by accident by two hikers in New Mexico. Its legs were short and thick to help support and steady its huge body, which may have weighed as much as 110 tons (100 tonnes).

Size: 49 feet (15 m) long
Order: Eusauropoda
Family: Euhelopodidae
Range: Asia (China)
Pn: yoo-HEL-oh-pus

Euhelopus

Euhelopus was a close relative of *Camarasaurus*, although it lived on the other side of the world. Its body shape was very similar, but its neck was much longer and contained as many as 17 to 19 vertebrae. (*Camarasaurus* had only 12 vertebrae.) Its teeth were large and spoon shaped, suitable for eating tough plants, such as ferns and horsetails.

Barapasaurus

This sauropod is one of the oldest so far known. It had a typical sauropod body and some of the bones in its backbone and neck were hollow. Six incomplete skeletons have been found so far in southern India, but no skull.

Size: 49 feet (15 m) long
Order: Eusauropoda
Family: Cetiosauridae
Range: Asia (India)
Pn: ba-RA-pa-SAW-rus

Size: 41 feet (12.6 m) long
Order: Eusauropoda
Family: Dicraeosauridae
Range: Africa (Tanzania)
Pn: die-KRAY-oh-SAW-rus

Dicraeosaurus

Dicraeosaurus was small compared to most members of its family and had a much shorter neck and larger head. Its name means "forked lizard" and comes from the forked spines that stuck out from its vertebrae. These may have helped to strengthen the backbone.

Amargasaurus

This small diplodocid had two rows of spines growing up from its backbone. These may have helped to protect the dinosaur from predators. Or they may have been covered with skin to make a sail-like structure to help the dinosaur absorb or lose heat.

Size: 33 feet (10 m) long
Order: Saurischia
Family: Dicraeosauridae
Range: South America (Argentina)
Pn: a-MAR-ga-SAW-rus

Size: 70 feet (21.3 m) long
Order: Saurischia
Family: Diplodocidae
Range: North America (Colorado, Oklahoma, Utah, Wyoming)
Pn: a-PAT-oh-SAW-rus

Apatosaurus

Although *Apatosaurus* would have moved on all fours, it may have been able to rear up on its back legs and bring its forelegs down to crush an enemy. Marks on the bones show that large muscles powered the tail, allowing the dinosaur to lash it from side to side to ward off attackers.

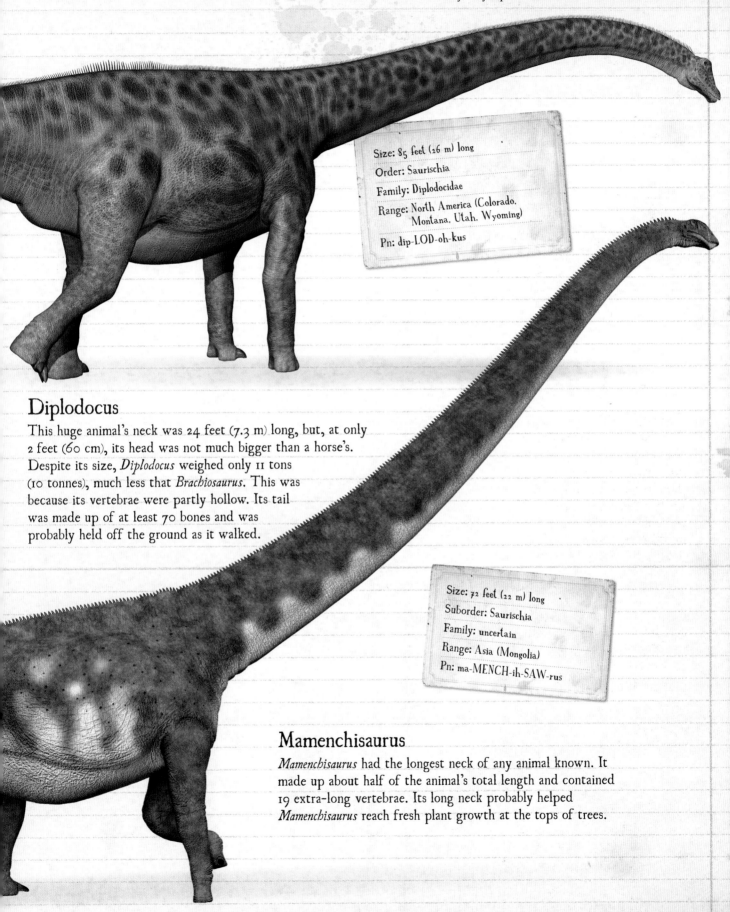

Size: 85 feet (26 m) long

Order: Saurischia

Family: Diplodocidae

Range: North America (Colorado, Montana, Utah, Wyoming)

Pn: dip-LOD-oh-kus

Diplodocus

This huge animal's neck was 24 feet (7.3 m) long, but, at only 2 feet (60 cm), its head was not much bigger than a horse's. Despite its size, *Diplodocus* weighed only 11 tons (10 tonnes), much less that *Brachiosaurus*. This was because its vertebrae were partly hollow. Its tail was made up of at least 70 bones and was probably held off the ground as it walked.

Size: 72 feet (22 m) long

Suborder: Saurischia

Family: uncertain

Range: Asia (Mongolia)

Pn: ma-MENCH-ih-SAW-rus

Mamenchisaurus

Mamenchisaurus had the longest neck of any animal known. It made up about half of the animal's total length and contained 19 extra-long vertebrae. Its long neck probably helped *Mamenchisaurus* reach fresh plant growth at the tops of trees.

DISCOVERING DINOSAURS

Most of what is known about dinosaurs comes from fossils, which may have lain untouched for millions of years. Sometimes fossils are found by chance, but usually they are uncovered by dinosaur experts called paleontologists. Before the fossils are moved, a detailed plan must be drawn, showing the position of each one. This may help the experts reconstruct the skeleton. Each bone is then minutely examined for clues. For example, tiny marks or roughened areas on the bone show where muscles were attached. Scientists also compare dinosaurs with similar creatures living today to work out how they may have looked and behaved.

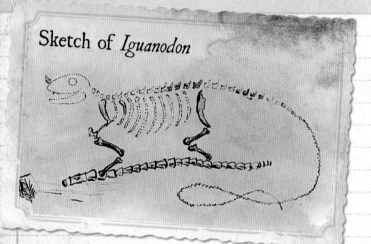

Sketch of *Iguanodon*

An artist's impression of what *Baryonyx* may have looked like.

SKETCH

This sketch was a very rough attempt at a reconstruction of *Iguanodon*, not a sketch of the fossil remains as found.

An expert technician painstakingly removes the fossilized rib cage of an *Albertosaurus* dinosaur from its plaster cast.

REBUILDING A SKELETON

It is rare that a whole skeleton of a dinosaur is discovered. Usually, missing parts have to be reconstructed using what knowledge scientists have of similar creatures. Only about 60 percent of the bones of the dinosaur *Baryonyx* have been found.

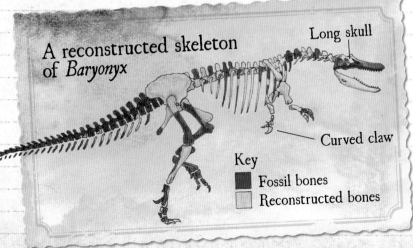

A reconstructed skeleton of *Baryonyx*

Long skull

Curved claw

Key
■ Fossil bones
□ Reconstructed bones

Paleontologists use
special tools

Bones are
embedded
in rock

BONEHEADS AND OTHER PLANT EATERS

Bonehead dinosaurs may have lived in herds, much like the mountain goats of today. Like goats, they fed on plants and led peaceful lives for much of the time, but males probably fought fierce battles with rivals in the mating season. Much of the impact of their head-butting contests was taken by the tough bony dome on the head. Most bonehead fossils date from the Late Cretaceous and have been found in North America and central Asia. Like boneheads, fabrosaurs and heterodontosaurs were plant-eating dinosaurs and moved upright on long, slender legs.

Lesothosaurus

Small and lizardlike, this fabrosaur had long legs, short arms and a slender tail. It moved upright on its back legs and could probably speed across the African plains to escape from enemies. A plant eater, it had sharp, pointed teeth, shaped like little arrowheads, which it used to chop tough leaves.

Size: 3 feet (90 cm) long

Order: Ornithischia

Family: uncertain

Range: southern Africa

Pn: less-OH-toe-SAW-rus

Pisanosaurus

Few fossils have been found of this little dinosaur, but it may be one of the earliest of the ornithischian, or bird-hipped, dinosaurs. It lived during the Late Triassic Period, and it seemed to have been lightly built and probably moved fast.

Size: 3 feet (90 cm) long

Order: Ornithischia

Family: Pisanosauridae

Range: South America (Argentina)

Pn: pee-SAN-oh-sAW-rus

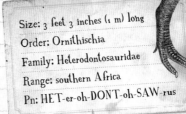

Size: 3 feet 3 inches (1 m) long

Order: Ornithischia

Family: Heterodontosauridae

Range: southern Africa

Pn: HET-er-oh-DONT-oh-SAW-rus

Heterodontosaurus

Although similar to the fabrosaurs in appearance, *Heterodontosaurus* had quite different teeth. Unlike most other reptiles, it had three kinds: small pointed teeth, which it used for nipping off leaves, larger back teeth for chewing, and two pairs of large canine teeth.

Prenocephale

Like other boneheads, *Prenocephale* was a plant eater and probably fed on leaves and fruit. It walked on two legs and had five-fingered hands, three-toed feet, and a long heavy tail. The large dome on its head was surrounded with a row of bony spikes and bumps.

Size: 8 feet (2.5 m) long
Order: Homalocephaloidea
Family: Pachycephalosauridae
Range: Asia (Mongolia)
Pn: pren-oh-KEF-a-lee

Pachycephalosaurus

The largest of the boneheads, this dinosaur had a huge dome on the top of its head made of solid bone, up to 10 inches (25 cm) thick. This dome probably acted like a crash helmet to protect the dinosaur's head when it took part in battles with rival males. The domes of males seem to have grown larger with age.

Size: 13 feet (4 m) long
Order: Homalocephaloidea
Family: Pachycephalosauridae
Range: North America (Alberta)
Pn: PAK-ee-KEF-a-loh-SAW-rus

Homalocephale

The homalocephalid family of boneheads did not have large domes on their heads. But the skull was heavy and thickened and the head was covered with bony knobs. *Homalocephale* also had unusually broad hips, which may have taken some of the impact when rival males fought.

Size: 6 feet 6 inches (2 m) long
Order: Homalocephaloidea
Family: Pachycephalosauridae
Range: North America (Alberta)
Pn: steg-O-ser-as

Stegoceras

The thickened skull of *Stegoceras* was covered with lumps and knobs. When two males began a head-butting battle, they kept their heads lowered and neck, body and tail held straight out. The tail would have helped to balance the weight of the head.

Size: 10 feet (3 m) long
Order: Homalocephaloidea
Family: Homacephalidae
Range: Asia (Mongolia)
Pn: home-ah-loh-KEF-ah-lee

HYPSILOPHODONTS

Hypsilophodonts were fast-running plant eaters that probably lived in herds like deer today. When danger threatened, they could have escaped at high speed, running upright on their long, slender back legs. A highly successful group, hypsilophodonts lived from the Late Jurassic to the end of the Cretaceous. Fossils have been found so far in North America, Europe, Asia, Antarctica and Australia. All members of the family had tall, grooved cheek teeth for grinding up plant food.

Size: 4 feet 6 inches (1.4 m) long
Order: Euornithopoda
Family: uncertain
Range: North America (Utah, Wyoming)
Pn: oth-ni-EL-ee-a

Size: 5 feet (1.5 m) long
Order: Euornithopoda
Family: Hypsilophodontidae
Range: North America (South Dakota),
       Europe (England, Portugal)
Pn: hip-see-LOAF-oh-don

Hypsilophodon

Scientists once believed that this dinosaur lived in trees, because its body shape looked similar to today's tree kangaroos. However, further study has shown that its feet are not suitable for grasping trees and that it was perfectly adapted for fast movement on land.

Othnielia

A typical hypsilophodont, *Othnielia* had long legs, a lightweight body, and short arms with five-fingered hands. Originally known as *Nanosaurus*, it was renamed in honor of the 19th-century American fossil collector Professor Othniel Charles Marsh to commemorate his work on dinosaurs.

Dryosaurus

One of the largest of the hypsilophodonts, *Dryosaurus* was also one of the earliest. Like other members of its family, it had long legs that were built for speed, with shinbones that were much longer than its thighbones.

Size: 10 feet (3 m) long
Order: Ornithischia
Family: Hypsilophodontidae
Range: Western North America,
       Africa, Europe (England,
       Romania), possibly Australia
Pn: DRY-oh-SAW-rus

Size: 11 feet 6 inches (3.5 m) long
Order: Euornithopoda
Family: Thescelosauridae
Range: North America (Alberta, Montana, Saskatchewan, Wyoming)
Pn: thes-kel-oh-SAW-rus

Leaellynasaura

Fossils of this dinosaur were found in 1987 in the south of Australia. This region was once part of polar Gondwana, so the dinosaur must have been adapted to survive the freezing temperatures. Its eye sockets and the part of its brain devoted to vision were unusually large, suggesting it had excellent sight.

Thescelosaurus

Bulkier than most of its relatives, *Thescelosaurus* also had teeth in the front of its upper jaw. The structure of its legs, with shinbones and thighbones of the same length, suggests that it was slower moving than other hypsilophodonts. But it did have rows of bony studs on its back that may have helped to protect it from enemies.

Size: 6 feet 6 inches–10 feet (2–3 m) long
Order: Euornithopoda
Family: uncertain
Range: Australia
Pn: LEE-el-in-a-SAW-ra

Size: 8 feet (2.5 m) long
Order: Euornithopoda
Family: uncertain
Range: North America (Alberta)
Pn: PARX-oh-SAW-rus

Parksosaurus

Parksosaurus was one of the last of the hypsilophodonts, surviving until the end of the Cretaceous. Although similar to its relatives, it had bigger eyes than most and had special bones to support its large eyeballs. *Parksosaurus* probably fed close to the ground, nipping off leaves with its narrow, beaked jaws.

143

IGUANODONTS

Large, plant-eating dinosaurs, iguanodonts appeared in the Jurassic and spread all over the world. They were bulky, big-boned animals with sturdy legs and hooflike nails on their feet. Each short arm had a five-fingered hand, which could be spread wide and used for walking when on all fours. The thumb took the form of a spike and could be used against attackers. Three of the other fingers bore hooflike nails, and the small fifth finger could be bent across the palm and used for grasping food.

Size: 24 feet (7.3 m) long
Order: Iguanodontia
Family: Rhabdodontidae
Range: Australia (Queensland)
Pn: MUT-a-BUR-a-SAW-rus

Vectisaurus

A close relative of *Iguanodon*, *Vectisaurus* lived at the same time and in the same area. The only difference between the two, apart from size, was that *Vectisaurus* had spines growing upward from its backbone that were long enough to form a definite ridge along the back.

Size: 13 feet (4 m) long
Order: Ornithopoda
Family: Iguanodontidae
Range: Europe (England)
Pn: VECK-ti-SAW-rus

Muttaburrasaurus

Found in Australia in 1981, fossils of this iguanodont show that it had a bony bump on its skull just in front of the eyes. No one knows exactly what this was used for but it could have been used in displays to attract mates.

Iguanodon

Iguanodon was the second dinosaur to be discovered — part of a leg bone was found in 1809 in southern England. Fossilized footprints suggest that *Iguanodon* lived in herds and was probably slow moving. It would have spent most of its time on four legs but could have reared up on two to feed on plants.

Size: 30 feet (9 m) long
Order: Ornithischia
Family: Iguanodontidae
Range: Europe (Belgium, England, Germany), North America (Utah), Africa (Tunisia), Asia (Mongolia)
Pn: ig-WA-no-don

Rhabdodon

When standing upright on their back legs, iguanodonts, such as *Rhabdodon*, would have held their long tail straight out behind to help balance the heavy weight of the body. This iguanodont lived on a group of volcanic islands located where central Europe is now.

Size: 13 feet (4 m) long
Order: Iguanodontia
Family: Rhabdodontidae
Range: Europe (France, Romania)
Pn: RAB-doh-don

Ouranosaurus

Ouranosaurus had a row of spines running down the center of its back. These spines would have been covered with skin to form a finlike structure that may have helped the dinosaur control its temperature — when the fin was turned to the sun it would have absorbed heat.

Size: 23 feet (7 m) long
Order: Iguanodontia
Family: uncertain
Range: Africa (Nigeria)
Pn: OO-ran-oh-SAW-rus

Size: 20 feet (6 m) long
Order: Iguanodontia
Family: uncertain
Range: Asia (China)
Pn: pro-BAK-troh-SAW-rus

Probactrosaurus

Like all iguanodonts, *Probactrosaurus* had a strong toothless beak for chopping mouthfuls of plant food. Farther back in the jaws were ridged teeth for grinding food down. New teeth grew as old ones wore out.

145

FAMILY LIFE

Like reptiles and birds today, most dinosaurs would have laid hard-shelled eggs in which their young grew. Although many fossil eggs have been found, few can be definitely identified as belonging to a particular species. Those that can be identified show that some dinosaurs looked after their eggs and young. In a nest belonging to *Troodon*, for example, eggs were arranged in a circle with the tips pointing in toward the center. One fossilized *Oviraptor* was found incubating its clutch.

These fossilized eggs belonging to *Oviraptor* were discovered in the Gobi Desert, Mongolia. Other clutches have been found, some containing as many as 22 eggs.

A CARING MOTHER

Fossilized eggs belonging to the duck-billed dinosaur *Maiasaura* (see page 150) were discovered arranged in circles in the middle of a nest mound. The mother probably lay next to the nest to guard her eggs from predators.

Adult feeds her young

Nest mound

BATTLING BONEHEADS

Dinosaurs, such as boneheads (see pages 140–141), probably lived in herds. In the breeding season males may have fought fierce head-butting battles to win females or leadership of the group. Some herding animals, such as mountain goats, do the same today.

A duck-billed dinosaur's egg was about 7 inches (18 cm) long and had a tough, waterproof shell. Fossils show that the baby duckbill would have been too weak to move far and would have stayed in the nest for a few weeks to be fed by its parents.

Dinosaur egg

Lambeosaurus

Parasaurolophus

Corythosaurus

Hypacrosaurus

KEEPING IN TOUCH

Many plant-eating dinosaurs lived in herds. This would have helped to protect them from predators. Duck-billed dinosaurs, or hadrosaurs, may have made special calls to keep in touch with others or to attract mates. Their crests may also have acted as echo chambers to make the calls louder, and helped dinosaurs recognize others of their own species.

DUCK-BILLED DINOSAURS

Also known as hadrosaurs, duck-billed dinosaurs get their name from their long, flattened beak. One of the largest and most varied of Late Cretaceous dinosaur groups, hadrosaurs were particularly common in North America and Asia. All had long back legs and shorter front legs. They probably spent much of their time on all fours while feeding, but could rear up on their back legs to run away from attackers. They are thought to have lived in herds and nested in groups. Although some hadrosaurs had flat heads, many had a strangely shaped crest on the top of the head.

Size: 30 feet (9 m) long
Order: Iguanodontia
Family: Hadrosauridae
Range: North America (Alberta, Montana, New Mexico)
Pn: KRITE-oh-SAW-rus

Kritosaurus

No one knows exactly why flat-headed dinosaurs, such as *Kritosaurus*, had bony humps on their snouts. It is possible that only the males had humps and that they used them in courtship displays.

Size: 13 feet (4 m) long
Order: Iguanodontia
Family: Hadrosauridae
Range: Asia (Mongolia, China)
Pn: bak-troh-SAW-rus

Bactrosaurus

This is the earliest known duck-billed dinosaur. The group appeared in the Late Cretaceous at the same time as flowering plants spread throughout the world. This plentiful food supply — and their efficient plant-grinding jaws for making use of it — may have been the reason for the great success of the duckbills.

Hadrosaurus

This duckbill was the first dinosaur to be discovered in North America. Its bones were found in New Jersey and it was reconstructed and named in 1858. Like *Kritosaurus*, *Hadrosaurus* was a flat-headed duckbill. It had no crests but there was a large hump made of bone on its snout.

Size: 30 feet (9 m) long

Order: Iguanodontia

Family: Hadrosauridae

Range: North America (Montana, New Jersey, New Mexico, South Dakota)

Pn: HAD-roh-SAW-rus

Edmontosaurus

Like all hadrosaurs, *Edmontosaurus* had a toothless beak for cropping plants. Behind it, in both the upper and lower jaws, were as many as a thousand tightly packed teeth for grinding down food. As teeth became worn, they were replaced with new ones. The neck was strong yet bendy, allowing the dinosaur to gather low-growing plants from a wide area around it without having to move.

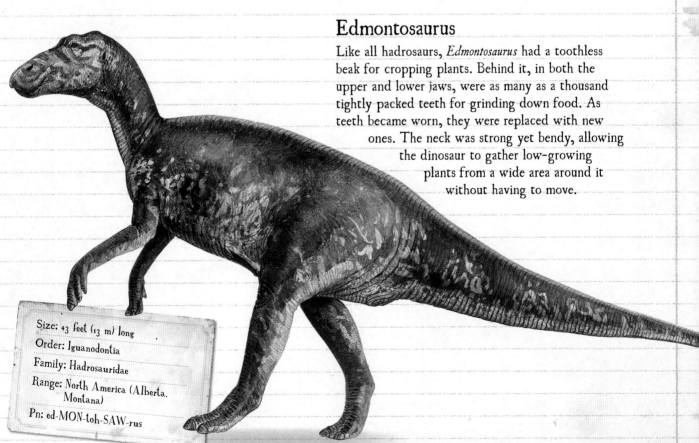

Size: 43 feet (13 m) long

Order: Iguanodontia

Family: Hadrosauridae

Range: North America (Alberta, Montana)

Pn: ed-MON-toh-SAW-rus

149

Maiasaura

The discovery of a complete *Maiasaura* nest site in Montana proved that dinosaurs were social animals. The females nested in groups and may even have returned to the same site year after year like turtles and many birds today. It is possible that the dinosaurs also shared the care of the young, some remaining on guard while others fed.

Size: 30 feet (9 m) long
Order: Iguanodontia
Family: Hadrosauridae
Range: North America (Montana)
Pn: my-ah-SAW-rah

Size: 26 feet (8 m) long
Order: Iguanodontia
Family: Hadrosauridae
Range: North America (Alberta)
Pn: PRO-sore-oh-LOAF-us

Prosaurolophus

This duckbill had a low crest of bone running from the tip of the flat snout up to the top of the head. It ended in a small bony knob. Like all duckbills, *Prosaurolophus* had a toothless beak at the front of its head for gathering plant food.

Size: 33 feet (10 m) long
Order: Iguanodontia
Family: Hadrosauridae
Range: North America (Alberta)
Pn: an-at-oh-SAW-rus

Anatosaurus

Two "mummified" bodies of *Anatosaurus* dinosaurs have provided rare clues to their diet. The stomach contents include pine needles, twigs, seeds and fruit. Like other hadrosaurs, it may have stood up on its back legs to gather food from trees.

Shantungosaurus

One of the biggest hadrosaurs known, *Shantungosaurus* had a particularly long tail, measuring up to almost half the total body length. Deep and flattened in shape, the tail was held out behind to help balance the body weight when the dinosaur walked upright. *Shantungosaurus* may have weighed as much as 5 tons (4.5 tonnes).

Size: 43 feet (13 m) long
Order: Iguanodontia
Family: Hadrosauridae
Range: Asia (China)
Pn: shan-TUNG-oh-SAW-rus

Size: 30 feet (9 m) long
Order: Iguanodontia
Family: Hadrosauridae
Range: North America (Alberta, California), Asia (Mongolia)
Pn: SORE-oh-LOAF-us

Saurolophus

The face of this duckbill curved upward from its broad snout to the tip of the bony crest on the top of the head. A fleshy nose sac, which helped make the dinosaur's calls louder, may have been attached to the crest.

Size: 30 feet (9 m) long

Order: Iguanodontia

Family: Hadrosauridae

Range: North America (Alberta, New Mexico, Utah)

Pn: par-a-SORE-oh-LOAF-us

Parasaurolophus

A spectacular, backward-pointing crest, more than 6 feet (1.8 m) long, topped the head of this dinosaur. The crest was hollow inside and may have acted like an echo chamber to make the dinosaur's booming calls louder. When the dinosaur held its head up, the crest may have fitted into a small notch in the backbone.

Size: 30 feet (9 m) long

Order: Iguanodontia

Family: Hadrosauridae

Range: North America (Alberta, Montana)

Pn: ko-RITH-oh-SAW-rus

Size: up to 20 feet (6 m) long

Order: Iguanodontia

Family: uncertain

Range: North America (Texas)

Pn: pro-toe-HAD-ross

Protohadros

Discovered in Texas, which would have been covered with marshland at the time, *Protohadros* is the oldest, most primitive duckbill known. The fact that it was found in the United States means that duckbills may not have first evolved in Asia as scientists previously believed.

Corythosaurus

A spectacular fan-shaped crest crowned the head of this duckbill. Crests of several different sizes have been found. Smaller crests may have belonged to young animals or females.

Tsintaosaurus

A tall horn grew from the top of this duckbill's head. It pointed straight up from between the eyes and had a notched tip. There has been much disagreement among experts about the position and use of this horn. Some think there may have been a flap of skin attached that was used like a flag for signaling to other members of the herd or in courtship rituals.

Size: 33 feet (10 m) long

Order: Iguanodontia

Family: Hadrosauridae

Range: Asia (China)

Pn: SIN-tow-SAW-rus

Lambeosaurus

Like all members of its family, *Lambeosaurus* would have moved around on all fours as it fed. But if threatened, it could probably rear up on its back legs to run away. It had two structures on its head: a tall hollow crest at the front and a solid bony spike pointing backward.

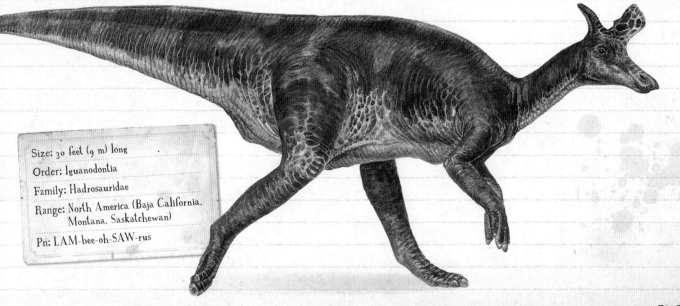

Size: 30 feet (9 m) long

Order: Iguanodontia

Family: Hadrosauridae

Range: North America (Baja California, Montana, Saskatchewan)

Pn: LAM-bee-oh-SAW-rus

STEGOSAURS

Stegosaurs were large, plant-eating dinosaurs. A typical stegosaur had a small head, huge body, and heavy tail lined with long sharp spikes. The most extraordinary features of these dinosaurs were the rows of large triangular plates on the back. There are several different ideas about their use, but many experts believe that they helped to control body temperature. The plates may have been covered with skin rich in blood vessels. When the stegosaur turned toward the sun, its blood would have been warmed as it passed through the plates. When the animal turned away from the sun or into a breeze, the plates would have lost heat, so cooling the body.

Lexovisaurus

Some experts believe that the bony plates on stegosaurs were not used for controlling body temperature but for helping the dinosaurs recognize their own species and attract mates. The arrangement of plates and spines was different in each species. *Lexovisaurus* had two rows of large thin plates.

Size: 16 feet (5 m) long
Order: Thyreophora
Family: Stegosauridae
Range: Europe (England)
Pn: lex-OH-vi-SAW-rus

Scutellosaurus

This dinosaur was an early form of stegosaur. Lining its back and sides were rows of bony studs that may have helped to protect the animal from attackers. Its tail was about half its total length and could have been held out to balance the weight of the body when the dinosaur ran on two legs.

Size: 4 feet (1.2 m) long
Order: Thyreophora
Family: uncertain
Range: North America (Arizona)
Pn: skoot-EL-oh-SAW-rus

Kentrosaurus

Smaller than *Stegosaurus*, *Kentrosaurus* was almost as well armored with bony plates and spikes. If attacked, the stegosaur could lash out with its spiked tail and wound its attacker. Long spikes at hip level provided extra protection against enemies.

Size: 16 feet (5 m) long
Order: Thyreophora
Family: Stegosauridae
Range: Africa (Tanzania)
Pn: KEN-tro-SAW-rus

Miragaia

Along with the typical stegosaur features
of a small head, large body, powerful tail,
and plates running along its back, *Miragaia*
had a much longer neck than any other
stegosaur. The neck contained at least
17 vertebrae, twice as many as
some other stegosaurs.

Size: 20 feet (6 m) long

Order: Thyreophora

Family: Stegosauridae

Range: Europe (Portugal)

Pn: Mi-ra-GUY-a

Stegosaurus

One of the largest and best
known stegosaurs, *Stegosaurus*
had a double row of bony plates
on its back, some measuring up
to 2 feet (60 cm) high. The heavy
tail was armed with spikes up to
3 feet 3 inches (1 m) long.

Size: 30 feet (9 m) long

Order: Thyreophora

Family: Stegosauridae

Range: North America (Colorado,
Oklahoma, Utah, Wyoming)

Pn: STEG-oh-SAW-rus

CRETACEOUS TIMES

The biggest change that took place during the Cretaceous Period, which began 146 million years ago, was the appearance of the first flowering plants. Small herbs, bushes and deciduous trees took over from horsetails and cycads and became the dominant greenery on the Earth. There was more plant food than ever, allowing huge herds of plant eaters, such as horned dinosaurs and duckbills, to thrive. With flowering plants came pollinating insects and many more species of mammals and birds.

Pteranodon, a flying reptile (pterosaur)

Magnolia

CRETACEOUS NORTH AMERICA

In this scene in what is now Montana, a duck-billed dinosaur bellows her alarm as she returns to her nest to find an agile *Troodon* stealing her eggs. Lizards and an early mammal scuttle by, while a tyrannosaur stalks nearer to a group of feeding horned dinosaurs.

Albertosaurus, a tyrannosaur

Sycamore

Small mammal

Moss

Centrosaurus, a horned dinosaur

Troodon

Lizard

CONTINENTS

In the Cretaceous, the world's landmasses continued to drift apart until, by the end of the period, they were close to their positions today. As the land broke into smaller pieces, there were greater differences between the dinosaurs in different continents as they evolved in isolation.

Montana — North America

Europe

Asia

PACIFIC OCEAN

ATLANTIC OCEAN

EQUATOR

TETHYS OCEAN

South America

Africa

India

Australia

Antarctica

Early oystercatcher

Conifer

KEY TO MAP

Ocean

Landmass

Sea-covered continent

Corythosaurus

Corythosaurus, a duck-billed dinosaur

Lizard

Troodon, a bird relative (maniraptoran)

ARMORED DINOSAURS

Two groups of heavily armored dinosaurs were common in the Cretaceous Period: nodosaurs and ankylosaurs. In both, the neck, back, sides, and tail were covered with flat plates of bone, set into the thick leathery skin. Nodosaurs had narrow skulls and long spikes that stuck out at the sides of the body. Ankylosaurs had broader skulls and a heavy ball of bone, like a club, at the end of the tail. If attacked, an ankylosaur could swing it from side to side and cause severe damage to its attacker.

Euoplocephalus

Like other ankylosaurs, this dinosaur had a heavy bony club at the end of its tail that could have weighed more than 60 pounds (27 kg). Powerful muscles at the hips helped *Euoplocephalus* swing its clubbed tail from side to side against any attacker.

Size: 18 feet (5.5 m) long
Order: Thyreophora
Family: Ankylosauridae
Range: North America (Alberta)
Pn: you-op-loh-KEF-ah-lus

Saichania

Like most ankylosaurs, *Saichania* had a network of air passages inside its skull. These may have helped to cool or moisten air before it reached the lungs. This was important, because Mongolia at this time was hot and humid.

Size: 23 feet (7 m) long
Order: Thyreophora
Family: Ankylosauridae
Range: Asia (Mongolia)
Pn: sy-KAHN-ee-a

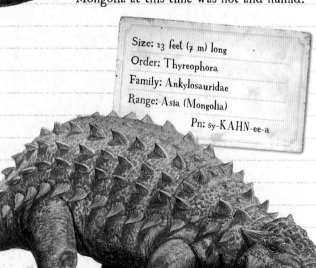

Polacanthus

Few fossils of this dinosaur have been found, but it is thought to have had large spines protecting its shoulders and tail. Smaller spiny plates guarded the sides and a mass of bone covered the hips. Like other nodosaurs, it may have crouched down when attacked, relying on its armor for defense.

Size: 13 feet (4 m) long
Order: Thyreophora
Family: Nodosauridae
Range: Europe (England)
Pn: pol-a-KAN-thus

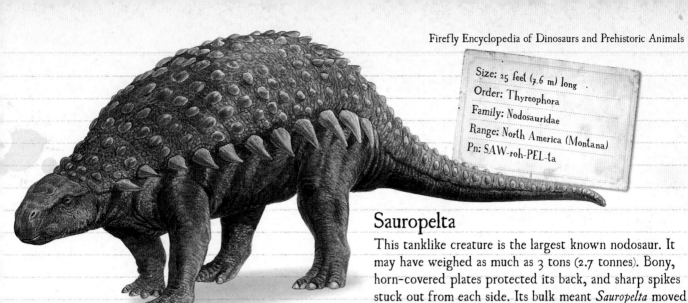

Size: 25 feet (7.6 m) long .
Order: Thyreophora
Family: Nodosauridae
Range: North America (Montana)
Pn: SAW-roh-PEL-ta

Sauropelta

This tanklike creature is the largest known nodosaur. It may have weighed as much as 3 tons (2.7 tonnes). Bony, horn-covered plates protected its back, and sharp spikes stuck out from each side. Its bulk meant *Sauropelta* moved slowly, but its armor would have given it protection.

Panoplosaurus

This heavily armored nodosaur had broad plates of bone across its neck and shoulders, whereas the rest of the back was covered in smaller bony studs. Huge spikes guarded each side, and even the head was protected with thick pieces of bone.

Size: 15 feet (4.5 m) long
Order: Thyreophora
Family: Nodosauridae
Range: North America (Alberta, Montana, South Dakota, Texas)
Pn: pan-o-ploe-SAW-rus

Hylaeosaurus

Hylaeosaurus was one of the earliest dinosaurs to be described and named. A fossil was found in southern England in the 1820s by Gideon Mantell, one of the first dinosaur experts. The bones are still imprisoned in the block of limestone in which they were found.

Size: 20 feet (6 m) long .
Order: Thyreophora
Family: Nodosauridae
Range: Europe (England)
Pn: hy-lee-oh-SAW-rus

Talarurus

Like all armored dinosaurs, *Talarurus* ate plants, which it cropped with the toothless beak at the front of its jaws. The club on the end of its tail was made from two large balls of bone joined together. Thin, bony rods strengthened the tail to support the heavy club.

Size: 16 feet (5 m) long .
Order: Thyreophora
Family: Ankylosauridae
Range: Asia (Mongolia)
Pn: tal-a-ROO-rus

159

HORNED DINOSAURS

There were three main groups of horned dinosaurs. First came the "parrot dinosaurs," or psittacosaurs, of the Early Cretaceous. These lightly built dinosaurs had distinctive parrotlike beaks. In the Late Cretaceous came the protoceratopids, which had heavier bodies and the beginnings of the bony neck frills that developed so dramatically in the later ceratopsians. The ceratopsians were the most common large plant eaters in Late Cretaceous western North America. These armored dinosaurs had sharp horns on massive heads and a bony frill at the back of the neck.

Bagaceratops

This little protoceratopid had a squat body and long tail, supported on four solid legs. At the back of its neck was a bony ridge, and there was a short horn halfway along its snout. Unlike other members of its family, it had no teeth in its upper beak.

Size: 3 feet 3 inches (1 m) long
Order: Ceratopsia
Family: uncertain
Range: Asia (Mongolia)
Pn: BAG-a-SER-a-tops

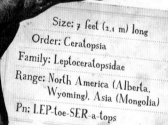

Size: 7 feet (2.1 m) long
Order: Ceratopsia
Family: Leptoceratopsidae
Range: North America (Alberta, Wyoming), Asia (Mongolia)
Pn: LEP-toe-SER-a-tops

Leptoceratops

This was one of the few protoceratopids to be found in North America. Most of the family lived in Asia. Its back legs were built for running and it could probably move on four legs or two. The five-clawed fingers on its hands could have been used for picking leaves and passing them to the mouth.

Microceratops

The smallest horned dinosaur is only preserved as an incomplete fossil of what is probably a juvenile. The characteristics of the adult are unknown and the name *Microceratops* was earlier given to a wasp, so this dinosaur was renamed *Microceratus* in 2008.

Size: 2 feet (60 cm) long
Order: Ceratopsia
Family: uncertain
Range: Asia (China, Mongolia)
Pn: mik-roh-SERRA-tops

Montanaceratops

Although it had a definite horn on its snout, *Montanaceratops* was a protoceratopid, not a member of the more advanced ceratopsian family. Its tail was unusually deep and flexible and could probably have been moved rapidly from side to side. The tail may have been used as a courtship signal in the mating season or as a way of recognizing its own species.

Size: 10 feet (3 m) long
Order: Ceratopsia
Family: Protoceratopsidae
Range: North America (Montana)
Pn: mon-tan-oh-SERRA-tops

Size: 20 feet (6 m) long
Order: Protoceratopsidae
Family: Ceratopsidae
Range: North America (Alberta)
Pn: AN-ki-SER-a-tops

Anchiceratops

This horned dinosaur lived near the end of the Late Cretaceous and was slightly more streamlined than some of its relatives. Its body was longer and its bony neck frill narrower. Like other horned dinosaurs, it fed on plants, which it gathered with its sharp, toothless beak.

Centrosaurus

Like other horned dinosaurs, *Centrosaurus* had thick pillarlike legs with heavy bones to support the bulky body. The short, wide toes were fanned out to help spread the weight. Despite the size of its head and bony neck frill, a mobile neck joint made sure that *Centrosaurus* could turn its head quickly and easily.

Size: 20 feet (6 m) long
Order: Ceratopsia
Family: Ceratopsidae
Range: North America (Alberta, Montana)
Pn: SEN-troh-saw-rus

Size: 17 feet (5.2 m) long
Order: Ceratopsia
Family: Ceratopsidae
Range: North America (Alberta)
Pn: KAZ-mo-saw-rus

Chasmosaurus

This horned dinosaur had a huge bony neck frill that stretched from the back of the skull to cover its neck and shoulders. A spectacular frill like this could have been used to ward off enemies as well as to attract females.

Pentaceratops

Like *Chasmosaurus*, this horned dinosaur had a huge neck frill, which was fringed with small spines. There were several large openings in the bony surface to make the frill lighter. The name of this dinosaur means "five-horned face," because scientists thought it had horns on its cheeks as well as on its snout. In fact, these were just elongated cheekbones.

Size: 20 feet (6 m) long
Order: Ceratopsia
Family: Ceratopsidae
Range: North America (New Mexico)
Pn: PEN-ta-SER-a-tops

Psittacosaurus

A parrotlike toothless beak covered with horn is the reason for this dinosaur's name, which means "parrot lizard." This dinosaur fed on plants, which it cropped with its strong beak. It had bony ridges on the sides of its head but no neck frill like the later ceratopsians.

Size: 8 feet (2.5 m) long
Order: Ceratopsia
Family: Psittacosauridae
Range: Asia (China, Mongolia, Siberia)
Pn: si-TAK-oh-SAW-rus

Size: 30 feet (9 m) long
Order: Ceratopsia
Family: Ceratopsidae
Range: North America (Alberta, Colorado, Montana, Saskatchewan, South Dakota, Wyoming)
Pn: try-SER-ah-tops

Triceratops

One of the largest and most common horned dinosaurs, *Triceratops* weighed as much as 10 tons (9 tonnes). Its skull alone was more than 6 feet (1.8 m) long. Like others in its family, *Triceratops* probably lived in large herds. Rival males may have fought one another, locking horns and pushing with their head shields.

Size: 25 feet (7.6 m) long
Order: Ceratopsia
Family: Ceratopsidae
Range: North America (Montana, South Dakota, Texas, Utah, Wyoming)
Pn: TOR-oh-SAW-rus

Torosaurus

The skull of this dinosaur is one of the largest known of any land animal, living or extinct. Including the enormous neck frill, which extended from the back of the head, it measured more than 8 feet (2.5 m). With this and the three pointed horns on its snout, *Torosaurus* was a challenge for any predator.

WHY DID THE DINOSAURS DISAPPEAR?

No one knows exactly what caused the mass extinctions that destroyed many of the Earth's creatures, including the dinosaurs, 65 million years ago. There is no doubt that a massive meteorite from outer space hit the Gulf of Mexico at that time. This caused widespread damage and may have triggered climate change. In common with previous mass extinction events, there were vast eruptions and outpourings of lava and gas, which also had an impact on global climates.

VOLCANIC ERUPTIONS

Volcanic eruptions that took place in India at the end of the Cretaceous Period caused a massive outpouring of lava, as shown in the rock layers of the Deccan Traps (see left). They prove that there were extraordinary events on the Earth at this time that may have caused the death of the dinosaurs.

Dromaeosaurus, a bird relative (maniraptoran), feeding on *Edmontosaurus*, a duck-billed dinosaur

CLIMATE CHANGE

Even a small volcanic eruption can cause local climate change, and in the Late Cretaceous there was an enormous amount of volcanic activity. These eruptions would have thrown huge quantities of ash and dust into the air, causing the climate to change and destroying plants and animals.

Quetzalcoatlus, a flying reptile (pterosaur)

This scene in the area now known as Montana shows the effect of increased volcanic activity. Debris has darkened the sky and blocked out sunlight. Plants are dying and with them plant eaters. Meat eaters survive for a while by scavenging.

Edmontonia, an armored dinosaur

Triceratops, a horned dinosaur

Pachycephalosaurus, a bonehead dinosaur

METEORITE IMPACT?

A meteorite, measuring at least 6 miles (10 km) across, struck the earth at the end of the Cretaceous Period and caused the death of the dinosaurs. Huge amounts of debris thrown up by the impact would have darkened the skies for many years, causing a long cold period and the death of plants. Plant-eating dinosaurs would have soon starved to death, followed by the meat eaters that fed on them.

CRATER

An important piece of evidence for the meteorite theory includes the discovery of a vast crater near the north coast of Mexico. This computer-generated image shows the meteorite crater now underwater and buried under a deep layer of rock. The blue area at the bottom of the picture shows the channel made by the meteorite as it landed.

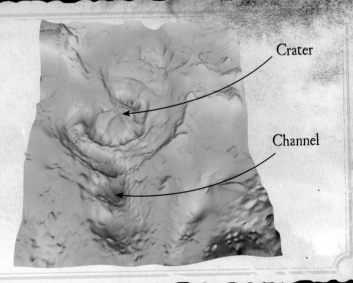

Crater

Channel

Other evidence to show that there may have been a meteorite impact can be seen in rocks all over the world from the end of the Cretaceous Period. They contain a rare chemical element that can only have come from outer space.

WHAT DIED AND WHAT SURVIVED?

Died	Survived
Ammonites	Crocodiles
Pterosaurs	Mammals
Dinosaurs	Birds
	Amphibians
Plesiosaurs	Insects

When the dinosaurs disappeared, groups such as ammonites, pterosaurs and marine reptiles also died forever. Creatures that managed to survive the mass extinction included other kinds of reptiles, such as crocodiles, lizards and snakes, as well as birds, mammals, amphibians and insects.

AVIAN DINOSAURS

Birds are thought to have evolved from two-legged dinosaurs called theropods during the Jurassic Period. In fact, recent revelations, including the discovery that many theropods were covered with feathers, have blurred the dividing line between dinosaurs and birds.

BIRDS

The living birds are a large group of highly successful tetrapods, most of which have arms modified as wings for flying. The living birds today number over 9,000 species. They evolved from a group of small feathered theropod dinosaurs. Fossils such as *Archaeopteryx* preserve a mixture of reptilian and birdlike features. By Cretaceous times a number of primitive bird groups had evolved, most of which are now extinct.

Size: up to 11 feet 6 inches (3.5 m) tall
Order: Dinornithiformes
Family: Dinornithidae
Range: New Zealand
Pn: din-OR-nis MAX-i-mus

Harpagornis moorei

This eagle may not have been much larger than many of its modern relatives, the eagles and Old World vultures, but it was stronger and more heavily built. *Harpagornis moorei* coexisted with moas in New Zealand, and became extinct at about the same time — perhaps as recently as the 17th century.

Size: possibly 3 feet 6 inches (1 m) tall
Order: Accipitriformes
Family: Accipitridae
Range: New Zealand
Pn: har-pag-OR-nis MORE-eye

Dinornis maximus

Dinornis maximus was the tallest bird that ever existed. It was one of about a dozen types of flightless moa that survived in New Zealand until around 1800. Moas were bulky, long-necked birds, and in the absence of other browsing mammals, fed off the rich supplies of seeds and fruits.

Emeus crassus

This moa, only half the height of *Dinornis*, had broad feet and massive lower legs, which were out of all proportion to its body size. A slow-moving animal, it must have provided easy prey for the moa hunters. The modern kiwi, the bird that is the emblem of New Zealand, is regarded by some paleontologists as a highly specialized moa. The three living species are tiny in comparison to their extinct relatives.

Size: 5 feet (1.5 m) tall
Order: Dinornithiformes
Family: Emeidae
Range: New Zealand
Pn: e-MAY-us CRASS-us

Size: up to 10 feet (3 m) tall
Order: Aepyornthiformes
Family: Aepyornithidae
Range: Madagascar
Pn: EYE-pee-OR-nis TIE-tan

Aepyornis titan

This species is the largest of the extinct genus *Aepyornis* and weighed up to 1,100 pounds (500 kg). The common name — elephant bird — stems from Arabian tales of the "rukhkh," which could carry off an elephant. *Aepyornis'* legs ended in three widely spread, stumpy toes. The long, thick thighbones show that it was not a runner. *Aepyornis,* eggs were over 1 foot (30 cm) long and could hold $2\frac{1}{4}$ gallons (9 l). It had no special defenses — no teeth, no talons and no wings. Size and strength were protection against predators. When man arrived in Madagascar, less than 1,500 years ago, species of *Aepyornis* were still alive. It may have become extinct as late as the 17th century.

Size: 3 feet 3 inches (1 m) tall
Order: Columbiformes
Family: Raphidae
Range: Mauritius
Pn: RAF-us COO-cul-AH-tus

Size: 4 feet (1.2 m) tall
Order: Neornithes
Family: Pelagornithidae
Range: North America (California)
Pn: OST-ee-oh-don-TOR-nis OR-ee

Osteodontornis orri

Osteodontornis orri is one of the "bony-toothed," gliding seabirds. *Osteodontornis'* body was heavily built, with legs and feet like a huge petrel. The long, narrow wings, designed for constant gliding flight, had a wingspan in some of the larger species of up to 20 feet (6 m), and its bill was as long as a modern pelican. The head, with its heavy, long, pelican-like bill, probably rested back on the shoulders in flight, like a modern heron's.

Raphus cucullatus

Raphus cucullatus, also known as the dodo, was a giant, terrestrial pigeon that became another casualty of man. Flightless and slow moving, it was easy prey to sailors who stopped off on islands in the Indian Ocean. The size of a modern turkey, it had a fat body and a waddling gait, and it was so ill-equipped to defend itself that it did not even flee the hungry sailors, leading to the extermination of the species by the 17th century.

Hesperornis regalis

This large, flightless bird differed from other toothed seabirds in having lost its wings almost completely. It swam with powerful kicks of its large, webbed feet, set well back on the body, propelling itself along in the manner of a modern grebe. *Hesperornis regalis* could have chased fast-moving fish and squid underwater.

Size: 6 feet (1.8 m) tall

Order: Ornithurae

Family: uncertain

Range: North America (Kansas)

Pn: HES-per-ORN-is re-GAR-lis

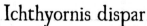

Ichthyornis dispar

The toothed jaws of this ancient bird were originally thought to belong to a mosasaur — a contemporary, fish-eating marine lizard. This reptile was preserved in the same rocks, and had similar jaws and teeth to those of *Ichthyornis*. *Ichthyornis dispar* and others of its genus had a general structure like that of a large, modern sea tern, but with a proportionally bigger head and bill. The large sternum suggests strong flight.

Size: 8 inches (20 cm) tall

Order: Ornithurae

Family: uncertain

Range: North America (Kansas, Texas)

Pn: ick-thee-YORN-is dis-par

Size: 3 feet 3 inches (1 m) tall

Order: Ornithurae

Family: uncertain

Range: Europe (England), North America (Utah, Wyoming), South America (Patagonia)

Pn: pres-bee-YOR-nis per-VAY-tus

Presbyornis pervetus

Presbyornis, a long-legged, long-necked bird, was so slenderly built that paleontologists first thought it was a flamingo, until it was discovered that its head and bill were similar to those of modern ducks. From the abundant remains of both bones and eggs, it seems that *Presbyornis pervetus* flocked together on the shallow margins of lakes, nesting in great, open colonies.

Pinguinus impennis

Another member of the ciconiiformes, the great auk, *Pinguinus impennis*, lost its final battle against extinction on a small island off Iceland in 1844. For years, it had been relentlessly hunted by sailors for its flesh, its eggs and the fat beneath its skin, which was used to provide oil for lamps. Despite its name, the great auk was not a large bird, being only about half as tall again as the razorbill, the modern auk that it most resembled. It differed only in that it had become flightless. Although unrelated to the modern penguins of the southern hemisphere, today's penguins are named after it.

Size: 1 foot 8 inches (50 cm) tall.

Order: Charadriiformes

Family: Alcidae

Range: Small islands off western Europe (British Isles, Iceland), North America (Greeland, Maine to Labrador)

Pn: ping-IN-us im-PEN-is

Size: 5 feet (1.5) m tall

Order: Dendrornithes

Family: Teratornithidae

Range: South America (Argentina)

Pn: Ar-gen-TAV-is mag-NIF-i-cens

Argentavis magnificens

Argentavis magnificens had huge wings compared with its body size. Although only some of its bones have been found, estimates place its wingspan at about 24 feet (7.3 m) — twice the wingspan of the longest-winged living bird, the wandering albatross. A bird of this size did not fly by flapping its wings. It would have conserved its energy by gliding from one food source to another, using as few wingbeats as possible. Launching itself from high places, it used the rising thermal currents of warm air during the day to keep it aloft. As with the modern albatross, its initial takeoff technique was probably awkward.

Neocathartes grallator

Originally thought to be a New World vulture modified for running, *Neocathartes* appears to be a flesh-eating member of another group, the bathornithids. It was capable of flight, although it is probable that it spent most of its time hunting on the ground.

Size: 1 foot 6 inches (45 cm) tall

Order: Gruiformes

Family: Bathornithidae

Range: North America (Wyoming)

Pn: nee-oh-cath-ART-ays grall-AY-tor

Limnofregata azygosternum

Limnofregata azygosternum appears to have been an ancestor of the modern frigate birds. Today, these are specialized seabirds, related to pelicans, and almost wholly adapted to an aerial existence. However, 50 million years ago, they were only just evolving, and *Limnofregata* may be a halfway stage in their development.

Size: 5 feet (1.5 m) tall

Order: Gruiformes

Family: Phorusrhacidae

Range: South America (Patagonia)

Pn: for-us-RAK-us in-FLAT-us

Size: up to 1 foot (30 cm) tall

Order: Neornithes

Family: Fregatidae

Range: North America (Wyoming)

Pn: LIM-no-freg-ART-a az-ee-gost-ER-num

Phorusrhacos inflatus

Phorusrhacos inflatus was a medium-sized member of a family of flightless birds that became the dominant predators in South America during the Tertiary Period. All the phorusrhacids had strong running legs, small, useless wings, and large heads, equipped with great, eaglelike beaks. Some species were giants, and stood 10 feet (3 m) tall; the head of one species was over 1 foot 6 inches (45 cm) long.

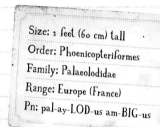

Palaelodus ambiguus

This medium-sized, long-legged shorebird is related to the modern wading and water birds, seabirds, and birds of prey. Paleontologists know little about what the head and bill of *Palaelodus* would have looked like, although the structure of its legs suggests it dived and swam underwater to feed, behaving in a way similar to a modern diving duck.

Size: 2 feet (60 cm) tall
Order: Phoenicopteriformes
Family: Palaeolodidae
Range: Europe (France)
Pn: pal-ay-LOD-us am-BIG-us

Size: 7 feet (2.1 m) tall
Order: Neornithes
Family: Diatrymidae
Range: Europe (Belgium, England, France),
North America (New Jersey, New
Mexico, Wyoming)
Pn: dye-a-TRIM-a ji-GANT-ee-a

Diatryma gigantea

Diatryma gigantea was a giant flightless bird that lived during the Paleocene and Eocene, when North America and Europe were joined together. Like other members of its family, it was heavily built with tiny wings, incapable of flight. Its stout legs were armed with strong, clawed feet. The bird's large head (with its massive, hooked beak) was almost the size of that of a modern horse. Some paleontologists suggest that the diatrymids became the dominant carnivores in the northern hemisphere.

SYNAPSIDS

The first animals to show mammal characteristics were small, lizardlike creatures that evolved during the Carboniferous Period. These creatures were known as synapsids, or mammal-like reptiles. One important feature of synapsids was tooth differentiation. This allowed a more efficient processing of food and release of the energy it contains. These creatures were so successful that they made up nearly three-quarters of all the tetrapods on land. A later group of synapsids called the therapsids evolved during the late Permain times, surviving to live alongside the dinosaurs before becoming extinct.

PELYCOSAURS

The reptilian ancestors of the mammals — the pelycosaurs and therapsids — and the mammals themselves all share the same type of synapsid skull. The single, large opening behind each eye socket allowed the development of longer jaw muscles, which resulted in stronger jaws that could deal with large prey. Pelycosaurs were the earliest of the synapsid (early relative of mammals) reptiles to evolve. They first appeared during the Late Carboniferous Period, some 300 million years ago, when reptiles were first colonizing the land. Like the early reptiles, the pelycosaurs started as small, lizardlike creatures. They evolved into many different types of a much heavier build, with strong jaws and teeth of different sizes and shapes.

Size: 1 foot 8 inches (50 cm) long
Order: Eupelycosauria
Family: Ophiacodontidae
Range: North America (Nova Scotia)
Pn: arc-ee-oth-IRIS

Archaeothyris

This small, lizardlike ophiacodont is the earliest known pelycosaur. Its remains were found in the same Late Carboniferous (Pennsylvanian) locality as those of the first known reptile, the anapsid *Hylonomus*. *Archaeothyris* was already more advanced than the other early anapsid reptiles. Its jaws were strong, and its sharp teeth suggest it had a varied, carnivorous diet.

Size: up to 12 feet (3.6 m) long
Order: Eupelycosauria
Family: Ophiacodontidae
Range: North America (Texas)
Pn: off-ee-a-COH-don

Ophiacodon

Ophiacodon shows the rapid evolution of features within the pelycosaur group. Its skull had changed from the small, low shape of its earlier relative *Archaeothyris* (above) to a deep, narrow shape. This allowed more space for longer jaw muscles to develop. With hind limbs that were longer than its forelimbs and set somewhat more directly beneath the body, *Ophiacodon* was probably a better runner than *Archaeothyris*.

Dimetrodon

The spectacular "sail" on the back of *Dimetrodon* has earned it the popular name of the "finback," and is believed to be an early method of controlling body temperature. The framework for the sail was provided by the elongated spines of the animal's back vertebrae, which were up to 3 feet 3 inches (1 m) long in the center. In life, a sheet of skin covered the spines, and this was probably richly supplied with blood vessels. Like a solar heater, the sail would have absorbed heat and warmed the blood, which then coursed through the body.

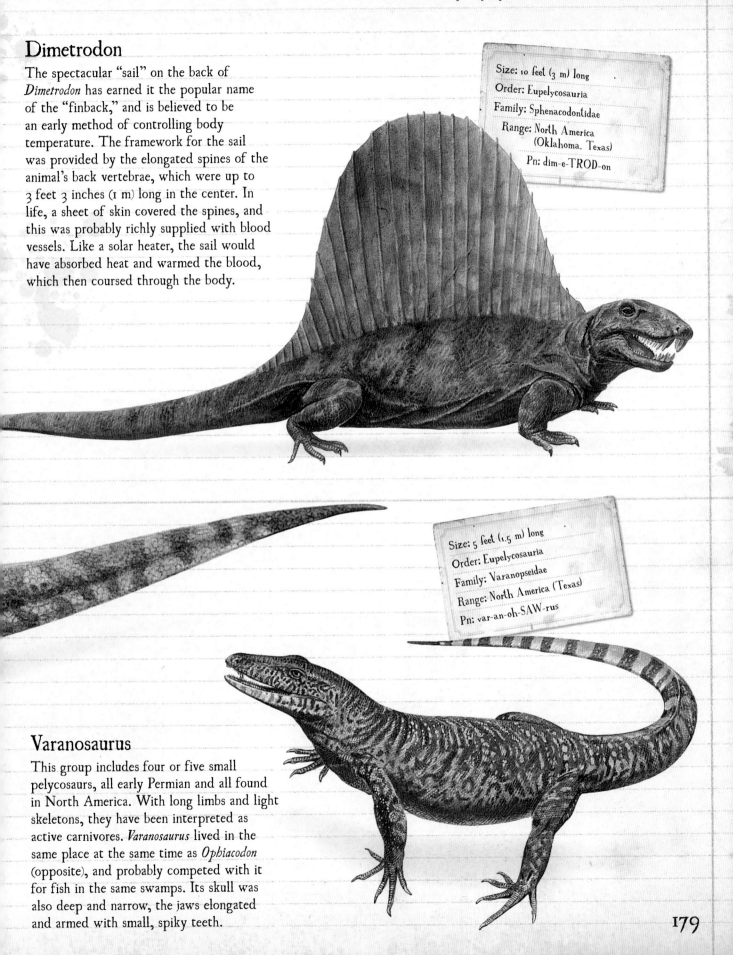

Size: 10 feet (3 m) long
Order: Eupelycosauria
Family: Sphenacodontidae
Range: North America
(Oklahoma, Texas)
Pn: dim-e-TROD-on

Size: 5 feet (1.5 m) long
Order: Eupelycosauria
Family: Varanopseidae
Range: North America (Texas)
Pn: var-an-oh-SAW-rus

Varanosaurus

This group includes four or five small pelycosaurs, all early Permian and all found in North America. With long limbs and light skeletons, they have been interpreted as active carnivores. *Varanosaurus* lived in the same place at the same time as *Ophiacodon* (opposite), and probably competed with it for fish in the same swamps. Its skull was also deep and narrow, the jaws elongated and armed with small, spiky teeth.

Casea

The caseids, represented by *Casea*, were the last family of pelycosaurs to evolve, in Early Permian times. They became the most abundant of the plant-eating pelycosaurs, and thrived almost to the end of the Permian. *Casea* was one of the smaller members; some of its more imposing relatives reached lengths of 10 feet (3 m) and weights of more than 1,320 pounds (600 kg). All of the caseids had deep, bulky bodies, in which the rib cage was enormously expanded in order to accommodate the long, plant-digesting gut.

Size: 4 feet (1.2 m) long

Order: Caseasauria

Family: Caseidae

Range: Europe (France),
North America (Texas)

Pn: cas-EE-a

Edaphosaurus

Edaphosaurus had a large sail on its back, similar to that of *Dimetrodon*. It differed in that the extended vertebral spines of *Edaphosaurus* had crosspieces of bone along their length. As well as serving to regulate body temperature, it is possible that the sail could also have served for display purposes — either of courtship or of threat — and it may have been brightly colored. This bulky pelycosaur was not an active creature, nor was it built for speed.

Size: 10 feet (3 m) long

Order: Eupelycosauria

Family: Edaphosauridae

Range: Europe (Czech Republic),
North America (Texas)

Pn: ee-daf-o-SAW-rus

THERAPSIDS

The therapsids were advanced synapsid reptiles and the direct ancestors of the mammals. The dicynodonts were the most successful and wide-ranging group of plant-eating therapsids. They evolved during the Late Permian Period and survived to the end of the Triassic Period — a span of almost 50 million years. The only group of therapsids that outlived the dicynodonts were the cynodonts. The advanced development of the dicynodonts' skulls and jaws was the main factor in the animals' success. The synapsid openings at the back of the skull were enlarged in dicynodonts, to allow for longer, stronger muscles to operate the creatures' jaws. The hinge between the lower jaw and the skull also permitted the jaws to move forward and backward with a strong, shearing action.

Lycaenops

Lycaenops, or "wolf face," was a small, lightly built carnivore, with long running legs. It was a member of the gorgonopsians, the dominant predators of the Late Permian. It may have hunted in packs, and probably preyed on large, plant-eating therapsids, such as *Moschops*. The canines were particularly long, and the front part of the skull was deep to accommodate their roots.

Size: 3 feet 3 inches (1 m) long
Order: Therapsida
Family: Gorgonopsidae
Range: Africa (South Africa)
Pn: ly-KINE-ops

Size: 5 feet (1.5 m) long
Order: Therapsida
Family: Phthinosuchidae
Range: Europe (Russia)
Pn: ff-THIN-o-SOOK-us

Phthinosuchus

Only the skull of this primitive therapsid is known. It is strikingly similar to that of a sphenacodont, but with larger synapsid openings behind the eyes and more prominent canine teeth. Paleontologists believe it to be intermediate in structure between the pelycosaurs and the therapsids.

Size: 1 foot (30 cm) long
Order: Therapsida
Family: uncertain
Range: Africa (South Africa)
Pn: gal-e-KIR-us

Size: 13 inches (33 cm) long
Order: Therapsida
Family: Cistecephalidae
Range: Africa (South Africa)
Pn: sist-e-ke-FAL-us

Galechirus

This tiny lizardlike reptile is thought to be an early member of the dicynodonts — the most abundant and successful group of the plant-eating therapsids. However, *Galechirus'* teeth suggest that it was actually an insectivore.

Cistecephalus

Dicynodonts adapted to many lifestyles. Some were semiaquatic, whereas others browsed in the coniferous forests. Some, such as *Cistecephalus*, lived underground. This creature had a wedge-shaped, flattened head, a short body and strong, stumpy forelimbs with broad toes, like those of a modern mole. It probably used its powerful limbs to dig into the soil to find worms, snails, and insects.

Size: 3 feet 3 inches (1 m) long
Order: Dicynodontia
Family: Lystrosauridae
Range: Africa (South Africa),
       Antarctica, Asia (China, India),
       Europe (Russia)
Pn: LISS-tro-SAW-rus

Lystrosaurus

The wide distribution of this sturdy, herbivore provides further evidence that during Late Permian and Triassic times India and all the southern continents were united as one landmass, Gondwana. *Lystrosaurus* used to be regarded as a kind of reptilian "hippopotamus" that wallowed in shallows, browsing on waterweeds. New analysis shows that it probably fed on more resistant vegetation and may have burrrowed.

Dicynodon

Dicynodon had the characteristic pair of canine tusks in its upper jaw, which gives the dicynodont group its name, "two dog teeth." It may have used these strong tusks to uproot plants. Another group of herbivorous reptiles, the pareiasaurs, were contemporaries of *Dicynodon*. Some of these were elephantine beasts, heavily armored and with a full set of leaf-shaped teeth in their jaws. This was a different dentition to that of the horny-beaked, virtually toothless dicynodonts.

Size: 4 feet (1.2 m) long

Order: Therapsida

Family: Dicynodontidae

Range: Africa (South Africa, Tanzania)

Pn: dik-eye-NO-don

Robertia

Although *Robertia* was among the first dicynodonts to evolve, it had already evolved the characteristic specialized canine "dog teeth." At the front of its jaws was a turtlelike beak, and the only teeth that remained were a pair of tusklike canines in the upper jaw. *Robertia* had a notch in the jaw in front of the canine teeth, into which tough stems and roots could presumably be inserted, then severed by the sharp beak.

Size: 1 foot 6 inches (45 cm) long

Order: Therapsida

Family: Pylaecephalidae

Range: Africa (South Africa)

Pn: rob-ERT-ee-a

Ericiolacerta

This lizardlike creature was an active insectivore, judging from its small teeth and long, slim limbs. The abundant plant life of early Triassic Africa — horsetails, ferns, conifers, and early cycads — that supported the great populations of dicynodonts also provided home and food for many insects and other invertebrates. These, in turn, were a source of suitable prey for small therocephalians, such as *Ericiolacerta*.

Size: 8 inches (20 cm) long

Order: Therapsida

Family: Ericolacertidae

Range: Africa (South Africa)

Pn: eric-ee-o-lac-ERT-a

Kannemeyeria

This dicynodont was a well-adapted land-living herbivore. Its limb girdles formed massive plates of bone to support the heavy, bulky body. *Kannemeyeria's* massive head was lightweight due to the great size of the openings for the eyes, nostrils and jaw muscles. Mouthfuls of leaves and roots would have been torn up by the powerful, horny beak and ground down by the shearing action of the toothless jaws.

Size: up to 10 feet (3 m) long

Order: Therapsida

Family: Kannemeyeriidae

Range: Africa (South Africa), Asia (India), South America (Argentina)

Pn: KAN-eh-MAY-er-ee-a

Size: 1 foot 7 inches (48 cm) long
Order: Therapsida
Family: Traversodontidae
Range: South America (Argentina)
Pn: mass-e-to-NATH-us

Oligokyphus

Oligokyphus and other members of its herbivorous family, the tritylodonts, were the last group of cynodonts to appear in the Late Triassic. *Oligokyphus* was like a modern weasel in appearance, with a long, slim body and tail. Its forelegs, as well as its hind legs, were placed directly beneath the body, as they are in mammals. This little cynodont had achieved a fully upright, four-legged posture, unlike all other therapsids.

Massetognathus

Of the dozen or so cynodont families, only three included herbivores. The traversodonts, represented by *Massetognathus*, were plant eaters, with a distinctive dentition. The teeth of the lower jaw fitted into those of the upper jaw. There was also a gap between the cheek teeth and the small canines toward the front of the jaws, which probably had the same function as in living rodents and rabbits.

Size: 1 foot 8 inches (50 cm) long
Order: Therapsida
Family: Tritylodontidae
Range: Europe (England)
Pn: OL-ig-oh-KY-fus

Size: 2 feet (60 cm) long
Order: Therapsida
Family: Procynosuchidae
Range: Africa (South Africa)
Pn: proc-in-oh-SOOK-us

Procynosuchus

Although not a typical cynodont, *Procynosuchus* is interesting because, despite being one of the earliest and most primitive members of the group, it was specialized for living in water. The rear of its body and tail were more flexible than was usual among cynodonts, and could obviously be flexed from side to side, in a crocodile-style swimming motion.

MAMMALS

The first true mammals appeared during the late Triassic. These early animals were small, shrewlike creatures, such as *Megazostrodon* and *Ptilodus*. Few of these early mammals evolved to be bigger than a dog, particularly because the land at the time was dominated by the powerful dinosaurs. Instead, many were nocturnal creatures, feeding on insects and worms at night, when the predatory dinosaurs were less active. With the extinction of the dinosaurs some 65 million years ago, these small mammals then evolved into the animals that dominate the land today.

WHAT IS A MAMMAL?

Mammals are warm-blooded, hairy vertebrates (animals with a backbone), that feed their young with milk produced by mammary glands. Most mammals give birth to live young, although today's echidnas and platypuses lay eggs. Most mammals keep their bodies at a constant temperature so they can be active for long periods. To produce the energy needed for such a high level of activity, they need to eat a great deal of food. The group includes animals living in a variety of habitats from water to land to air.

Mammals first appeared in the late Triassic Period, about 220 million years ago, when the earth was dominated by reptiles and, in particular, dinosaurs. Following the disappearance of the dinosaurs some 65 million years ago, mammals began to increase in diversity as new habitats of tropical rain forests, temperate woodlands, savanna and prairie grasslands emerged.

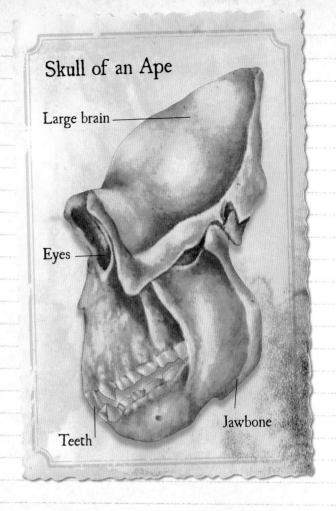

Skull of an Ape

Large brain

Eyes

Teeth

Jawbone

BRAINS

The active lifestyles of mammals call for a high degree of control over their nervous systems. For this reason, mammals have large and complex brains capable of rapidly processing information transmitted from the eyes, nose and ears.

HAIR

Hair on mammals usually takes the form of a dense fur coat. This retains body heat, for mammals are warm-blooded. By maintaining a regular body temperature, mammals can be active for long periods, regardless of external conditions.

Warmth of fur

Epigaulus

TYPES OF MAMMAL

Among the most ancient of mammal orders, marsupials give birth to small, undeveloped young that are then nurtured and suckled in a skin pouch.

Marsupials
Procoptodon

Bats and rodents
Icaronycteris

Bats are the only mammals to have evolved powered flight. Rodents are the largest mammal order today.

Whales, dolphins and porpoises (cetaceans) are thoroughly adapted to living in the sea. They are warm-blooded and still suckle their young.

Cetaceans
Zygorhiza

Carnivores
Dinofelis

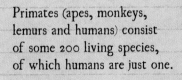

The diverse carnivore (meaning "meat eating") order ranges from cats, mongooses and dogs to weasels, otters and sea lions.

Hoofed mammals
Diadiaphorus

An abundant and varied group, hoofed mammals are large plant eaters that root and browse among vegetation or crop grass.

Apes and monkeys
Oreopithecus

Primates (apes, monkeys, lemurs and humans) consist of some 200 living species, of which humans are just one.

YOUNG

Most mammals give birth to live young, which are then fed with a regular supply of highly nutritious milk. This gives mammals a distinct evolutionary advantage because, with nothing to do but sleep and suckle, infant mammals can grow fast.

PRIMITIVE MAMMALS

The most primitive mammals belong to this group of "first mammals." Some modern classifications make a greater separation between the living mammal groups (the therians) and the extinct groups. However, the interrelationships between the primitive mammal groups are far from clear, largely because so much of the fossil material just consists of teeth remains. Nevertheless, it is still thought that they all evolved from the cynodonts, a group of synapsid reptiles. The only surviving primitive mammals are the monotremes: echidnas, or spiny anteaters, and the duck-billed platypuses, all of which are found only in Australasia. Reflecting their reptilian ancestry, they all lay eggs.

Crusafontia

The dryolestid *Crusafontia* is known only from a few teeth. Paleontologists believe that *Crusafontia* probably resembled a tiny squirrel and it may have reproduced the way a marsupial does — giving birth to very immature young, then suckling them in a pouch for the first few weeks of their lives.

Size: 4 inches (10 cm) long
Order: Dryolestida
Family: Dryolestidae
Range: Europe (Portugal)
Pn: croos-a-FONT-ee-a

Size: 5 inches (12 cm) long
Order: Haramiyida
Family: Haramiyidae
Range: Europe (England. Germany)
Pn: Har-a-MEE-ya

Haramiya

Haramiya is known from only a few isolated teeth. This fragmentary evidence suggests that it was somewhat like a miniature vole, and crushed its food with its broad cheek teeth. It may have lived on low-growing vegetation, possibly on the fruit of cycadlike plants.

Zalambdalestes

Zalambdalestes looked very like the modern elephant shrew. It had a long upturned snout and powerful little legs, the back pair longer than the front. The legs had greatly elongated foot bones. It may have run in the undergrowth, catching insects with its long incisor teeth.

Size: 8 inches (20 cm) long
Infraclass: Eutheria
Family: Zalambdalestidae
Range: Asia (Mongolia)
Pn: zal-am-dal-EST-es

Ptilodus

Apart from its long, prehensile (capable of grasping) tail, *Ptilodus* was similar to a modern squirrel in appearance and may have lived in a similar way—scampering around in the branches of trees. The lower premolar teeth were very large and bladelike, and *Ptilodus* may have used them to strip the husks from tough nuts and seeds.

Size: 1 foot 8 inches (50 cm) long
Order: Multituberculata
Family: Ptilodontidae
Range: North America (the Rockies, New Mexico to Saskatchewan)
Pn: til-oh-dus

Size: 1 foot (30 cm) long
Order: Didelphimorphia
Family: Alphadontidae
Range: North America (Alberta to New Mexico)
Pn: ALF-a-don

Alphadon

Primitive marsupials such as *Alphadon* were probably very similar to modern opossums. They were omnivores, and ate a wide range of foods including insects, small vertebrates and fruit. They were probably also tree dwellers, able to climb well, using feet equipped with opposable toes, which could be brought together to give a good grip.

Purgatorius

Little is known about this animal except for what can be deduced from the single molar tooth discovered in rocks in Montana. However, even such a tiny piece of evidence is important because it belonged to the earliest known primate. The tooth resembles the molars of a modern lemur. Small in size, *Purgatorius* was most probably an insect eater.

Size: possibly 4 inches (10 cm) long
Order: Primates
Family: uncertain
Range: North America (Montana)
Pn: purg-a-TOR-ee-us

MARSUPIALS

The marsupials — including the familiar kangaroos and koalas of Australia, and the opossums of North America — are among the most ancient of all of the orders of mammals. They evolved during the Late Cretaceous, between 100 and 75 million years ago. The unique feature of marsupials is their method of reproduction. Placentals (the vast majority of mammals, including humans) nurture their young via a placenta within a womb and do not give birth until the young have reached a relatively advanced stage. But marsupials give birth to very small and immature young — little more than embryos. These are then suckled, usually in a pouch on the belly, and grow to maturity outside the mother's body. The marsupials are more closely associated with the primitive egg-laying monotremes. The marsupials seem to have evolved in North or South America, and one group migrated via Antarctica (then much warmer) to Australia.

Size: 5 feet 6 inches (1.7 m) long

Order: Diprotodontia

Family: Thylacoleonidae

Range: Australia (New South Wales, Queensland, Western and Southern Australia)

Pn: thy-LAC-ol-ay-o

Thylacoleo

This "marsupial lion" had a short, catlike face. Projecting front incisors were modified into killing teeth and looked like the canines in the placental carnivores. The back teeth formed powerful meat-shearing blades. It probably had a meat-eating diet and preyed on the giant kangaroos and wombats of the time.

Palorchestes

The nasal bones in the skull of this animal suggests that it probably had some kind of trunk. In that case, *Palorchestes* would have looked like a giant marsupial tapir. *Palorchestes'* front legs were strong, and each had five toes equipped with huge claws. This has led experts to believe that this creature may have fed by pulling down branches in order to reach the leaves.

Size: 8 feet (2.5 m) long

Suborder: Diprotodontia

Family: Palorchestes

Range: Australia

Pn: pal-ork-est-es

Size: 2 feet 6 inches (80 cm) long
Order: Marsupialia
Family: Borhyaenidae
Range: South America (Patagonia)
Pn: clad-os-ICT-is

Cladosictis

Cladosictis was a primitive carnivorous marsupial that may have resembled an otter in shape and size, with a long body and tail and short limbs. It probably scampered through the undergrowth, seeking out and catching small mammals and reptiles, and swam in rivers after fish. It may even have eaten reptiles' or birds' eggs and insects. The teeth were similar to that of carnivorous placental mammals.

Size: 16 inches (40 cm) long
Order: Marsupialia
Family: Argyrolagidae
Range: South America (Patagonial)
Pn: Ar-gi-ro-LAG-us

Argyrolagus

Just like modern kangaroo rats and other desert rodents (to which it is no relation), *Argyrolagus* moved quickly over open country on its slim, two-toed hind legs, balanced by its long heavy tail. The head was somewhat rodentlike, but it had a pointed snout.

Procoptodon

Extinct kangaroos tended to be generally larger than the modern forms, with some different features. *Procoptodon* was the largest of these kangaroos and was distinctive because of the short face.
Unlike modern kangaroos, each hind foot had only a single long, functional toe.

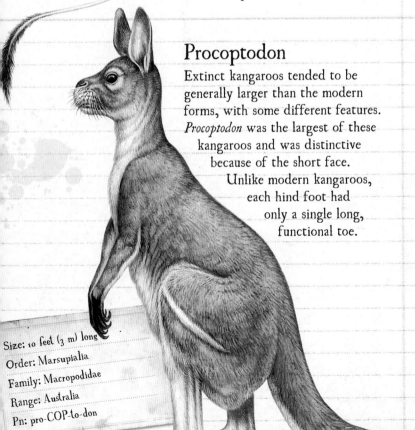

Size: 10 feet (3 m) long
Order: Marsupialia
Family: Macropodidae
Range: Australia
Pn: pro-COP-to-don

Size: possibly 6 inches (15 cm) long
Order: Marsupialia
Family: Necrolestes
Range: South America (Patagonia)
Pn: nec-ro-LES-tes

Necrolestes

All that is known of this little creature is a single specimen of the tip of the jaws with an oddly upturned snout. This may have ended in fleshy folds, like the tentacles surrounding the nostrils of the living star-nosed mole. *Necrolestes* may have eaten insects or worms and lived as a burrower — hence its ghoulish name, which means "grave robber."

GLYPTODONTS, ANTEATERS, ARMADILLOS AND SLOTHS

The edentates are represented today by the anteaters, tree sloths and armadillos. The name of the cohort (a grouping of many orders) means "without teeth," but in fact only the anteaters are completely toothless. The other members have teeth, although these have become reduced to just a few rudimentary pegs, often without roots or a protective enamel covering. The edentates comprise some of the world's most bizarre mammals. In addition to the living anteaters with their elongated snouts and the armadillos with their flexible suits of armor, the edentates include several strange, extinct groups.

Size: 1 foot 6 inches (45 cm) long
Order: Palaeanodonta
Family: Matacheiromyidae
Range: North America (Wyoming)
Pn: met-ACK-air-OM-is

Metacheiromys

With its short legs, sharp claws, and long, heavy tail, *Metacheiromys* may have resembled a modern mongoose. However, it had a long, narrow head, more like that of an armadillo. It had strong canines, but had lost almost all of its cheek teeth. Horny pads grew in their place, which the animal doubtless used to crush its prey.

Size: 3 feet (1 m) long
Order: Xenarthra
Family: Megatheriidae
Range: South America (Patagonia)
Pn: HAP-al-ops

Hapalops

By Miocene times, some 20 million years ago, ground sloths had become well established in South America. *Hapalops* was an early Miocene member of the group, and it was small in comparison with its later relatives.

Doedicurus

In addition to its armored suit, *Doedicurus* possessed a powerful weapon at the end of its tail — a bony club covered in spikes at the end of a stiff shaft. This remarkable structure bore a striking resemblance to the maces carried by medieval knights.

Size: 13 feet (4 m) long
Order: Cingulata
Family: Glyptodontidae
Range: South America (Patagonia)
Pn: do-DIC-oo-rus

Glossotherium

This great ground sloth was a bulky creature, with a large head and heavy tail. Its long, clawed feet were turned inward, as they are in its relatives, so it walked on its knuckles, gorilla style. It seems to have lived on desert shrubs. The great ground sloths died out only 11,000 years ago.

Size: 13 feet (4 m) long
Order: Xenarthra
Family: Mylodontidae
Range: North America (California)
Pn: gloss-o-THER-ee-um

Megatherium

This gigantic creature is the largest known ground sloth. It was as large as a modern elephant and probably weighed as much as 3 tons (3 tonnes). Its head was deep and bearlike, and its jaws were equipped with strong muscles for grinding up its plant food between the few remaining, peg-shaped teeth.

Size: 20 feet (6 m) long
Order: Pilosa
Family: Megatheriidae
Range: South America (Patagonia, Bolivia, Peru)
Pn: Meg-a-THER-ee-um

Eurotamandua

The myrmecophagids, or "true anteaters" (to distinguish them from the completely unrelated marsupial anteaters), are highly specialized for exploiting a diet of ants and termites. Little is known about their evolution. With its long tubular snout, toothless jaws, powerful forelimbs and huge claws, this was undoubtedly an anteater.

Size: 1 foot 8 inches (50 cm) long
Order: Pholidota
Family: Manidae
Range: Europe (Germany)
Pn: eo-MAN-is

Size: 3 feet (90 cm) long
Order: Afredentata
Family: Myrmecophagidae
Range: Europe (Germany)
Pn: euro-ta-MAN-doo-a

Eomanis

A well-preserved fossil shows that *Eomanis*, the earliest known pangolin, looked very much like the pangolins of today. It may have been able to close its eyes, ears and nostrils as a protection against ant stings, as the modern species is able to do. Its diet consisted of both plant matter and insects.

195

INSECTIVORES AND CREODONTS

A wide range of animals have traditionally been classed as insectivores, although new research has put this in doubt. The extinct angalids (rabbitlike mammals) were once considered insectivores, but are now associated with elephant shrews. Almost all insectivores are small and nocturnal or crepuscular (active at dusk or dawn), a successful group that has adapted to a range of habitats and lifestyles. The creodonts, dominant flesh-eating mammals, evolved a great number of forms, which all disappeared some 7 million years ago.

Size: 1 foot (30 cm) long

Order: Anagalida

Family: Anagalidae

Range: Asia (Mongolia)

Pn: ANA-gal-ay

Anagale

Anagale looked similar to a modern rabbit, but it had a long tail and, probably, short ears. It also ran around instead of jumping rabbit style. *Anagale*'s hind legs were longer than the forelegs, and they were equipped with spadelike claws. It probably searched through the soil for grubs and worms.

Size: 10 inches (25 cm) long

Order: Dermoptera

Family: Plagiomenidae

Range: North America (Montana)

Pn: PLAN-e-ther-ee-um

Planetetherium

Dermopterans are also known as "flying lemurs," although they are neither lemurs nor can they fly. The surviving modern animals, colugos, can glide from tree to tree using their outstretched skin membrane. *Planetetherium* had incisor teeth that were divided to make a forward-pointing comb, probably used for scraping food or grooming.

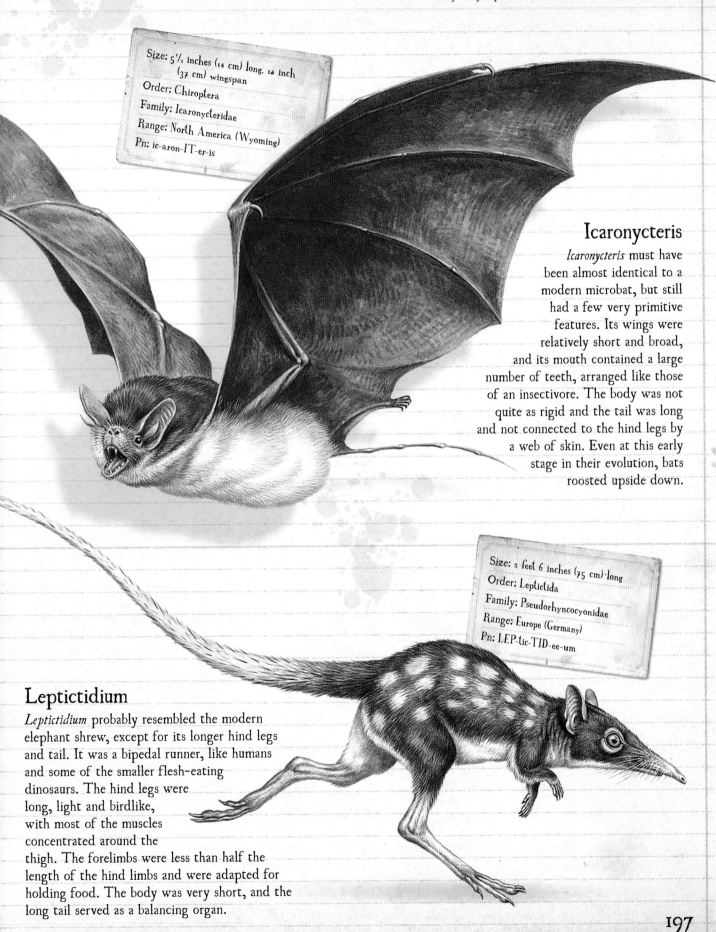

Size: 5½ inches (14 cm) long, 14 inch (37 cm) wingspan
Order: Chiroptera
Family: Icaronycteridae
Range: North America (Wyoming)
Pn: ic-aron-IT-er-is

Icaronycteris

Icaronycteris must have been almost identical to a modern microbat, but still had a few very primitive features. Its wings were relatively short and broad, and its mouth contained a large number of teeth, arranged like those of an insectivore. The body was not quite as rigid and the tail was long and not connected to the hind legs by a web of skin. Even at this early stage in their evolution, bats roosted upside down.

Size: 2 feet 6 inches (75 cm) long
Order: Leptictida
Family: Pseudorhyncocyonidae
Range: Europe (Germany)
Pn: LEP-tic-TID-ee-um

Leptictidium

Leptictidium probably resembled the modern elephant shrew, except for its longer hind legs and tail. It was a bipedal runner, like humans and some of the smaller flesh-eating dinosaurs. The hind legs were long, light and birdlike, with most of the muscles concentrated around the thigh. The forelimbs were less than half the length of the hind limbs and were adapted for holding food. The body was very short, and the long tail served as a balancing organ.

Size: 10 feet (3 m) long

Order: Creodonta

Family: Oxyaenidae

Range: Asia (Mangolia)

Pn: sar-KAS-to-don

Sarkastodon

Around 35 million years ago, Central Asia boasted some huge mammals, such as rhinoceroses. As result, the creodonts grew to a great size, too. *Sarkastodon* was one of the largest creodonts, bigger than the biggest bear. The teeth were large and thick, like those of a modern grizzly bear. *Sarkastodon* probably ate a wide range of foods.

Miacis

The miacids were the earliest true carnivores (meaning "meat eaters") to appear 60 million years ago. Scampering through the branches, this animal must have looked like a modern pine marten. The shape of its limbs and its flexible shoulder and elbow joints indicate that it was well adapted for moving through the trees of its native tropical swamp forest.

Size: 8 inches (20 cm) long

Order: Carnivora

Family: Miacoidea

Range: Europe (Germany)

Pn: my-A-cis

Chapalmalania

The procyonids traveled south from North America via the Central American land bridge. Once in South America, they evolved into a number of specialized forms. *Chapalmalania* was a gigantic raccoon that must have looked like a giant panda. It was so large that its remains were first thought to be those of a bear. Like the panda, it probably had a specialized diet of local plants.

Size: 5 feet (1.5 m) long

Order: Carnivora

Family: Procyonidae

Range: South America (Argentina)

Pn: CHAP-al-mal-AN-ee-a

Hyaenodon

Hyaenodon was a widespread and long-lived genus including many species, from animals the size of a weasel to species as large as a hyena. Its long, slim legs indicate that *Hyaenodon* could run, although perhaps not very fast. It may have been hyenalike in habits, actively hunting down other animals, but also scavenging dead ones.

Potamotherium

Potamotherium is the earliest known otter, and like its modern counterpart it had a long, sinuous body and short legs. It probably leaped through the riverside undergrowth, with its back arched and its head close to the ground. *Potamotherium*'s sense of smell was not well developed, but its hearing and sight seem to have been acute, helping it to hunt down its fish prey in the water. It was without a doubt an excellent swimmer.

Plesictis

This tree-living hunter had big eyes, perhaps for nocturnal hunting, and a long tail for balance. It was similar to the modern cacomistle (*Bassaricus sumichrasti*) and may have been its direct ancestor. It probably led much the same lifestyle, scampering through the trees. Like other procyonids, the cusps of its teeth were blunt and the molars were square in cross section, indicating that it was probably omnivorous, eating eggs, insects, and plant matter, as well as hunting for small mammals and birds.

MUSTELIDS AND BEARS

Mustelids probably evolved from the miacids (earliest true carnivores) in the early Tertiary Period. Modern members of the family include weasels, stoats, badgers and otters, civets, genets and mongooses — all slim, long-bodied hunters. The amphicyonids were a family of "bear-dogs" that existed from the Eocene Epoch 50 million years ago to Miocene times, about 5 million years ago. Amphicyonids were a varied and successful group of large hunting animals. When the creodonts declined, the amphicyonids replaced them in the ecosystems and were then themselves replaced by the "true dogs" during Pliocene times (some 5 million years ago). The amphicyonids' common name, "bear-dogs," refers to their similarity to both of these creatures.

Hemicyon

Despite its great size, *Hemicyon* was lightly built for a bear. Indeed, it was more like a heavy dog, and its name means "half-dog." It was probably more carnivorous than most other bears, so it would likely have been an active hunter. It had powerful legs and was probably a swift runner, hunting in open plains and possibly roaming in packs.

Size: 5 feet (1.5 m) long
Order: Carnivora
Family: Hemicyonidae
Range: Asia (Mongolia), Europe (France, Spain), North America (USA)
Pn: HEM-ee-SIGH-on

Size: 6 feet 6 inches (2 m) long
Order: Carnivora
Family: Ursidae
Range: Africa (Namibia), Asia (China), Europe (France)
Pn: AG-ree-oh-THER-ee-um

Agriotherium

Although bears are no longer found in Africa, they were in the past. *Agriotherium* lived in southwestern Africa. *Agriotherium* was a very large bear, even larger than the Kodiak bear. It was also very primitive and looked like a dog in some ways. However, its teeth had developed the typical bear pattern, so it is safe to assume that it was omnivorous.

Size: 6 feet 6 inches (2 m) long
Order: Carnivora
Family: Ursidae
Range: Europe (Austria, Germany, Netherlands, Spain, UK, Russia)
Pn: ER-sus SPEL-ay-us

Ursus spelaeus

The genus *Ursus* is represented today by the brown, or grizzly, bear, the polar bear and the American black bear. But in Pleistocene times, the cave bear, *Ursus spelaeus*, was a particularly numerous and impressive species. It lived in Europe during the height of the last ice age and often escaped the worst of the winters by hibernating in caves. Many bears seem to have congregated together for this long, annual sleep, judging from the piles of fossil bones found together.

Amphicyon

Amphicyon was a typical "bear-dog." It probably looked like a large bear with the sharp teeth of a wolf. It had a thick neck, strong legs and a heavy tail. It may have led a similar life to that of a modern brown or grizzly bear, eating a wide range of plant and animal foods, and killing its prey with powerful blows from its strong forefeet. *Amphicyon* must have been a fearsome adversary for any other creature living on the plains of the northern hemisphere.

Size: 6 feet 6 inches (2 m) long
Order: Carnivora
Family: Amphicyonidae
Range: Europe (France, Germany), North America (Nebraska)
Pn: AM-phi-SIGH-on

DOGS AND HYENAS

The canids — including the modern foxes, jackals, coyotes, wolves and dogs — are a successful group of "all-rounders." They have become adapted to an enormous range of habitats and a wide variety of diets. As members of the order Carnivora, the Canidae family are related to the otters and weasels, cats and mongooses, and to the seals, sea lions and walruses. The earliest canids were almost entirely restricted to North America, not colonizing other continents until as recently as 6 million years ago. They have evolved a superb sense of smell, good vision and acute hearing. They can also chase swift-moving prey for considerable distances.

Size: 2 feet 6 inches (80 cm) long
Order: Carnivora
Family: Canidae
Range: North America (Nebraska)
Pn: phlay-oh-SIGH-on

Phlaocyon

Just as *Hesperocyon* superficially resembled a member of the cat family, so *Phlaocyon* looked more like a member of the raccoon family. However, several features of its skull suggest it did belong to the dog family, though it was a very primitive member.

Cynodesmus

Cynodesmus was one of the first canids that looked like a modern dog. It was roughly the size and shape of the coyote of today's North and Central America. Its face, however, was shorter (the long snout of typical dogs was to develop much later in their evolution).

Size: 3 feet 3 inches (1 m) long
Order: Carnivora
Family: Canidae
Range: North America (Nebraska)
Pn: sigh-no-DES-mus

Hesperocyon

An active little animal, looking like a mongoose or civet, *Hesperocyon* was one of the earliest canids. With its long flexible body and tail and its short, weak legs, it may not have looked much like a dog. However, the arrangement of its teeth show without a doubt it was a primitive canid.

Size: 2 feet 6 inches (80 cm) long
Order: Carnivora
Family: Canidae
Range: North America (Nebraska)
Pn: HES-per-oh-SIGH-on

Cerdocyon

The dog family evolved in North America, migrating into South America some 2 million years ago. Among the invaders was the early fox *Cerdocyon*, which lives on in the form of the common zorro or crab-eating fox found across South America.

Size: 2 feet 6 inches (80 cm) long
Order: Carnivora
Family: Canidae
Range: South America (Argentina)
Pn: ker-do-SIGH-on

Size: 4 feet 6 inches (1.4 m) long
Order: Carnivora
Family: Canidae
Range: North America (California)
Pn: CAN-is DI-rus

Canis dirus

The genus of dogs called *Canis* includes the nine living species of wolves, coyotes, jackals, and dogs — both wild dogs and every domestic breed, from Great Dane to Chihuahua. Many more species existed in the past, one of the best known being *C. dirus*, the dire wolf. This prehistoric wolf was much like its modern counterpart, but it was more heavily built. It was probably a scavenger rather than a hunter.

Size: 4 feet (1.2 m) long
Order: Carnivora
Family: Canidae
Range: Africa (Morocco), Europe (Greece)
Pn: IC-tee-THER-ee-um

Size: 2 feet 6 inches (80 cm) long
Order: Carnivora
Family: Canidae
Range: North America (Nebraska)
Pn: OS-tee-oh-BOR-us

Ictitherium

Ictitherium was one of the earliest hyenas and probably looked more like a civet (a relative of the mongooses and genets) in build and appearance. It also had teeth similar to those of a civet, which were well suited to an insectivorous diet, instead of the formidable bone-crunching teeth of hyenas.

Osteoborus

Osteoborus was a member of the borophagines, scavenging dogs that first appeared about 8 million years ago. Its heavy build and bulbous forehead gave it a bearlike appearance, although huge, bone-crushing premolar teeth reflected its scavenging hyena-like habits.

203

CATS AND MONGOOSES

The nimravids were the earliest cats to evolve, and are sometimes called false sabertooths to distinguish them from the true sabertooths, grouped in the Felidae family. The felids contain the modern cat family and such familiar creatures as the lion, tiger, leopard, and domesticated cat. They are the most highly specialized of mammalian hunters, hunting by stealth. The family of small carnivores, the viverrids, contains the modern civets, genets and mongooses. They are mostly long-bodied, short-legged animals and omnivores with a varied diet.

Nimravus

This false sabertooth was a contemporary of other sabertooths in Europe and North America and competed with them for food and habitat. *Nimravus*, with its sleek body, was probably not unlike the modern caracal of Africa and Asia, although it had a longer back and more doglike feet.

Size: 4 feet (1.2 m) long

Order: Carnivora

Family: Nimravidae

Range: Europe (France), North America (Colorado, Nebraska, North and South Dakota, Wyoming)

Pn: nim-RAV-us

Size: up to 11 feet 6 inches (3.5 m) long

Order: Panthera

Family: Felidae

Range: Africa (South Africa), Asia (India), Europe (England), North America (California)

Pn: pan-THER-a

Panthera

Panthera leo, the modern lion, is found today in parts of Africa and western India. Its canine teeth are used to kill prey by biting through the neck and throttling it. *Panthera leo spelaea*, a cave lion of Europe, was about 25 percent bigger than the modern lion and the largest cat that ever lived.

Size: 4 feet (1.2 m) long

Order: Carnivora

Family: Felidae

Range: North America (California),
South America (Argentina)

Pn: smil-oh-don

Size: 4 feet (1.2 m) long

Order: Carnivora

Family: Felidae

Range: Africa (South Africa), Asia
(China, India), Europe (France),
North America (Texas)

Pn: Dy-noh-FEE-liss

Smilodon

Smilodon was the classic sabertooth cat.
Unlike most other cats, it had a short tail,
like that of a modern bobcat. Its whole body
was powerfully built, with the muscles of its
shoulders and neck arranged to produce a
powerful downward lunge of its massive head.
The jaw opened to an angle of over 120 degrees,
allowing the huge pair of saber teeth in its
upper jaws to be driven into the victim.

Dinofelis

Dinofelis was a panther-size cat, with flattened canines
that were short compared with the sabertooths,
scimitar-tooths or dirk-tooths, but longer than those of
the biting cats. It is a matter of debate as to which
subfamily of the felids *Dinofelis* belongs. It first became
extinct in Eurasia and North America, but survived in
Africa until mid-Pleistocene times.

Size: 3 feet (90 cm) long

Order: Carnivora

Family: Viverridae

Range: Africa (Kenya)

Pn: KAN-yoo-its

Kanuites

The viverrids have changed remarkably little during
their evolution, and *Kanuites* probably looked similar
to the existing genets. It had a long tail and
perhaps retractable claws like those of a
cat. It was probably omnivorous
and may have lived in trees as
well as on the ground.

205

SEALS, SEA LIONS AND WALRUSES

The order Carnivora also includes a successful group of marine carnivores, grouped together as the pinnipeds. They include the modern sea lions, walruses, and seals. All have feet modified into flippers or pinnae. The desmostylians were an order of strange aquatic mammals that have been described as "sea horses." Members of this order were about the size of a pony. The sirenians, or sea cows, are the only mammals to have become fully adapted aquatic plant eaters, represented today by three species of manatee and one species of dugong.

Size: 5 feet (1.5 m) long
Order: Carnivora
Family: Enliarctidae
Range: North America (Pacific coast)
Pn: En-al-ee-ARC-tos

Enaliarctos

This primitive sea mammal represents an early stage in the adaptation of a land-dwelling carnivore to a marine lifestyle. *Enaliarctos* is almost halfway between an otter and a sea lion. Its teeth still bore meat-shearing blades like those of a dog and its body was streamlined and otterlike, with distinct legs and a tail.

Acrophoca

Acrophoca may have been the ancestor of the modern leopard seal. It was a fish eater, but with less developed flippers, probably not as well adapted to an aquatic life, spending much of its time on or near the shore.

Size: 5 feet (1.5 m) long
Order: Carnivora
Family: Phocidae
Range: South America (Peru)
Pn: AC-ro-PHOC-a

Size: 5 feet 6 inches (1.7 m) long
Order: Carnivora
Family: Desmatophocidae
Range: Asia (Japan), North America (California, Oregon)
Pn: des-mat-o-phoc-a

Desmatophoca

The typical streamlined shape of the modern sea lion had begun to appear with *Desmatophoca*. As in its living relatives, its forelimbs were stronger than the hind limbs, and the feet were modified to form paddles, with elongated, splayed-out fingers held together by webs of skin. Although *Desmatophoca* still had a tail, it was much shorter than that of other sea lions.

Size: 20 feet (6 m) long
Order: Sirenia
Family: Dugongidae
Range: Europe (France)
Pn: RYE-tee-OH-dus

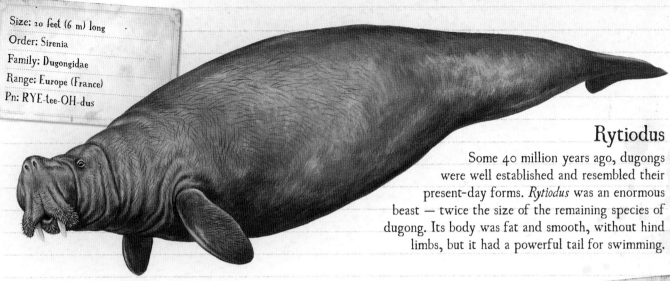

Rytiodus

Some 40 million years ago, dugongs were well established and resembled their present-day forms. *Rytiodus* was an enormous beast — twice the size of the remaining species of dugong. Its body was fat and smooth, without hind limbs, but it had a powerful tail for swimming.

Size: possibly 5 feet (1.5 m) long
Order: Sirenia
Family: Prorastomidae
Range: West Indies (Jamaica)
Pn: pro-RAST-o-mus

Imagotaria

Imagotaria is classed as a walrus, but it probably looked and behaved like a sea lion. The canine teeth, used by sea lions to catch fish, had begun to enlarge, but *Imagotaria* had not yet formed the tusks or broad shell-crusher back teeth used by walruses.

Size: 6 feet (1.8 m) long
Order: Carnivora
Family: Odobenidae
Range: North America (Pacific Coast)
Pn: i-mag-o-TAR-ee-a

Prorastomus

Prorastomus is the most primitive sirenian known. Only its skull and parts of its backbone and ribs have been discovered. Its skull indicates that it was not specialized for an aquatic lifestyle and it is probable that *Prorastomus* was still essentially a land dweller.

Desmostylus

Built like a hippopotamus, and perhaps behaving in a similar way, too, *Desmostylus* had a thickset body and stout legs with broad feet and hoofed toes. It must have had an amphibious lifestyle, paddling in coastal shallows and sinking down to the seabed in search of food.

Size: 6 feet (1.8 m) long
Order: Desmostylus
Family: Desmostylidae
Range: Asia (Japan), North America (Pacific coast)
Pn: des-mos-STIL-us

207

WHALES, DOLPHINS AND PORPOISES

The whales, dolphins and porpoises, sea creatures of magnificence and intelligence, are members of the only mammal order to have become thoroughly adapted to living their whole lives in the oceans. Their sleek, streamlined bodies and fishlike shape allow them to swim with ease, but deny them any kind of life on land. However, they have retained the basic mammalian features of warm-bloodedness, the ability to suckle their young and the necessity to breathe air. Living species are found throughout the oceans of the world, and there are also freshwater dolphins in South America, India and China. Many modern species are, however, threatened with extinction.

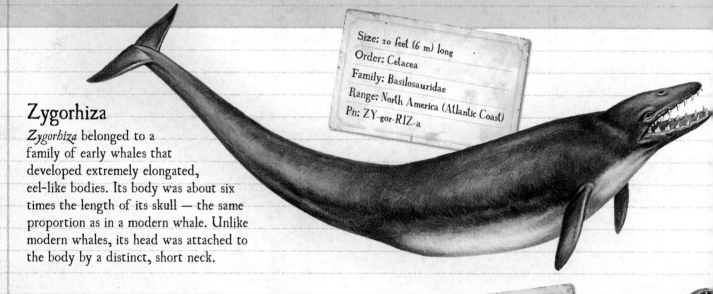

Zygorhiza

Zygorhiza belonged to a family of early whales that developed extremely elongated, eel-like bodies. Its body was about six times the length of its skull — the same proportion as in a modern whale. Unlike modern whales, its head was attached to the body by a distinct, short neck.

Size: 20 feet (6 m) long
Order: Cetacea
Family: Basilosauridae
Range: North America (Atlantic Coast)
Pn: ZY-gor-RIZ-a

Pakicetus

Pakicetus is the earliest known whale. Although only part of its skull has been found, it has such primitive features it is probable that the rest of its body had few adaptations to a marine existence and was probably seal-like in appearance.

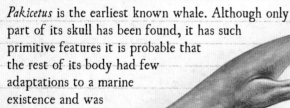

Size: 6 feet (1.8 m) long
Order: Cetacea
Family: Pakicetidae
Range: Asia (Pakistan)
Pn: PAK-i-KET-us

Size: 8 feet (2.5 m) long
Order: Cetacea
Family: Protocetidae
Range: Africa and Asia (Mediterranean area)
Pn: PRO-to-KET-us

Protocetus

Protocetus, which lived some 8 million years after *Pakicetus*, had become much more whalelike in appearance. Its body was more streamlined, its forelegs were flat and paddlelike, but the hind legs were greatly reduced and of little use in swimming.

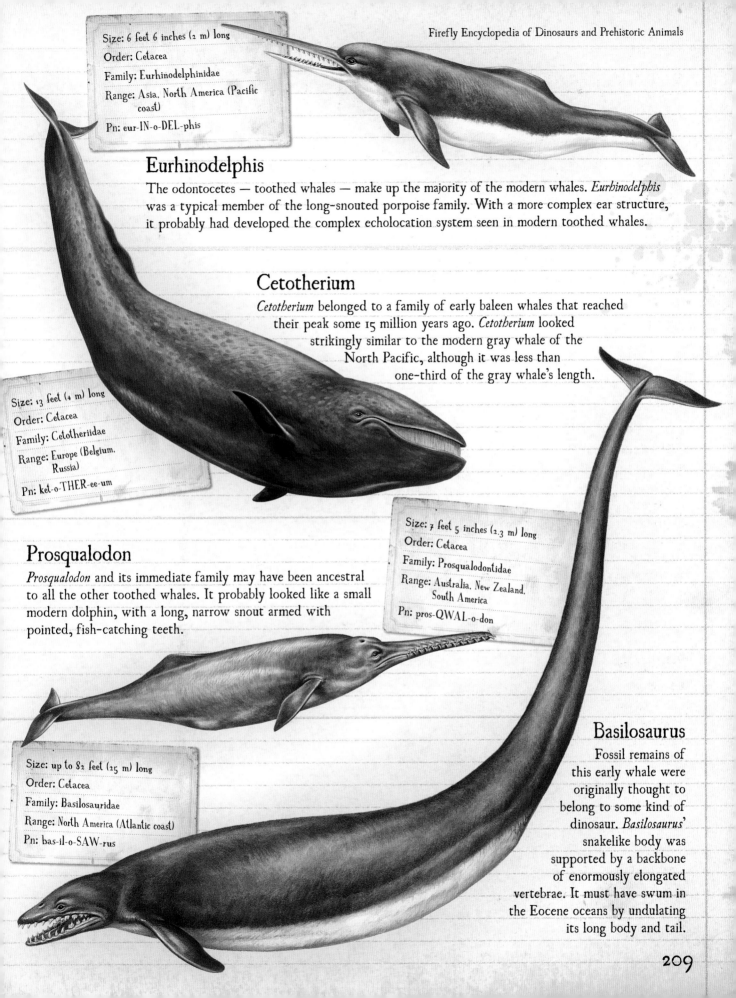

Size: 6 feet 6 inches (2 m) long
Order: Cetacea
Family: Eurhinodelphinidae
Range: Asia, North America (Pacific coast)
Pn: eur-IN-o-DEL-phis

Eurhinodelphis

The odontocetes — toothed whales — make up the majority of the modern whales. *Eurhinodelphis* was a typical member of the long-snouted porpoise family. With a more complex ear structure, it probably had developed the complex echolocation system seen in modern toothed whales.

Cetotherium

Cetotherium belonged to a family of early baleen whales that reached their peak some 15 million years ago. *Cetotherium* looked strikingly similar to the modern gray whale of the North Pacific, although it was less than one-third of the gray whale's length.

Size: 13 feet (4 m) long
Order: Cetacea
Family: Cetotheriidae
Range: Europe (Belgium, Russia)
Pn: ket-o-THER-ee-um

Prosqualodon

Prosqualodon and its immediate family may have been ancestral to all the other toothed whales. It probably looked like a small modern dolphin, with a long, narrow snout armed with pointed, fish-catching teeth.

Size: 7 feet 5 inches (2.3 m) long
Order: Cetacea
Family: Prosqualodontidae
Range: Australia, New Zealand, South America
Pn: pros-QWAL-o-don

Basilosaurus

Fossil remains of this early whale were originally thought to belong to some kind of dinosaur. *Basilosaurus'* snakelike body was supported by a backbone of enormously elongated vertebrae. It must have swum in the Eocene oceans by undulating its long body and tail.

Size: up to 82 feet (25 m) long
Order: Cetacea
Family: Basilosauridae
Range: North America (Atlantic coast)
Pn: bas-il-o-SAW-rus

EARLY ROOTERS AND BROWSERS

Most ungulates ("hoofed animals") are large plant eaters that root and browse among vegetation or crop grass. Early rooters and browsers were a diverse group, most of which ate leaves, shoots, and roots, though some evolved into scavengers. Specialized grazers, such as horses, cattle and deer, evolved from these early ungulates. They rose to dominance during the Miocene, moving from the forest to the developing grasslands.

Chriacus

This agile climbing animal may have scampered through tropical forests of North America, eating insects, small animals, and fruit. Its hind limbs were those of a climbing animal.

Size: 3 feet (1 m) long
Order: Mesonychia
Family: Triisodontidae
Range: North America (Wyoming)
Pn: cry-ACK-us

Size: 13 feet (4 m) long
Order: Mesonychia
Family: Triisodontidae
Range: Asia (Mongolia)
Pn: AN-drew-SAR-cus

Andrewsarchus

With a gigantic skull nearly 3 feet (1 m) in length, *Andrewsarchus* was the largest known terrestrial carnivorous mammal. Its teeth were very large and adapted for crushing and tearing food.

Trogosus

From a distance, the squat body, short head and flat feet of this large animal would have given it the appearance of a modern bear. However, as soon as *Trogosus* opened its mouth, its huge chisel-like incisors would have made it appear more like a gigantic rat or rabbit.

Size: 7 feet 6 inches (3 m) long.
Order: Cimolesta
Family: Coryphodontidae
Range: Widespread in North America, Europe, eastern Asia
Pn: cor-ee-PHO-don

Size: 4 feet (1.2 m) long
Order: Cimolesta
Family: Esthonychidae
Range: North America (Wyoming)
Pn: tro-GOS-us

Coryphodon

Coryphodon was a large animal with canine tusks similar to those of a hippopotamus. These were especially well developed in the male. Like a hippopotamus, too, *Coryphodon* probably lived in swamps and marshes.

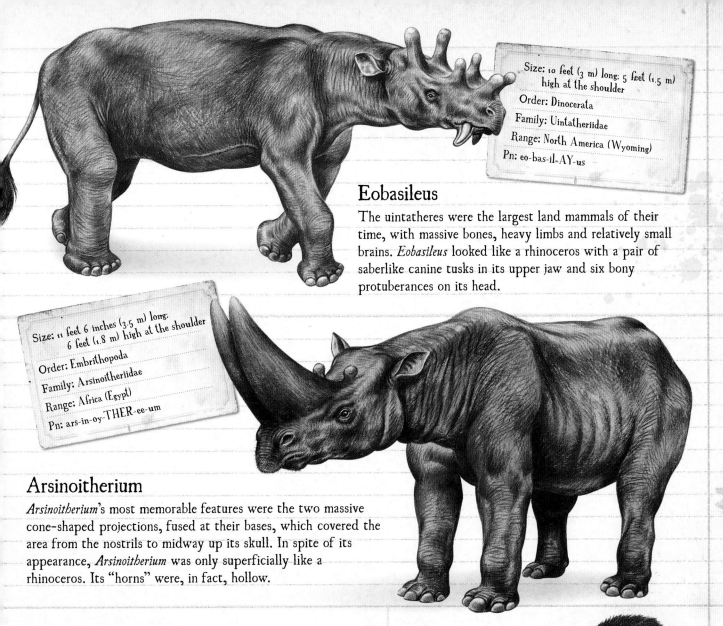

Size: 10 feet (3 m) long; 5 feet (1.5 m) high at the shoulder
Order: Dinocerata
Family: Uintatheriidae
Range: North America (Wyoming)
Pn: eo-bas-il-AY-us

Eobasileus

The uintatheres were the largest land mammals of their time, with massive bones, heavy limbs and relatively small brains. *Eobasileus* looked like a rhinoceros with a pair of saberlike canine tusks in its upper jaw and six bony protuberances on its head.

Size: 11 feet 6 inches (3.5 m) long; 6 feet (1.8 m) high at the shoulder
Order: Embrithopoda
Family: Arsinoitheriidae
Range: Africa (Egypt)
Pn: ars-in-oy-THER-ee-um

Arsinoitherium

Arsinoitherium's most memorable features were the two massive cone-shaped projections, fused at their bases, which covered the area from the nostrils to midway up its skull. In spite of its appearance, *Arsinoitherium* was only superficially like a rhinoceros. Its "horns" were, in fact, hollow.

Stylinodon

With its short, powerful digging forelimbs and strong claws, *Stylinodon* was probably the size of a bear, with a body like an aardvark and a piglike face. It had no incisor teeth in its jaws, but the canine teeth had become greatly developed into huge, rootless, gnawing chisels.

Size: 5 feet 3 inches (1.6 m) long
Order: Hyracoidea
Family: Pliohyracidae
Range: Europe (Caucasus)
Pn: k-vab-eb-i-HY-rax

Size: 4 feet 3 inches (1.3 m) long
Order: Taeniodonta
Family: Stylinodontidae
Range: North America (Wyoming, Colorado, Utah)
Pn: sty-LIN-o-don

Kvabebihyrax

With its stout body and small eyes set high upon the skull, *Kvabebihyrax* must have looked more like a small hippopotamus than a modern hyrax. The snout was short, and a pair of very large incisor teeth projected downward.

ELEPHANTS AND MASTODONTS

The African and Indian elephants are the only two surviving species of a once-diverse group called the proboscids. From their origins in northern Africa, their evolution involved an increase in size, the development of long pillarlike legs to support the immense weight, and an extension of a proboscis or trunk, accompanied by the massive enlargement of the head. The trunk or tusks originally enabled the animal to reach food on the ground, but they also function in display and courtship. Two million years ago, mammoths and mastodonts flourished over the northern continents, only to suffer mass extinction with the advance of the ice age.

Moeritherium

This pig-size, low-slung animal resembled a tapir or a pygmy hippopotamus more than an elephant. The external nostrils were at the front of the skull, which implies that it did not even possess a trunk, though it may have had a broad, thick upper lip that helped it to root about among swamp vegetation.

Size: 2 feet (60 cm) high
Order: Proboscidea
Family: Moeritheriidae
Range: Africa (Egypt, Mali, Senegal)
Pn: mow-er-rith-ER-ee-um

Size: 13 feet (4 m) high
Order: Proboscidea
Family: Deinotheriidae
Range: Europe (Germany, Bohemia), Asia (India), Africa (Kenya)
Pn: dine-o-THER-ee-um

Deinotherium

The most remarkable feature of this elephant was its lower jaw, which curved downward at a right angle, giving rise to two huge curved tusks. The animal may have used its bizarre tusks for foraging for food — stripping the bark from trees or digging up tubers. The Deinotheres thrived unchanged throughout the Pliocene, and then vanished altogether about 2 million years ago.

Gomphotherium

Gomphotheres were the dominant large mammals of the Miocene until they were gradually replaced by elephants about 5 million years ago. This four-tusked mastodont was wide ranging; its remains have been discovered on four continents.

Size: 10 feet (3 m) high

Order: Proboscidea

Family: Gomphotheriidae

Range: Europe (France), Africa (Kenya), Asia (Pakistan), North America (Nebraska)

Pn: gom-pho-THER-ee-um

Phiomia

Phiomia evolved alongside its smaller, distant relative *Moeritherium. Phiomia* probably browsed in forests of the Fayum area, whereas *Moeritherium* wallowed in the swamps. The upper and lower jaws were long, the flattened tusks of the lower jaw forming a spoon-shaped extension used for gathering food.

Size: 8 feet (2.5 m) high

Order: Proboscidea

Family: Gomphotheriidae

Range: Africa (Egypt)

Pn: phee-OM-ee-a

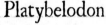

Platybelodon

Platybelodon was another shovel-tusked browsing mastodont, which lived in Europe and Asia. The shovel arrangement of its tusks was short and broad, and they were indented at each side to make room for the tusks of the upper jaw. *Platybelodon* evidently enjoyed wading through shallow rivers and dredging waterweeds.

Size: 10 feet (3 m) high

Order: Proboscidea

Family: Gomphotheriidae

Range: Europe (Caucasus Mountains), Asia (Mongolia), Africa (Kenya)

Pn: plat-ee-bel-O-don

Elephas falconeri

The genus *Elephas* includes the modern Indian elephant, *E. maximus*. The earliest members of the genus arose in Africa about 5 million years ago, and radiated out into Europe and Asia. *Elephas falconeri* stood less than 3 feet (90 cm) in height and lived on the Mediterranean islands. Similar dwarf elephants arose on islands in Southeast Asia.

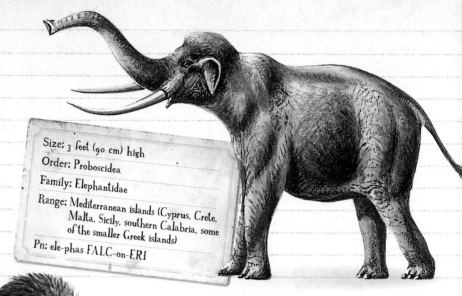

Size: 3 feet (90 cm) high

Order: Proboscidea

Family: Elephantidae

Range: Mediterranean islands (Cyprus, Crete, Malta, Sicily, southern Calabria, some of the smaller Greek islands)

Pn: ele-phas FALC-on-ERI

Size: 15 feet (4.5 m) high

Order: Proboscidea

Family: Elephantidae

Range: Europe (England, Germany)

Pn: mam-UTH-us trog-ON-ther-ee

Elephas antiquus

Modern elephants belong to the Elephantidae family. True elephants differ from their earlier relatives, the mastodonts, because they have lost the tusks of the lower jaw and have different teeth. *Elephas antiquus* was a large, long-legged and straight-tusked elephant. The tusks were long and straight, and slightly curved at the tip.

Size: 12 feet (3.7 m) high

Order: Proboscidea

Family: Elephantidae

Range: Europe

Pn: ele-phas ant-IK-was

Mammuthus trogontherii

The mammoths were a wide-ranging group of plant-eating animals that were well adapted to colder climates. *Mammuthus trogontherii* was one of the largest mammoths and, living in much colder conditions than its ancestors, was probably the first to develop a hairy coat. It roamed in herds across the cold grasslands, consuming the coarse grasses that grew there.

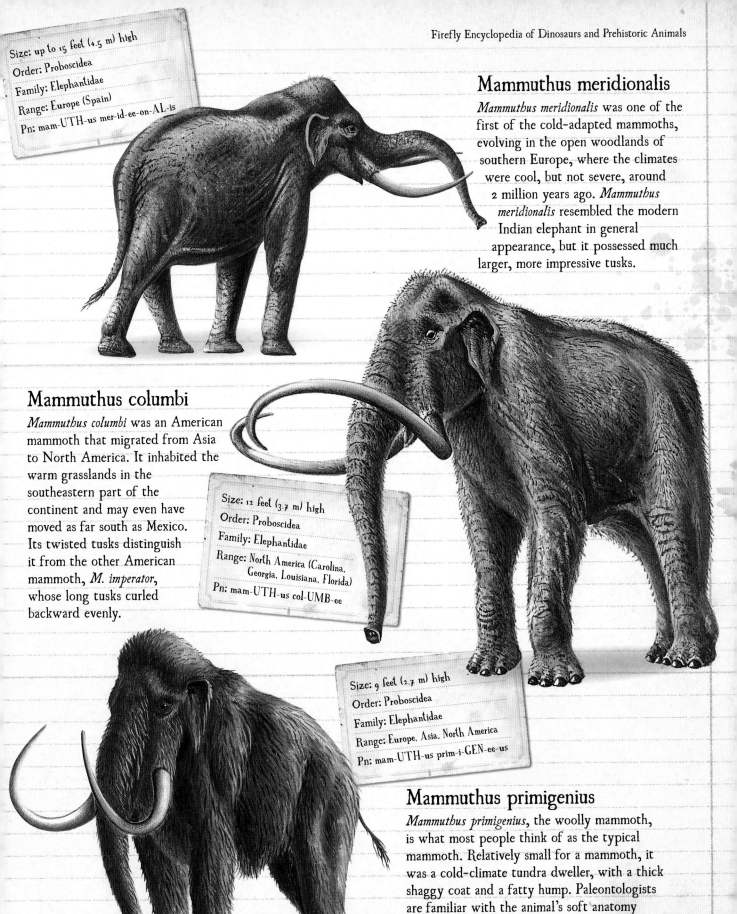

Size: up to 15 feet (4.5 m) high
Order: Proboscidea
Family: Elephantidae
Range: Europe (Spain)
Pn: mam-UTH-us mer-id-ee-on-AL-is

Mammuthus meridionalis

Mammuthus meridionalis was one of the first of the cold-adapted mammoths, evolving in the open woodlands of southern Europe, where the climates were cool, but not severe, around 2 million years ago. *Mammuthus meridionalis* resembled the modern Indian elephant in general appearance, but it possessed much larger, more impressive tusks.

Mammuthus columbi

Mammuthus columbi was an American mammoth that migrated from Asia to North America. It inhabited the warm grasslands in the southeastern part of the continent and may even have moved as far south as Mexico. Its twisted tusks distinguish it from the other American mammoth, *M. imperator*, whose long tusks curled backward evenly.

Size: 12 feet (3.7 m) high
Order: Proboscidea
Family: Elephantidae
Range: North America (Carolina, Georgia, Louisiana, Florida)
Pn: mam-UTH-us col-UMB-ee

Size: 9 feet (2.7 m) high
Order: Proboscidea
Family: Elephantidae
Range: Europe, Asia, North America
Pn: mam-UTH-us prim-i-GEN-ee-us

Mammuthus primigenius

Mammuthus primigenius, the woolly mammoth, is what most people think of as the typical mammoth. Relatively small for a mammoth, it was a cold-climate tundra dweller, with a thick shaggy coat and a fatty hump. Paleontologists are familiar with the animal's soft anatomy and appearance in life, because several well-preserved remains have been found buried in frozen mud in Siberia and Alaska.

215

SOUTH AMERICAN HOOFED MAMMALS

During the Tertiary Era, South America supported as strange and unique a collection of mammals as Australia does today, and for many of the same reasons. Having once been part of a more or less unified landmass, continental drift and rising sea levels caused South America to become detached from North America and then from Africa and Antarctica. For about 50 or more million years, from Paleocene until Pliocene times, South American mammals were marooned on an island continent and given the opportunity to diversify. The following animals are meridiungulates: the descendants of stranded early rooters and browsers.

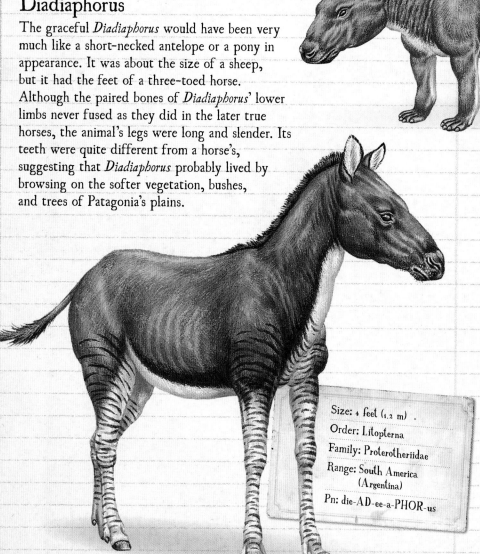

Diadiaphorus

The graceful *Diadiaphorus* would have been very much like a short-necked antelope or a pony in appearance. It was about the size of a sheep, but it had the feet of a three-toed horse. Although the paired bones of *Diadiaphorus'* lower limbs never fused as they did in the later true horses, the animal's legs were long and slender. Its teeth were quite different from a horse's, suggesting that *Diadiaphorus* probably lived by browsing on the softer vegetation, bushes, and trees of Patagonia's plains.

Size: Possibly 2 feet (60 cm) long
Order: Condylarthra
Family: Didolodontidae
Range: South America (Argentina)
Pn: di-DOL-o-dus

Size: 4 feet (1.2 m)
Order: Litopterna
Family: Proterotheriidae
Range: South America (Argentina)
Pn: die-AD-ee-a-PHOR-us

Didolodus

The teeth of this creature were so much like those of the earliest hoofed animals that in life *Didolodus* may have resembled one closely. A fleet-footed browser that scampered through the undergrowth of the forests and ate the leaves of low-growing trees and bushes, *Didolodus* — or something closely related to it — may have been ancestral to most of the other hoofed South American mammals.

Size: 10 feet (3 m) long
Order: Litopterna
Family: Macraucheniidae
Range: South America (Argentina)
Pn: mac-row-KEEN-ee-a

Macrauchenia

Macrauchenia was a later and larger version of *Thesodon* (below), from which it may have evolved. The lifestyle of *Macrauchenia* ("large neck") is an enigma. It had certain camel-like features, including size, posture, small head, and long neck. But its three-toed, hoofed feet were rhinoceros-like, and it probably bore a substantial trunk, too, because the nostrils enter the skull high up between the eyes.

Size: 6 feet 6 inches (2 m) long
Order: Litopterna
Family: Macraucheniidae
Range: South America (Argentina)
Pn: THES-o-don

Thesodon

Trotting across the Pampas plains, this browsing long-necked creature would have looked much like a modern guanaco. The main difference would have been in the feet, which in *Thesodon* were three-toed and so heavier. The position of its nostrils suggests that a trunk was also present, but this may have been no more prominent than the one carried by the living saiga antelope.

Thoatherium

The smallest of the known litopterns, *Thoatherium* probably resembled a small gazelle. The feet and legs were very long for the size of the animal's body, and it must have been a graceful runner. Although the paired bones of the lower limbs were reduced, they did not fuse. Its teeth, too, remained primitive, so it can be assumed that *Thoatherium* lived on foliage rather than grasses.

Size: 2 feet 4 inches (70 cm) long
Order: Litopterna
Family: Proterotheriidae
Range: South America (Argentina)
Pn: tho-ath-ER-ee-um

Trigonostylops

There are no remains of *Trigonostylops* other than its skull, so it is difficult to make any deductions about the animal's general appearance or its lifestyle. The teeth are very primitive and the large size of the lower canines suggest that its body was probably something like an *Astrapotherium* (opposite).

Size: Possibly 5 feet (1.5 m) long

Order: Astrapotheria

Family: Trigonostylopidae

Range: South America (Argentina)

Pn: trig-on-o-STY-lops

Pachyrukhos

Pachyrukhos had a short tail, hind limbs that were considerably longer than its front limbs, and very long hind feet. It evidently moved around by hopping and leaping, like a rabbit. Its teeth were adapted for a diet of nuts and tough plants. *Pachyrukhos* probably had long ears and large eye sockets. These features suggest that the animal was nocturnal.

Size: 1 foot (30 cm) long

Order: Notoungulata

Family: Hegetotheriidae

Range: South America (Argentina)

Pn: pac-ee-RUK-os

Size: 10 feet (3 m) long

Order: Pyrotheria

Family: Pyrotheriidae

Range: South America (Argentina)

Pn: py-ro-THER-ee-um

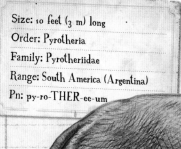

Pyrotherium

The remains of *Pyrotherium* were first found in the volcanic ash deposits of Deseado, Argentina: hence its name, which means "fire animal." In life, *Pyrotherium* probably looked like the early elephant *Barytherium*, its African contemporary. *Pyrotherium* had a massive body supported on pillarlike legs, short broad toes, a short thick neck, and a head equipped with a trunk and tusks.

Notostylops

Notostylops was a rabbitlike animal that lived in the undergrowth, consuming herbaceous plants and other types of low-growing vegetation. The animal's body was probably fairly generalized with few adaptations to fit it for any particular ecological niche. *Notostylops* would have had a short, deep face in order to accommodate the unusual rodentlike dentition that is characteristic of the family.

Size: 16 inches (40 cm) long
Order: Notoungulata
Family: Intatheriidae
Range: South America (Argentina)
Pn: PRO-tip-o-THER-ee-um

Size: 2 feet 6 inches (75 cm) long
Order: Notoungulata
Family: Notostylopidae
Range: South America (Argentina)
Pn: NOT-o-STY-lops

Protypotherium

Protypotherium was about the size of a rabbit. It had a long tail and legs, and its ratlike head tapered to a pointed muzzle. All 44 teeth were present, and did not show specializations for any particular food. The neck was short and the body long, and there was a long and quite thick tail. The long, slender legs ended in paws, which bore claws. *Protypotherium* probably ate leaves and scampered, rodentlike, over the Pampas.

Size: 8 feet (2.5 m) long
Order: Astrapotheria
Family: Astrapotheriidae
Range: South America (Argentina)
Pn: as-trap-o-THER-ee-um

Astrapotherium

Astrapotherium was a large animal. Its short head had a dome over the forehead created by enlarged air sinuses, and four tusks formed from canine teeth. The animal was probably largely aquatic, wallowing in shallow water and rooting around for water plants in a similar way to the rhinoceroses of the northern hemisphere.

219

Size: 4 feet 3 inches (1.3 m) long
Order: Notoungulata
Family: Isotemnidae
Range: South America (Argentina)
Pn: tom-as-HUX-lee-a

Thomashuxleya

Thomashuxleya was named for the 19th-century British naturalist and paleontologist Thomas Huxley. Robust and the size of a sheep, *Thomashuxleya* appears to have been an unspecialized animal, with few adaptations to any particular way of life. The head was quite large in relation to the body, and there were 44 teeth in the jaws.

Size: 3 feet 4 inches (1 m) long
Order: Notoungulata
Family: Notohippidae
Range: South America (Argentina)
Pn: rin-CHIP-us

Rhynchippus

Rhynchippus (meaning "snout horse") presents a classic example of the combined evolution of the South American ungulates with unrelated groups elsewhere in the world: in this case, with the horse. Its skeleton was not particularly horselike, but the teeth were similar to those of a grazing animal, such as a horse or a rhinoceros.

Scarrittia

In life, this bulky creature probably looked much like a lumbering, flat-footed rhinoceros. *Scarrittia* was a heavy animal with a long body and neck. It had stout legs, three-toed hoofed feet and a short tail. The animal's face was short and the jaws contained the full complement of 44 low-crowned, fairly unspecialized teeth.

Size: 6 feet 2 inches (2 m) long
Order: Notoungulata
Family: Leontiniidae
Range: South America (Argentina)
Pn: scar-RIT-ee-a

Homalodotherium

Unlike other notoungulates, the llama-size *Homalodotherium* had a claw instead of a hoof on the four "fingers" of each "hand." The animal's forelimbs were longer and heavier than the hind limbs. Higher at the shoulders than at the hips, it is likely that *Homalodotherium* was partly bipedal (using two legs). It probably browsed on the leaves of low branches, rearing up onto its hind legs.

Size: 6 feet 6 inches (2 m) long
Order: Notoungulata
Family: Homalodotheriidae
Range: South America (Argentina)
Pn: hom-a-lod-o-THER-ee-um

Size: 9 feet (2.7 m) long
Order: Notoungulata
Family: Toxodontidae
Range: South America (Argentina)
Pn: TOX-o-don

Toxodon

Toxodon was a rhinoceros-like animal, with a heavy, barrel-shaped body supported on short, stocky legs. However, the creature's three-toed, hoofed feet were small. Because the hind legs were longer than the front ones, the body sloped forward to the shoulders. The front of the head was broad, and it may have had a fleshy prehensile (capable of grasping) lip. Behind the snout the skull narrowed, then widened again. Its teeth suggest that *Toxodon* was a mixed browser and grazer.

Adinotherium

Adinotherium looked like a sheep-size, and less ungainly, version of *Toxodon*. The front legs were relatively longer, so the shoulders were about the same height as the hips, and there was no hump. *Adinotherium* also had a small horn on the skull. This was probably some kind of display structure.

Size: 5 feet (1.5 m) long
Order: Notoungulata
Family: Toxondontidae
Range: South America (Argentina)
Pn: ad-in-o-THER-ee-um

221

HORSES

Ungulates — hoofed mammals — represent the main group of large plant-eating land animals living today. Their earliest representatives were early rooters and browsers, which evolved with the formation of open grassy plains during the drier Miocene climates. The Perissodactyla or odd-toed ungulates contained many genera in the early Tertiary but are now confined to horses, tapirs and rhinoceroses. The even-toed Artiodactyla have far more representatives now than in any previous period, including deer, sheep, goats and cattle, pigs and peccaries, giraffes, hippopotamuses, and camels and llamas.

Size: 2 feet (60 cm) high at the shoulder

Order: Perissodactyla

Family: Equidae

Range: North America

Pn: mess-o-HIP-us

Size: 2 feet (60 cm) high at the shoulder

Order: Perissodactyla

Family: Equidae

Range: North America, later Asia, Europe

Pn: AN-ki-THER-ee-um

Mesohippus

With forests turning to more open country, the horses were no longer confined to scampering around the undergrowth and began to develop the capacity to trot and run. About the size of a greyhound, *Mesohippus* was larger than any of its predecessors.

Anchitherium

The evolution of the horse was not a simple straight-line affair, and a number of side branches developed that have left no descendants today. *Anchitherium* evolved in North America in Early Miocene times, becoming extinct in China some 5 million years ago.

Hyracotherium

Hyracotherium, the earliest known equid, is believed to be ancestral to the rest of the horse line. This creature, however, was tiny compared to modern horses. The relative size and complexity of its brain suggests that *Hyracotherium* was alert and intelligent, and this may have been a factor in the survival of the horse line as a whole.

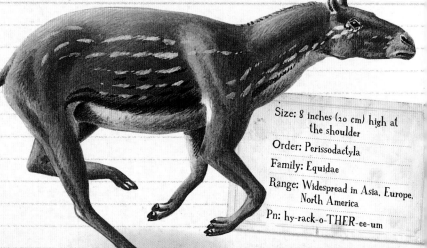

Size: 8 inches (20 cm) high at the shoulder

Order: Perissodactyla

Family: Equidae

Range: Widespread in Asia, Europe, North America

Pn: hy-rack-o-THER-ee-um

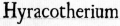

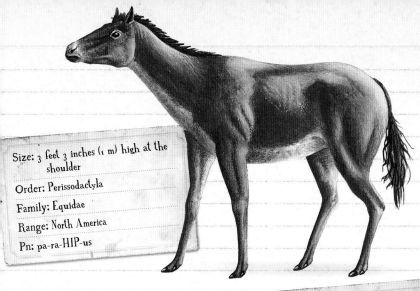

Parahippus

Parahippus represents an intermediate stage in the evolution of the horse. There were still three toes on the feet, and in appearance it was very similar to its ancestor *Mesohippus*. Its body was larger, though, as were its molars, which came to resemble millstones. This latter change is highly significant, as the tougher enamel coating on the teeth enabled *Parahippus* to grind down and masticate the newly evolved grasses on the plains.

Size: 3 feet 3 inches (1 m) high at the shoulder

Order: Perissodactyla

Family: Equidae

Range: North America

Pn: pa-ra-HIP-us

Size: 4 feet 6 inches (1.4 m) high at the shoulder

Order: Perissodactyla

Family: Equidae

Range: Widespread in North America, Europe, Asia, Africa

Pn: hip-AR-ee-on

Size: 4 feet 6 inches (1.4 m) high at the shoulder

Order: Perissodactyla

Family: Equidae

Range: South America

Pn: hip-i-DEE-on

Hipparion

Once the plains-living grazing horses had evolved, they too radiated into many different types. Of these, all but the *Equus* species are now extinct. *Hipparion* resembled the modern horse but had three toes, two of which were reduced and did not touch the ground.

Hippidion

Hippidion probably resembled a small donkey, with a fairly large head. However, its long, delicate nasal bones were distinct from those of other horses, suggesting that *Hippidion* continued to evolve in isolation from the mainstream of horse evolution.

Size: 3 feet 3 inches (1 m) high at the shoulder

Order: Perissodactyla

Family: Equidae

Range: North America (Nebraska)

Pn: MER-ee-CHIP-us

Merychippus

Herds of *Merychippus*, the earliest horse to feed exclusively on grass, once roamed the prairies of what is now Nebraska. Its premolar teeth had the same grass-grinding design as the molars. Tall teeth needed a deep jaw to contain them, so the head developed the heavy jawline of the modern horse.

TAPIRS AND BRONTOTHERES

Perissodactyls include two other groups of unusual extinct herbivores: the brontotheres and chalicotheres. The brontotheres are also called the titanotheres, or "thunder beasts," due to their great size. These rhinoceros-like creatures browsed on soft forest vegetation. Some forms evolved massive "horns" and large canines, and there was a common tendency to hugely increased bulk. What are often referred to as horns were in fact bony structures with a covering of thick skin. When climates became dryer and more open woodlands became plentiful, brontotheres became extinct and were replaced by the rhinoceroses. The chalicotheres, unlike the rest of the ungulates, evolved large claws on their toes instead of hooves. Other features suggest these animals were forest browsers and may have been able to rear up on their hind legs to feed on trees and shrubs.

Size: 1 feet 6 inches (45 cm) high at the shoulder

Order: Perissodactyla

Family: Brontotheriidae

Range: North America, Asia

Pn: Ee-oh-ti-TAN-ops

Eotitanops

If you could travel back through time, and glimpsed a group of *Eotitanops* scampering through the undergrowth, it would be impossible to tell *Eotitanops* from its distant cousin *Hyracotherium*. However, *Hyracotherium* gave rise to the elegant horses, but *Eotitanops* evolved into the huge, small-brained, lumbering, brontotheres that failed to see out the Oligocene.

Brontops

As the Eocene passed into the Oligocene, the brontotheres became very large — larger than any living rhinoceros — and developed the distinctive bony knobs on the snout. Skeletons of *Brontops* have been found with partly healed breaks in the ribs, which lends support to the theory that the skull outgrowths were used in fights among males for dominance. The breaks suggest that the animal had received a heavy blow in the flanks from a rival.

Size: 8 feet (2.5 m) high at the shoulder

Order: Perissodactyla

Family: Brontotheriidae

Range: North America

Pn: BRON-tops

Embolotherium

The head of *Embolotherium* is typical of the grotesque shapes developed by the later brontotheres. From the back of the skull it swept forward in a deep hollow and then up to a massive single "horn" on the nose. The eyes were situated well forward, just behind the nostrils and at the horn's base. As in other large brontotheres, the shallow skull left little room for much of a brain.

Size: 8 feet (2.5 m) high at the shoulder
Order: Perissodactyla
Family: Brontotheriidae
Range: Asia (Mongolia)
Pn: EM-bol-o-THER-ee-um

Size: 4 feet (1.2 m) high at the shoulder
Order: Perissodactyla
Family: Brontotheriidae
Range: North America
Pn: DOL-i-kor-IN-us

Dolichorhinus

Dolichorhinus resembled a small hornless rhinoceros with a particularly long head. Indeed, with its low-crowned teeth, which were only suitable for chewing soft forest leaves, it probably lived very much like one of the modern rhinoceroses. The four-toed front feet and three-toed hind feet of its ancestors were retained. The type of feet adapted for swift running, with reduced toes, as seen in the horses and antelopes, were never evolved in the brontotheres.

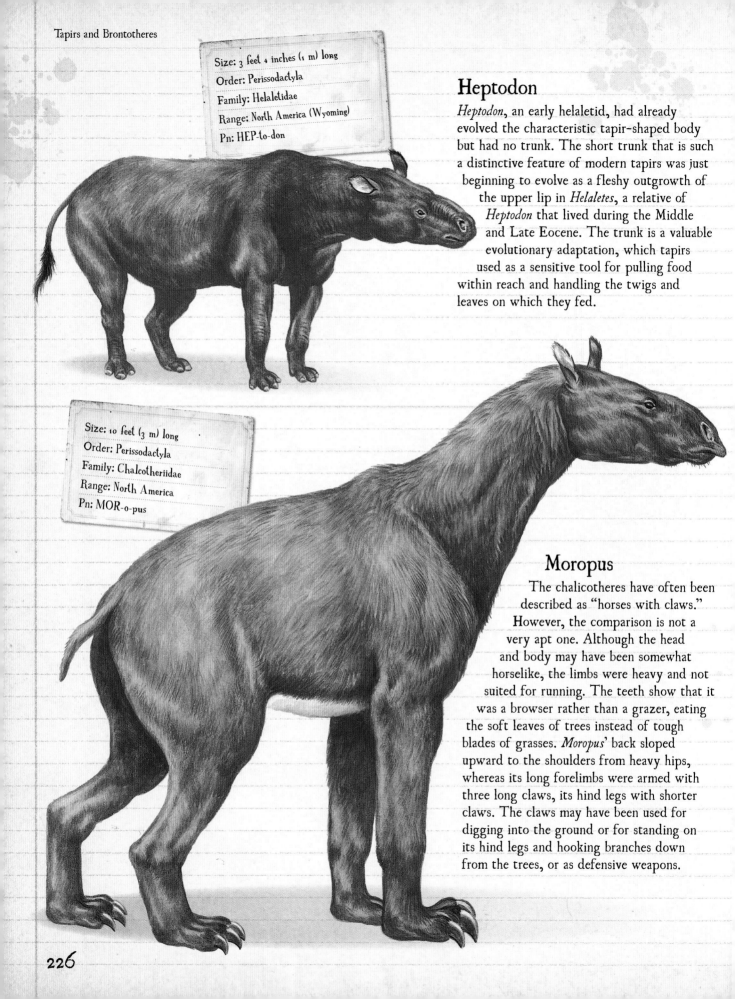

Size: 3 feet 4 inches (1 m) long

Order: Perissodactyla

Family: Helaletidae

Range: North America (Wyoming)

Pn: HEP-to-don

Heptodon

Heptodon, an early helaletid, had already evolved the characteristic tapir-shaped body but had no trunk. The short trunk that is such a distinctive feature of modern tapirs was just beginning to evolve as a fleshy outgrowth of the upper lip in *Helaletes*, a relative of *Heptodon* that lived during the Middle and Late Eocene. The trunk is a valuable evolutionary adaptation, which tapirs used as a sensitive tool for pulling food within reach and handling the twigs and leaves on which they fed.

Size: 10 feet (3 m) long

Order: Perissodactyla

Family: Chalcotheriidae

Range: North America

Pn: MOR-o-pus

Moropus

The chalicotheres have often been described as "horses with claws." However, the comparison is not a very apt one. Although the head and body may have been somewhat horselike, the limbs were heavy and not suited for running. The teeth show that it was a browser rather than a grazer, eating the soft leaves of trees instead of tough blades of grasses. *Moropus'* back sloped upward to the shoulders from heavy hips, whereas its long forelimbs were armed with three long claws, its hind legs with shorter claws. The claws may have been used for digging into the ground or for standing on its hind legs and hooking branches down from the trees, or as defensive weapons.

Brontotherium

The bones of this giant mammal are quite common in the Badlands of South Dakota and Nebraska. The local Sioux Indians associated them with the creatures of mythology — the great horses that galloped across the sky producing storms — and so the term brontothere, "thunder beast," was born. *Brontotherium* itself was one of the largest — larger than the living rhinoceroses. Its nasal horn was Y-shaped and swept upward higher than the back of the head. Powerful neck muscles were needed to support this creature's heavy head with its flamboyant ornamentation.

Size: 8 feet (2.5 m) high at the shoulder
Order: Perissodactyla
Family: Brontotheriidae
Range: North America
Pn: BRON-to-THER-ee-um

Size: 6 feet 6 inches (2 m) long
Order: Perissodactyla
Family: Tapiridae
Range: North America
Pn: MY-o-tap-IR-us

Miotapirus

The characteristic tapir features — a heavy body, short legs and tail, a large head with short flexible snout, and a short neck — appeared early in the evolution of perissodactyls and have remained unchanged ever since. *Miotapirus* was probably nocturnal, as are members of the living species *Tapirus*, and may have been just as versatile, adapting to many different environments — fossils of *Miotapirus* have been discovered in a range of sites from sea level up to heights of 15,000 feet (4,500 m).

227

RHINOCEROSES

R hinoceroses and their closest relatives are odd-toed ungulates, members of the Perissodactyla. Unlike the later horses, which have eliminated all the lateral digits and now have only one toe, most rhinoceroses have three toes, the center of weight-bearing passing through the middle or third toe.

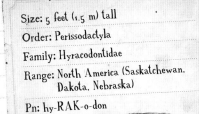

Size: 5 feet (1.5 m) tall
Order: Perissodactyla
Family: Hyracodontidae
Range: North America (Saskatchewan, Dakota, Nebraska)
Pn: hy-RAK-o-don

Size: 5 feet (1.5 m) long
Order: Perissodactyla
Family: Hyrachyidaeodon
Range: North America (Wyoming), Asia (China), Europe (France)
Pn: hy-RAK-ee-us

Hyracodon

Hyracodon was a lightly built, fast-running animal, not unlike a pony. As with the horses, the number of its toes was reduced, so that the foot was lightened and could be moved quickly, and all the leg muscles were concentrated near the top. The large and heavy head, however, seemed out of proportion to the body.

Hyrachyus

The hyrachids mark the transition between the tapirs and the rhinoceroses. *Hyrachyus* was a very similar creature to *Heptodon*, but it was a little larger and more heavily built. It was a common and widespread animal. Many species have been discovered, ranging from the size of a modern tapir to that of a modern-day fox.

Size: 26 feet (8 m) long
Order: Perissodactyla
Family: Hyracodontidae
Range: Asia (Pakistan, China)
Pn: in-DRIK-o-THER-ee-um

Indricotherium

It seems impossible that an animal as small, lightweight and fleet-of-foot as *Hyracodon* could have evolved into the largest land mammal known to have lived, but all of the evidence points in that direction. *Indricotherium* was an immense animal. It was twice the weight of the largest known mammoth and more than four times that of the heaviest modern elephant.

Metamynodon

Remains of *Metamynodon* are found in rocks that were formed from river sands and gravels, indicating that these beasts were mostly aquatic by nature. It was like a hippopotamus in appearance. It had a broad, flat head, a short neck and a massive barrel-shaped body. The front feet were unique among rhinoceroses in having four toes.

Size: 13 feet (4 m) long
Order: Perissodactyla
Family: Amynodontidae
Range: North America (Nebraska, South Dakota), Asia (Mongolia)
Pn: met-AM-ee-NO-don

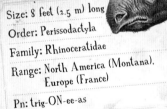

Size: 8 feet (2.5 m) long
Order: Perissodactyla
Family: Rhinoceratidae
Range: North America (Montana), Europe (France)
Pn: trig-ON-ee-as

Trigonias

The earliest well-preserved example of a rhinocerotid is *Trigonias*. It was already similar to the modern rhinoceroses in its general appearance, but *Trigonias* had no horn on the snout. There were also more teeth in the jaw than are found in the jaws of any modern rhinoceros, although the actual number seems to have varied between different species.

Teleoceras

Like the amynodontids, the rhinocerotids developed hippopotamus-shaped forms as well. *Teleoceras* was typical of these. It had a long and massive body but short and stumpy legs. *Teleoceras*' legs were so short, in fact, that the creature's body would at times have dragged on the ground.

Size: 13 feet (4 m) long
Order: Perissodactyla
Family: Rhinoceratidae
Range: North America (Nebraska)
Pn: tel-ee-o-SER-as

Size: 16 feet (5 m) long
Order: Perissodactyla
Family: Rhinoceratidae
Range: Europe (southern Russia), Asia (Siberia)
Pn: el-AS-mo-THER-ee-um

Elasmotherium

Elasmotherium was well adapted to the developing grasslands of the late Tertiary. Its teeth were like those of a huge horse, adapted for eating tough, abrasive grasses. The largest known of the true rhinoceroses, it was almost as big as a modern elephant. Its "horn" was a truly remarkable structure, 6 feet 6 inches (2 m) long and protruding from its forehead instead of its snout.

229

SWINE AND HIPPOPOTAMUSES

The artiodactyls are the even-toed ungulates, and are the most widespread and abundant of today's running, grazing animals. They usually have four or two weight-bearing toes on each foot forming the semicircular hoof, giving rise to the "cloven hoof" typical of pigs, deer and cattle. With the exception of the suines (pigs, peccaries and hippopotamuses), the artiodactyls all ruminate: that is, they "chew the cud" to improve the efficiency of digestion. The importance of the ungulates, particularly artiodactyls, to human evolution cannot be ignored. They were hunted, then several species were domesticated, which added to the resources available to humans.

Size: 20 inches (50 cm) long including tail
Order: Artiodactyla
Family: Dichobunidae
Range: Europe (France), North America (Wyoming), Asia (Pakistan)
Pn: dee-a-co-DEX-is

Size: 10 feet (3 m) long
Order: Artiodactyla
Family: Entelodontidae
Range: North America (Nebraska, South Dakota)
Pn: di-NO-yus

Diacodexis

The earliest known of the artiodactyls, *Diacodexis* had simple teeth, and all five toes were present (though as in most artiodactyls, the third and fourth were the longest). There may also have been small hooves on the toes. *Diacodexis* must have lived in forest undergrowth, browsing leaves from bushes.

Dinohyus

The entelodonts reached their maximum size in the omnivorous *Dinohyus*. This animal was much like *Archaeotherium*, but about the size of a bull. Although *Dinohyus'* bodily proportions were piglike, the evidence of its long and heavy skull suggests that its face must have been quite different.

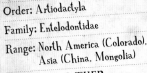

Size: 4 feet (1.2 m) long
Order: Artiodactyla
Family: Entelodontidae
Range: North America (Colorado), Asia (China, Mongolia)
Pn: ARK-ee-oh-THER-ee-um

Archaeotherium

Archaeotherium would have looked something like a modern warthog. Its skull was remarkably elongated, with long knobs of bone beneath the eyes and on the lower jaw. Like a pig, it could eat just about anything.

Elomeryx

The hippopotamus-like *Elomeryx* had a long body and short stumpy legs, with a head that was long and superficially resembled that of a horse. Its teeth, however, were quite different, with elongated canines well adapted to hooking up the roots of water plants, and spoon-shaped incisors ideally suited for digging in the mud. *Elemeryx*'s broad feet would have been useful for walking on soft mud.

Size: 5 feet (1.5 m) long

Order: Artiodactyla

Family: Anthracotheriidae

Range: Europe (France), North America (Dakota)

Pn: el-oh-MER-ix

Platygonus

Size: 3 feet 3 inches (1 m) long

Order: Artiodactyla

Family: Tayassuidae

Range: North America (Great Plains), South America

Pn: PLAT-ee-GON-us

Platygonus was larger than modern peccaries and had longer legs. Like its modern relatives, it was primarily a forest animal. It also inhabited the more open Great Plains region, a fact that may help to explain its long limbs suitable for running.

Size: 5 feet (1.5 m) long

Order: Artiodactyla

Family: Suidae

Range: Africa (Tanzania)

Pn: me-TRID-ee-oh-ko-AIR-us

Metridiochoerus

A contemporary of early humans, *Metridiochoerus* was a giant warthog that inhabited eastern Africa. Its head was large and heavy, and both its upper and lower canine teeth curled outward and upward to form great curved tusks.

Size: 14 feet (4.3 m) long

Order: Artiodactyla

Family: Hippopotamidae

Range: Asia, Africa, Europe

Pn: HIP-oh-POT-a-mus

Hippopotamus

The only obvious differences between a *Hippopotamus gorgops* of Pleistocene East Africa and the living species *H. amphibius* were the great size and particularly prominent eyes of the former. These eyes probably protruded, periscope-like, above the skull on stalks.

OREODONTS AND EARLY HORNED BROWSERS

Size: 1 foot (30 cm) long
Order: Artiodactyla
Family: Cainotheriidae
Range: Europe (Spain)
Pn: cain-o-THER-ee-um

Tylopods (meaning "padded foot") are a broad grouping of artiodactyls (even-toed ungulates). The suborder Tylopoda includes rabbitlike cainotheres, piglike merycoidodonts, and the camelids. In many important respects, they stand midway between the swines (pigs, peccaries and hippopotamuses) and the pecorans (giraffes, deer and cattle). Only the camelids — the camels, llamas and their closest relatives — still survive.

Cainotherium

Cainotherium was a small, rabbitlike animal, with hind limbs longer than the front limbs. The parts of the creature's brain that were associated with hearing and with smell were well developed. This feature implies that *Cainotherium* was probably equipped with long rabbitlike ears and probably had a sensitive nose as well. It probably browsed on a variety of vegetation.

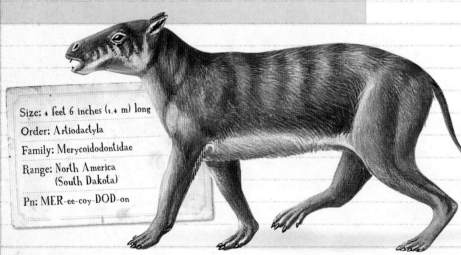

Size: 4 feet 6 inches (1.4 m) long
Order: Artiodactyla
Family: Merycoidodontidae
Range: North America (South Dakota)
Pn: MER-ee-coy-DOD-on

Merycoidodon

Merycoidodon, which was a typical member of its family, probably looked something like a pig or peccary, but with a longer body and shorter legs. Paleontologists believe that *Merycoidodon* probably would not have been able to run particularly well, because there was no fusion of its limb bones.

Brachycrus

Brachycrus was a merycoidodont that appeared quite late in North America. Although it was similar to *Merycoidodon*, it was somewhat smaller and considerably more specialized. Its skull and jaw were short — indeed, practically apelike — and the eye sockets faced forward.

Size: 3 feet 3 inches (1 m) long
Order: Artiodactyla
Family: Merycoidodontidae
Range: North America (Great Plains)
Pn: BRACK-ee-CRUS

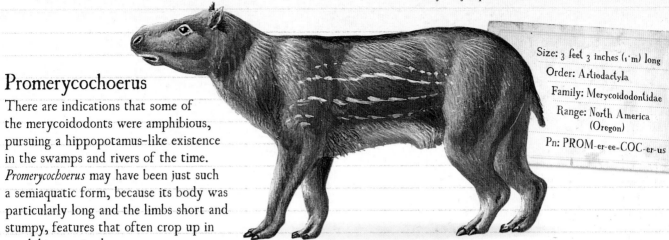

Promerycochoerus

There are indications that some of the merycoidodonts were amphibious, pursuing a hippopotamus-like existence in the swamps and rivers of the time. *Promerycochoerus* may have been just such a semiaquatic form, because its body was particularly long and the limbs short and stumpy, features that often crop up in amphibious animals.

Size: 3 feet 3 inches (1 m) long
Order: Artiodactyla
Family: Merycoidodontidae
Range: North America (Oregon)
Pn: PROM-er-ee-COC-er-us

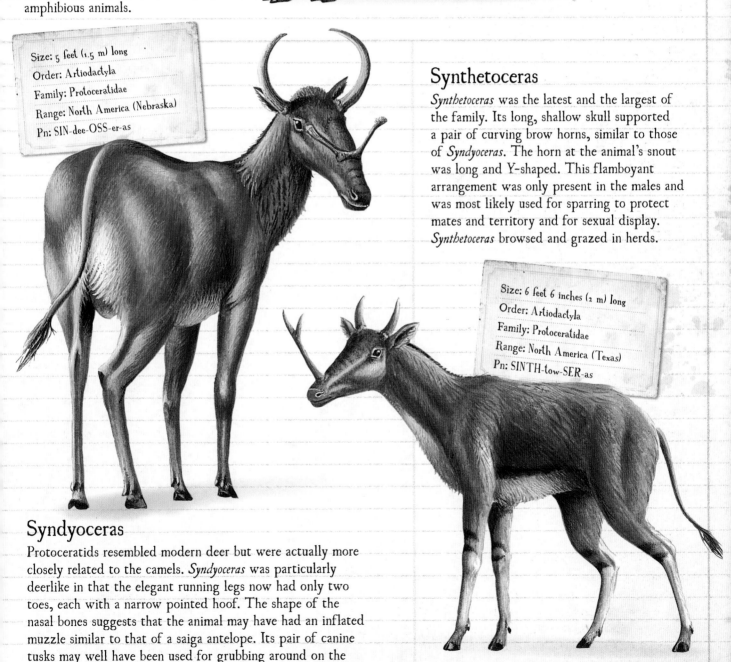

Size: 5 feet (1.5 m) long
Order: Artiodactyla
Family: Protoceratidae
Range: North America (Nebraska)
Pn: SIN-dee-OSS-er-as

Synthetoceras

Synthetoceras was the latest and the largest of the family. Its long, shallow skull supported a pair of curving brow horns, similar to those of *Syndyoceras*. The horn at the animal's snout was long and Y-shaped. This flamboyant arrangement was only present in the males and was most likely used for sparring to protect mates and territory and for sexual display. *Synthetoceras* browsed and grazed in herds.

Size: 6 feet 6 inches (2 m) long
Order: Artiodactyla
Family: Protoceratidae
Range: North America (Texas)
Pn: SINTH-tow-SER-as

Syndyoceras

Protoceratids resembled modern deer but were actually more closely related to the camels. *Syndyoceras* was particularly deerlike in that the elegant running legs now had only two toes, each with a narrow pointed hoof. The shape of the nasal bones suggests that the animal may have had an inflated muzzle similar to that of a saiga antelope. Its pair of canine tusks may well have been used for grubbing around on the ground in the search for food.

233

CAMELS

The modern camelids are found only where conditions are harsh. The camels are famed as "ships of the desert," capable of covering immense distances across difficult terrain in the most inhospitable of climates. Thanks to their extraordinary physiology, they can live for up to two months on rough grazing alone, without additional water. Modern camels are the remnants of a formerly widespread and diverse group, which first evolved some 40 million years ago in North America, becoming extinct there about 12,000 years ago. The South American camelids — the llamas and their relatives — are also found in challenging habitats, including that of the high Andes.

Size: 3 feet (90 cm) long
Order: Artiodactyla
Family: Camelidae
Range: North America (South Dakota)
Pn: poe-broth-ER-ee-um

Poebrotherium

Around 35 million years ago, the dense forests that once covered Dakota had given way to more open woodlands. Camelids became plentiful and began to look more like modern camels. At about the size of a sheep, *Poebrotherium* was larger than *Protylopus*. Its head, with a distinctive narrow snout, was a smaller version of a llama's, and it may have had the llama's prominent ears as well.

Size: 20 inches (80 cm) long
Order: Artiodactyla
Family: Oromerycidae
Range: North America (Utah, Colorado)
Pn: PROT-il-LOP-us

Size: 10 feet (3 m) high at the head
Order: Artiodactyla
Family: Camelidae
Range: North America (Colorado)
Pn: EYE-pee-CAM-el-us

Protylopus

As in most groups of ungulates, the first camelids were small, rabbit-size animals. The simple, low-crowned teeth were arranged along the jaw without any breaks, a primitive feature and one that indicates that the animal's diet was the soft leaves of the forest vegetation. The forelimbs, which were shorter than the hind limbs, had four toes.

Aepycamelus

The giraffelike camel was formerly known as *Alticamelus* because of its extraordinary height. The legs were long and stiltlike, and the two toes had very small hooves. *Aepycamelus*, then, had lost the running hooves of its ancestors and put in their place the broad pads of modern camels. *Aepycamelus*, with its extremely long legs, must have moved with a similar gait to modern camels and giraffes.

Size: 11 feet 6 in (3.5 m) high at the shoulder

Order: Artiodactyla

Family: Camelidae

Range: North America (Nebraska)

Pn: ti-tan-OT-i-LOP-us

Size: 6 feet 6 inches (2 m) high at the shoulder

Order: Artiodactyla

Family: Camelidae

Range: North America (California, Utah)

Pn: CAM-e-lops

Titanotylopus

Titanotylopus was one of the large camels that evolved in North America between 2 and 5 million years ago. It must have been taller than the elephants of the time, yet with its long neck and splayed two-toed feet, it was very similar to modern camels. However, it didn't have a hump; this evolved at a later time.

Camelops

Camelops, another giant of the late Cenozoic Era and a contemporary of early humans, appears to have been the last camel to have survived in North America. It probably looked very much like the modern Asian camel, but certain parts of its anatomy indicate that it was more closely related to the South American llamas.

Stenomylus

A number of side branches of the camel family evolved in the Miocene, but became extinct soon afterward. *Stenomylus* and its relatives were small gazellelike animals. They must have lived very much as African gazelles do today, browsing in herds on low vegetation and sprinting rapidly away from danger. The neck was long and the legs were slender. The two toes on each foot had small, deerlike hooves.

Size: 5 feet (1.5 m) long

Order: Artiodactyla

Family: Camelidae

Range: North America (Colorado)

Pn: pro-CAM-el-us

Size: 3 feet (90 cm) long

Order: Artiodactyla

Family: Camelidae

Range: North America (Nebraska)

Pn: sten-OM-mee-lus

Procamelus

Procamelus was either on the direct ancestral line to modern camels or very close to it. It was much larger than any of the earlier camels, approaching the size of a modern llama. The head was very long but the braincase was quite small. *Procamelus* still had incisors in the upper jaw, but only a single pair — and even these were reduced in size.

GIRAFFES, DEER AND CATTLE

Two surviving members of the giraffe family are the tall, long-necked, long-legged giraffe of the African savanna and the other smaller, darker okapi of the African tropical forest. The cervids, or true deer, were quite late to evolve and have become the principal browsing animals of the northern hemisphere and South America. The bovids, the true antelopes and cattle, still occupy a great range of habitats from forests and grasslands to swamps and even deserts. In North America, they survive today as bison, bighorn sheep, and mountain goats.

Size: 7 feet (2.2 m) high at the shoulder

Order: Artiodactyla

Family: Giraffidae

Range: India (sub-Himalayas), North Africa (Libya)

Pn: siv-ath-ER-ee-um

Sivatherium

Named in honor of Siva, or the Lord of the Beasts, who is one of the principal Hindu gods, this massive animal would have appeared more like a moose than a giraffe. The male, at least, was ornamented with a pair of huge branched ossicones on the top of its skull, and a smaller pair of conical ones around the eyes.

Size: 8 feet (2.5 m) long

Order: Artiodactyla

Family: Cervidae

Range: Widespread in Europe, Asia

Pn: meg-a-los-ER-os

Size: 6 feet (1.8 m) long

Order: Artiodactyla

Family: Giraffidae

Range: North Africa (Libya)

Pn: pro-lib-ee-THER-ee-um

Megaloceros

Often called the giant Irish elk, *Megaloceros* is not an elk (or moose) but is more akin to the fallow deer. Although many specimens have been unearthed in Ireland, *Megaloceros* ranged from the British Isles to Siberia and China.

Prolibytherium

In contrast to the small ossicones of the living giraffe and okapi species, *Prolibytherium* sported broad, leaf-shaped ossicones that reached a span of about 14 inches (35 cm). Otherwise, *Prolibytherium* probably resembled the modern okapi.

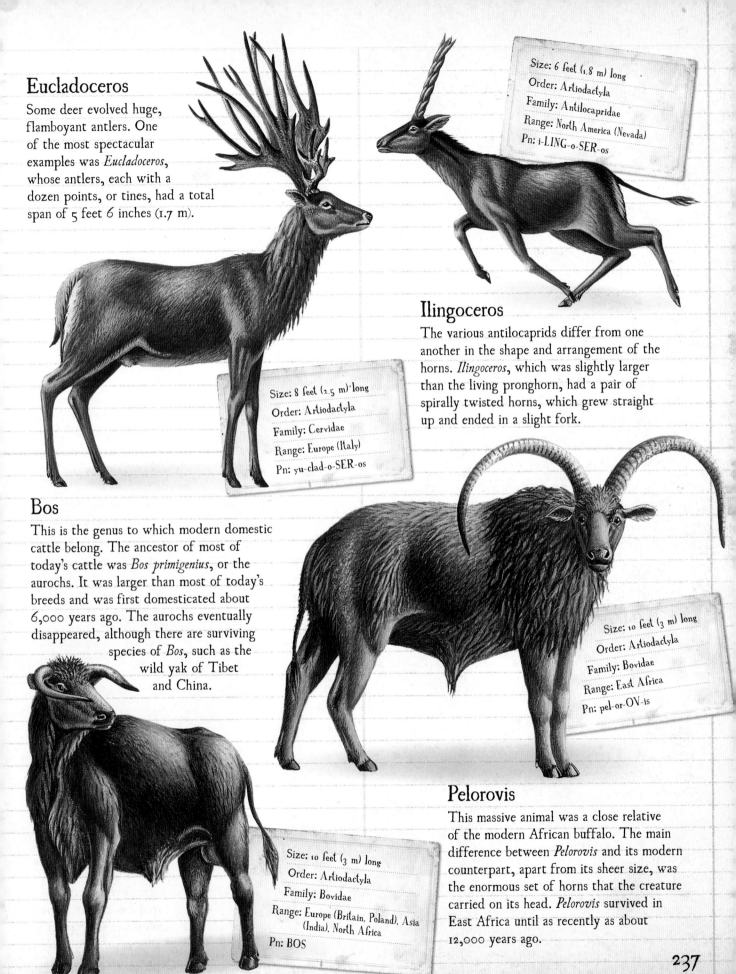

Eucladoceros

Some deer evolved huge, flamboyant antlers. One of the most spectacular examples was *Eucladoceros*, whose antlers, each with a dozen points, or tines, had a total span of 5 feet 6 inches (1.7 m).

Size: 8 feet (2.5 m) long
Order: Artiodactyla
Family: Cervidae
Range: Europe (Italy)
Pn: yu-clad-o-SER-os

Size: 6 feet (1.8 m) long
Order: Artiodactyla
Family: Antilocapridae
Range: North America (Nevada)
Pn: i-LING-o-SER-os

Ilingoceros

The various antilocaprids differ from one another in the shape and arrangement of the horns. *Ilingoceros*, which was slightly larger than the living pronghorn, had a pair of spirally twisted horns, which grew straight up and ended in a slight fork.

Bos

This is the genus to which modern domestic cattle belong. The ancestor of most of today's cattle was *Bos primigenius*, or the aurochs. It was larger than most of today's breeds and was first domesticated about 6,000 years ago. The aurochs eventually disappeared, although there are surviving species of *Bos*, such as the wild yak of Tibet and China.

Size: 10 feet (3 m) long
Order: Artiodactyla
Family: Bovidae
Range: East Africa
Pn: pel-or-OV-is

Size: 10 feet (3 m) long
Order: Artiodactyla
Family: Bovidae
Range: Europe (Britain, Poland), Asia (India), North Africa
Pn: BOS

Pelorovis

This massive animal was a close relative of the modern African buffalo. The main difference between *Pelorovis* and its modern counterpart, apart from its sheer size, was the enormous set of horns that the creature carried on its head. *Pelorovis* survived in East Africa until as recently as about 12,000 years ago.

RODENTS, RABBITS AND HARES

Rodents are a relatively early and primitive group in the evolution of mammals. They have diversified into several major types, including squirrels, beavers, rats, mice, gophers, chichillas, guinea pigs, and porcupines. They are the largest order of mammals today, making up 40 percent of all known living mammals. The lagomorphs — the pikas, rabbits, and hares — seem to be very like rodents, although they have two pairs of gnawing teeth in the front of the upper jaw instead of the single pair found in rodents. Lagomorphs swiftly became a widespread vegetarian group, exploiting grassy planes and shrubs.

Size: 1 foot (30 cm) long
Order: Rodentia
Family: Castoridae
Range: Europe (France, Germany)
Pn: STEN-ee-o-FIB-er

Steneofiber

Beavers are well represented in the fossil record from as far back as the Early Oligocene, around 35 million years ago. The early Miocene beaver *Steneofiber* was small and lived on and near freshwater lakes, much as most living beavers do today. It is unlikely, though, that it could have felled large trees, as its modern counterparts do. Many early species were more terrestrial, however, and some even burrowed.

Size: 1 foot (30 cm) long
Order: Rodentia
Family: Mylagaulidae
Range: North America (Great Basin)
Pn: epi-GOL-us

Epigaulus

Epigaulus is one of the oddest rodents known. It must have resembled a modern marmot, except that it possessed clawed hands that were broad and paddlelike, small eyes, and a pair of stout horns on the skull. No other known rodent had horns like these and their function is a mystery.

Size: 2 feet (60 cm) long
Order: Rodentia
Family: Ischyromyidae
Range: North America
Pn: ISK-ee-ROM-is

Ischyromys

Ischyromys is among the earliest known of the true rodents. Mouselike in appearance, this creature had many of the typical rodent head features, including the characteristic pair of upper incisors. The rest of the body was that of a typical rodent as well, with versatile forelimbs, strong hind limbs, and five clawed toes on each of its feet.

Palaeolagus

By the early Oligocene, the pikas had become compact animals with short legs and short ears, while the rabbits and hares developed longer legs and a running, then hopping, locomotion. *Palaeolagus* was similar to a modern rabbit, although its hind legs were shorter, suggesting that it was not yet the leaping animal of today.

Size: 10 inches (25 cm) long
Order: Lagomorpha
Family: Leporidae
Range: North America
Pn: PAL-ay-ol-AG-us

Size: 1 foot (30 cm) long
Order: Rodentia
Family: Eocardiidae
Range: South America
Pn: ee-oh-CARD-ee-a

Eocardia

Cavioids are the most typical South American rodents and are closely related to the guinea pigs and the capybara (large beaverlike rodents). Some cavioids became quite large, although *Eocardia* was more modest in size, reaching only 1 foot (30 cm) tall and resembling the present-day guinea pig in appearance.

Telicomys

Closely related to the guinea pigs and capybaras, *Telicomys* was probably the largest rodent that has ever lived. *Teliocomys* reached the size of a small rhinoceros, and would probably have looked like a hairy hippopotamus or a giant capybara.

Size: 7 feet (2.1 m) long
Order: Rodentia
Family: Dinomyidae
Range: South America
Pn: tel-ee-COM-is

Size: 1 foot (30 cm) long
Order: Rodentia
Family: Chapattimyidae
Range: Asia (Pakistan)
Pn: BER-ba-LOM-is

Birbalomys

Birbalomys is thought to be the most primitive rodent and probably close to the ancestry of the whole rodent group. It may have resembled the North African gundis, creatures somewhat like guinea pigs that today inhabit desert or semidesert habitats.

239

LEMURS AND MONKEYS

For more than 150 years, scientists have recognized that humans are related to the apes. More recently, it became evident that this relationship extended to the monkeys, lemurs and tarsiers, which are the survivors of a much more diverse group of fossil primates. The primates consist of some 200 living species. Within the order are the flying lemurs, the lemurlike adapids, the lemurids (lemurs), the tarsiers, as well as the platerrhines ("flat noses") or New World monkeys, and catarrhines ("downfacing noses") or Old World monkeys, apes and hominids. They evolved in North America or Eurasia 40 million years ago. The two lines diverged soon after, when a land bridge that linked North with South America once more disappeared.

Size: 2 feet 6 inches (80 cm) long
Order: Dermoptera
Family: Plesiadapidae
Range: North America (Rocky Mountains), Europe (France)
Pn: PLES-ee-a-DAP-is

Plesiadapis

Plesiadapis was squirrel-like in build and about the size of a modern beaver. It may have spent much of its time on the ground; however, it was also well adapted for scrambling in trees, with claws on long fingers and hands.

Size: 1 foot 4 inches (40 cm) long
Order: Primates
Family: Notharctidae
Range: North America (Wyoming)
Pn: noth-ARK-tus

Megaladapis

The largest known lemur, with a massive body and short limbs, *Megaladapis* must have weighed about 110 pounds (50 kg). Unlike its smaller relatives, it was probably a slow climber, clambering around in the tropical forest in search of leaves to eat. It was possibly finally wiped out by humans.

Notharctus

This adapid was probably much like a modern lemur, and it was highly adapted for living in trees. *Notharctus* had eyes directed forward, giving stereoscopic vision so it could judge distances accurately, long hind legs so it could jump from branch to branch, and a long heavy tail to balance it in its acrobatics.

Size: 5 feet (1.5 m) long
Order: Primates
Family: Megaladapidae
Range: Madagascar
Pn: meg-a-lad-AP-is

Size: 1 foot 4 inches (40 cm) long
Order: Primates
Family: Incertae sedis
Range: South America (Bolivia)
Pn: BRAN-is-EL-a

Branisella

This is the earliest known monkey to have lived on the South American continent, but little can be said with confidence about *Branisella*'s lifestyle and relationships, because the only fossil evidence of its existence are some fragments of jawbone. *Branisella*'s teeth were quite primitive, with many tarsier-like features.

Mesopithecus

Mesopithecus, which is also known as the "middle ape," was similar to the modern macaque monkey. It had long muscular arms and legs, and long, nimble fingers and toes. Its limbs could be used both for walking on the ground and for climbing in trees.

Size: 1 foot 4 inches (40 cm) long
Order: Primates
Family: Cercopithecidae
Range: Europe (Greece), Asia (Asia Minor)
Pn: MES-o-pi-THEK-us

Size: 3 feet 3 inches (1 m) long
Order: Primates
Family: Atelidae
Range: South America (Argentina)
Pn: TREM-a-SEB-us

Tremacebus

By the end of the Oligocene, New World monkeys had become very much like the modern forms. *Tremacebus*, which is sometimes known as *Homunculus* because of its miniature humanoid form, must have resembled today's only truly nocturnal owl monkey, the *Douroucouli*. *Tremacebus* is known from only a few specimens, including a skull, from Patagonia.

Theropithecus

The baboons are largely ground-dwelling monkeys that travel in family groups. They generally have doglike faces and consume a wide range of food. Although they tend to walk on all fours on the ground, they are still very good at climbing. *Theropithecus* was a large baboon, with a short face, and a large crest of bone running along the top of its skull that must have held strong jaw muscles.

Size: 4 feet (1.2 m) long
Order: Primates
Family: Cercopithecidae
Range: South and East Africa
Pn: THER-o-pi-THEK-us

241

APES

The only living hominoids (meaning "resembling humans") are the apes (pongids) and our own species, *Homo sapiens*. Living apes differ from Old World monkeys in having no tails, and arms and shoulders that are designed for hanging and swinging from branches. Between 16 and 10 million years ago, the earth really was the "planet of the apes," with many more species of apes distributed more widely across the world. Most of these species are now extinct.

Size: 4 feet (1.2 m) tall
Order: Primates
Family: Oreopithecidae
Range: Europe (Italy)
Pn: OR-ee-oh-pi-THEK-us

Oreopithecus

Oreopithecus, the "mountain ape," has been jokingly referred to as "the abominable coalman," because its remains were found in coal deposits in northern Italy, dated to about 14 million years ago, and because some of its features were almost human. *Oreopithecus* had a monkey's snout, apelike brow ridges and monkeylike anklebones.

Size: 1 foot (1.2 m) tall
Order: Primates
Family: Pliopithecidae
Range: Europe (France, Czech Republic)
Pn: PLEE-o-pi-THEK-us

Pliopithecus

It now seems unlikely that *Pliopithecus* gave rise to the gibbons, as was once thought. Nevertheless, there are distinct similarities between the two creatures and they probably share a common ancestor in early Miocene times. *Pliopithecus* lived between 16 and 10 million years ago, with some 30 different, but contemporaneous, species, most of which are now extinct. *Pliopithecus* was the size of a gibbon, with a long body and long hands and feet.

Size: 2 feet (60 cm) tall
Order: Primates
Family: Pliopithecidae
Range: East Africa (Kenya)
Pn: den-drop-i-THEK-us

Dendropithecus

It is now widely thought that an early relative of *Pliopithecus*, such as *Micropithecus* or *Dendropithecus*, was ancestral to the gibbons. Remains of the slimly built *Dendropithecus* ("tree ape") have been dated to about 15 million to 20 million years ago. Although it had shorter arms and a longer tail than *Pliopithecus*, *Dendropithecus* was more gibbonlike in other respects, including its diet.

Sivapithecus

With its orangutan-like face, chimpanzee-like feet, and rotating wrists, *Sivapithecus* appears to be an ape in the transition period between life in the trees and life on the ground. This reconstruction showing a tail is speculative and the one presented for the smaller *Ramapithecus* (see below) is more accurate.

Size: 5 feet (1.5 m) tall

Order: Primates

Family: Hominidae

Range: Southeast Europe, Asia, Africa (Kenya)

Pn: SI-va-pi-THEK-us

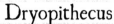

Size: 2 feet (60 cm) long

Order: Primates

Family: Hominidae

Range: Europe (France, Greece), Asia (Caucasus), Africa (Kenya)

Pn: dry-OP-i-THEK-us

Dryopithecus

The evolutionary lines that developed into the modern apes and *Homo sapiens* may have begun with the widespread *Dryopithecus* ("woodland ape"), which lived about 12 to 9 million years ago. *Dryopithecus* evolved in East Africa and migrated to Europe and Asia.

Size: 10 feet (3 m) tall

Order: Primates

Family: Hominidae

Range: Asia (China, Pakistan, India)

Pn: gi-GANT-o-pi-THEK-us

Ramapithecus

Although *Ramapithecus* has elbows similar to those of modern apes, the arm bones are quite primitive. The face and skull share several features with the orangutan, which implies a developmental relationship between the two.

Size: 4 feet (1.2m) tall

Order: Primates

Family: Hominidae

Range: Asia (Pakistan), Africa (Kenya)

Pn: RAM-a-pi-THEK-us

Gigantopithecus

This enormous creature was a veritable King Kong of the fossil apes. *Gigantopithecus* must have weighed something like 650 pounds (300 kg). A close relative of *Sivapithecus*, it is known mostly from fragmental remains of its jaws and teeth, which were about twice the breadth of a modern gorilla's teeth. It was a ground-dwelling ape and was probably gorilla-like in appearance.

243

HUMANS

The key features of human evolution, or "hominization," have included: changes in locomotion and posture, notably an upright stance, bipedal (two-legged) locomotion, legs longer than arms, and smaller big toes; the growth of the pelvis and of the birth canal to accommodate larger-brained babies; increased manual dexterity, due to lengthened thumbs and the "precision grip" — the ability to hold small objects between thumb and index finger; and modifications of the head. Compared with less evolved primates, hominids have smaller jaws and teeth. They have reduced ridges of bone over the eyes, their brains are larger relative to the rest of the body, and their brains are more complex. Cultural developments include the formation of groups, tool making, the harnessing of fire, and burial rituals.

Size: 4–5 feet (1.2–1.5 m)
Order: Primates
Family: Hominidae
Range: Africa (Ethiopia, Kenya, Tanzania, possibly South Africa), possibly Southeast Asia
Pn: HO-mo HAB-i-lis

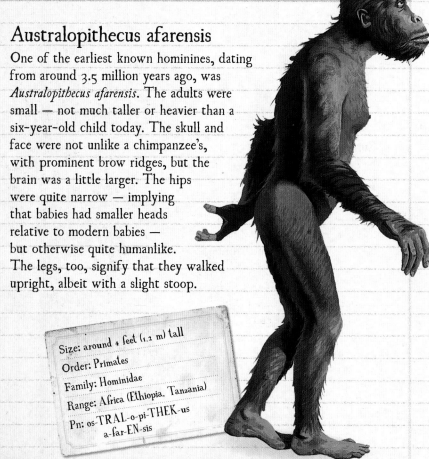

Australopithecus afarensis

One of the earliest known hominines, dating from around 3.5 million years ago, was *Australopithecus afarensis*. The adults were small — not much taller or heavier than a six-year-old child today. The skull and face were not unlike a chimpanzee's, with prominent brow ridges, but the brain was a little larger. The hips were quite narrow — implying that babies had smaller heads relative to modern babies — but otherwise quite humanlike. The legs, too, signify that they walked upright, albeit with a slight stoop.

Size: around 4 feet (1.2 m) tall
Order: Primates
Family: Hominidae
Range: Africa (Ethiopia, Tanzania)
Pn: os-TRAL-o-pi-THEK-us a-far-EN-sis

Homo habilis

By about 1.5 to 2 million years ago, several hominines existed alongside one another in East Africa. Some were close enough to modern humans to be placed in the genus *Homo*. *Homo habilis* was still quite short and light, with less massive brow ridges than its predecessors. Its head, too, was larger, as was its brain, but even so it was half the size of a modern human brain. However, the distinctive feature of *H. habilis*, or "handy human," is that it is one of the first hominines that is known to have used stone tools.

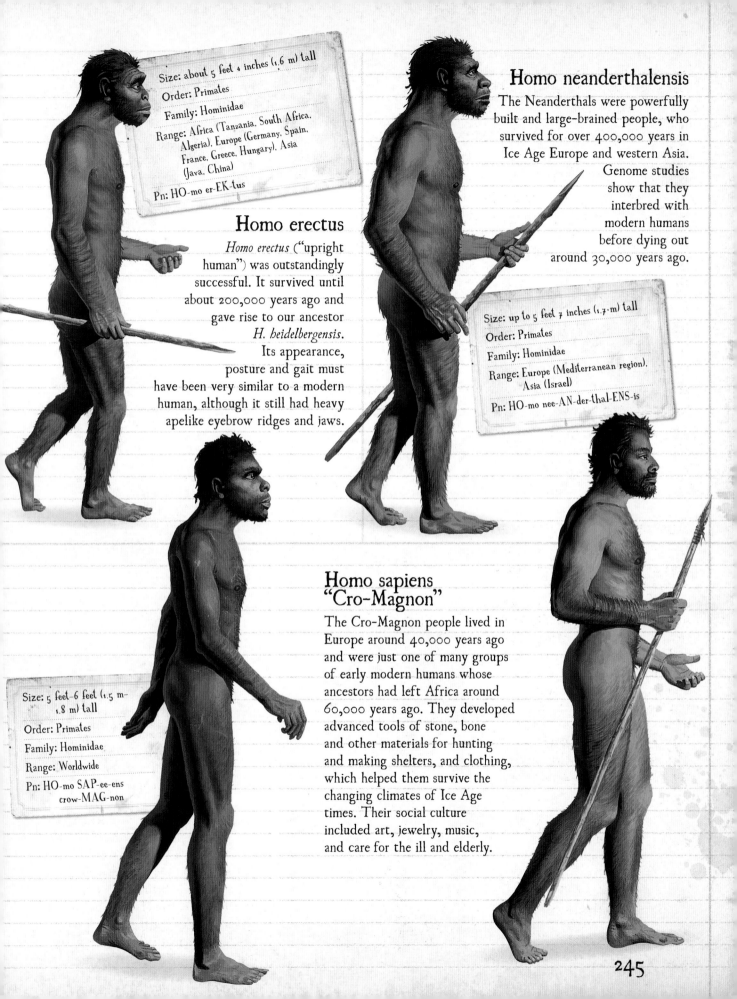

Size: about 5 feet 4 inches (1.6 m) tall

Order: Primates

Family: Hominidae

Range: Africa (Tanzania, South Africa, Algeria), Europe (Germany, Spain, France, Greece, Hungary), Asia (Java, China)

Pn: HO-mo er-EK-tus

Homo erectus

Homo erectus ("upright human") was outstandingly successful. It survived until about 200,000 years ago and gave rise to our ancestor *H. heidelbergensis*.
Its appearance, posture and gait must have been very similar to a modern human, although it still had heavy apelike eyebrow ridges and jaws.

Homo neanderthalensis

The Neanderthals were powerfully built and large-brained people, who survived for over 400,000 years in Ice Age Europe and western Asia.
Genome studies show that they interbred with modern humans before dying out around 30,000 years ago.

Size: up to 5 feet 7 inches (1.7 m) tall

Order: Primates

Family: Hominidae

Range: Europe (Mediterranean region), Asia (Israel)

Pn: HO-mo nee-AN-der-thal-ENS-is

Size: 5 feet–6 feet (1.5 m–1.8 m) tall

Order: Primates

Family: Hominidae

Range: Worldwide

Pn: HO-mo SAP-ee-ens crow-MAG-non

Homo sapiens "Cro-Magnon"

The Cro-Magnon people lived in Europe around 40,000 years ago and were just one of many groups of early modern humans whose ancestors had left Africa around 60,000 years ago. They developed advanced tools of stone, bone and other materials for hunting and making shelters, and clothing, which helped them survive the changing climates of Ice Age times. Their social culture included art, jewelry, music, and care for the ill and elderly.

245

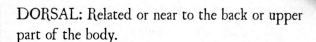

GLOSSARY

AGNATHANS: A group of jawless and toothless fishlike vertebrates.

AMPHIBIAN: A four-legged vertebrate animal that can live on land and in water but usually lays its eggs in water. Modern amphibians include frogs, toads, and salamanders.

ANAPSID: A member of a group of reptiles characterized by having no openings in the skull behind the eye, including turtles, tortoises, and some other primitive groups.

ARCHOSAUR: The group of reptiles to which dinosaurs and pterosaurs belonged. Crocodiles are the only surviving archosaurs.

ARTHROPODS: The biggest group of animals, which includes many extinct groups, as well as living groups, such as insects and spiders.

BIPEDAL: Capable of standing, walking or running on two legs.

CARNIVORE: An animal that eats the flesh of other animals in order to survive.

CARTILAGE: Gristly, flexible material that makes up the skeleton in many animals.

CHORDATE: Animals with a notochord or backbone.

CLUBMOSS: A type of plant that lived before flowering plants. Common in the Carboniferous Period, they are now almost extinct.

DIAPSID: A member of a major group of animals that includes the dinosaurs, extinct marine reptiles, lizards, snakes, and birds, characterized by a pair of openings in the skull immediately behind the eye socket.

DORSAL: Related or near to the back or upper part of the body.

EVOLUTION: The gradual development of all life from a common ancestor over time through genetic change and adpatation to the environment.

EXTINCTION: The complete dying out of a type of plant or animal.

FAMILY: A group of related species. For example, all the species of duck-billed dinosaurs, such as *Maiasaura*, belong to the family Hadrosauridae.

FOSSIL: The remains of an animal preserved in rock. Bones and teeth are more likely to form fossils than soft body parts. Impressions in mud, such as footprints, can also be fossilized.

GONDWANA: A supercontinent formed when Pangea broke up about 180 million years ago. Gondwana split to form the southern landmasses of South America, Africa, India, Australia and Antarctica.

HERBIVORE: An animal that eats plant matter only.

HOMINIDS: A family of primates that includes humans and their fossil ancestors, such as the australopithecines.

INSECTIVORES: A group of small and mainly nocturnal mammals that feed on insects.

INVERTEBRATE: An animal without a backbone.

LAURASIA: A supercontinent formed when Pangea broke up about 180 million years ago. Laurasia then split to form the northern landmasses of North America and Eurasia.

MAMMAL: A four-legged vertebrate animal that has hair on its body and feeds its young on milk produced in its own body. Mammals include animals such as cats, horses and humans.

MARSUPIAL: A mammal that gives birth to small, undeveloped young that are nurtured in a skin pouch on the mother's stomach.

MASS EXTINCTION: The disappearance of a large number of different species over a short period of time.

METEORITE: A lump of rock from outer space that enters the Earth's atmosphere and lands on Earth.

NOTOCHORD: A flexible rod running from head to tail. It forms the basis of the backbone in vertebrate animals.

OMNIVORE: An animal that is able to eat material of plant and animal origin.

ORDER: An order is a group of related families. For example, there are two orders of dinosaurs: the Ornithischia and the Saurischia. Some large orders are divided into smaller suborders.

ORNITHISCHIA: One of the two orders of dinosaurs. The orders differ in the structure of their hip bones (see pages 112–113).

PALEONTOLOGIST: A scientist who specializes in the study of fossils and ancient life.

PANGEA: A global supercontinent that formed about 240 million years ago and included all the world's land. It later split into two parts — Gondwana and Laurasia.

PREDATOR: An animal that hunts and kills other animals for food.

PRIMATES: A group of mammals that includes living monkeys, apes and humans.

REPTILE: A four-legged vertebrate animal that lays eggs with tough, leathery shells. Dinosaurs, pterosaurs, and ichthyosaurs were all reptiles. Modern reptiles include tortoises, snakes, lizards and crocodiles.

SAURISCHIA: One of the two orders of dinosaurs. The orders differ in the structure of their hip bones (see pages 112–113). Saurischians included plant-eating and meat-eating dinosaurs.

SPECIES: A term for a type of plant or animal. Members of the same species can mate and produce young that can themselves have young.

TETRAPODS: A major group of vertebrates including all four-limbed vertebrates. Their descendants include the amphibians, reptiles, mammals and birds.

THERAPSIDS: A group of reptilelike synapsid tetrapods that include the ancestors of the mammals.

THEROPOD: A diverse subgroup of saurischian dinosaurs, some of which were very large, walked on their hind limbs and were mostly meat-eating.

VERTEBRATE: An animal with a backbone. Mammals, birds, reptiles, amphibians and fish are all vertebrates.

INDEX

Canobius 52
capybaras 239
Carboniferous Period 8, 26–7, 28, 62,
72, 177
Carcharodontosaurus 119
carnivores
dinosaurs 30, 31, 112, 116–19, 120,
126–7, 128–9
mammals 186, 189, 200–7
skulls 129
synapsids 177
Carnotaurus 116, 117
cartilaginous fish 46–9
Casea 180
catarrhines 240
cats 37, 189, 202, 204–5
cattle 210, 222, 230, 232, 236–7
Caudipteryx 124
cavioids 239
Cearadactylus 104
Cenozoic era 9
Centrosaurus 156, 162
cephalopods 33
ceratopsians (Ceratopsia) 34, 35, 114,
160–3
ceratosaurs 116–17
Cerdocyon 203
Ceresiosaurus 88
cervids 236
Cetaceans 189
Cetotherium 209
chalicotheres 224
Chapalmalania 198
Charnia 14
Chasmosaurus 162
Cheirolepis 52
chelonians 75, 76
chinchillas 238
Chriacus 210
Cistecephalus 182
civets 200, 203
Cladoselache 46
Cladosictis 193
claudiosaurs 88–9
Claudiosaurus 89
climate change 16, 29, 36, 164–5, 166
clubmoss 26
Cobelodus 47
coelacanths 33
Coelodonta antiquitatus 36
Coelophysis 30, 31, 116, 117
Compsognathus 116
conifers 120, 121, 157

conodonts 20
continents
Cambrian Period 19
Carboniferous Age 27
Cretaceous Period 34, 35, 157
Devonian Period 25
Ediacaran Period 15
Jurassic Period 33, 121
Ordovician Period 21
Permian Age 28, 29
Silurian Period 22
South America 216
Triassic Period 30, 83
Cooksonia 23
coprolites 129, 132
corals 20, 21, 23
Coryphodon 210
Corythosaurus 147, 152, 157
coyotes 202, 203
Crassigyrinus 64
crater, meteorite 166
creodonts 196–9
Cretaceous Period 9, 34–5, 72, 110,
156–7, 166, 167
crinoids 96, 97
crocodiles 67, 74, 75, 83, 98, 102–3
Crocodylia 77, 102
Cro-Magnons 235
crurotarsans 98
Crurotarsi 77
Crusafontia 190
crust, Earth's 11
Cryolophosaurus 119
Cryptoclidus 92
Ctenurella 51
cycads 30, 121
Cyclomedusa 15
Cyclonema 21
Cymbospondylus 94
Cynaphagus 31
Cynodesmus 202
cynodonts 31, 80, 190

D

Dapedium 55
Dartmuthia 45
Deccan Traps 164
deer 37, 210, 222, 230, 232, 233, 236–7
Deinonychus 122
Deinosuchus 102
Deinotherium 212
Deltoptychius 49

Dendropithecus 242
Deodicurus 194
Desmatophoca 206
Desmatosuchus 31, 98
desmostylians 206
Desmostylus 207
Devonian Period 8, 24–5, 38
Diacodexis 230
Diadiaphorus 216
diapsids 75, 76
Diatryma gigantea 175
Dickensonia 14
Dicraeosaurus 135
Dicroidium 29
Dicynodon 29, 75, 183
dicynodonts 80, 181
Didiaphorus 189
Didolodus 216
Dilophosaurus 117
Dimetrodon 28, 179
Dimorphodon 96, 106
Dinofelis 189, 205
Dinohyus 230
Dinomischus 19
Dinornis maximus 170
Dinosauria 77, 114–15
dinosaurs 9, 30, 31, 32, 34, 110–67
after the dinosaurs 36–7
armored 9, 158–9
bird relatives 122–3
boneheads and other plant eaters 140–1
ceratosaurs 116–17
Cretaceous Period 156–7
disappearance of 9, 164–7
discovering 138–9
domination of 72
duck-billed 129, 146, 147, 148–53, 156
family life 146–7
family tree 114–15
feeding 128–9
footprints 132
fossils 132–3
horned 156, 160–3
hypsilophodonts 142–3
iguanodonts 144–5
Jurassic Period 120–1
movement 112–13
ostrich 124–5
prosauropods 130–1
sauropods 120, 128, 130, 134–7
stegosaurs 120, 154–5
tetanurans 118–19
Triassic Period 82

gymnosperms 26, 31
Gyroptychius 59

H

hadrosaurs 34, 128, 147, 148–53
Hadrosaurus 149
hair 188
Hallucigenia 18
Hapalops 194
Haramiya 190
hares 238–9
Harpagornis morei 170
head-butting 140–1, 147
Hemicyclaspis 43
Hemicyon 200
Henodus 89
Heptodon 226
herbivores
   dinosaurs 31, 37, 112, 120, 128–31,
      134–7, 140–5, 147, 148–56, 158–63
   synapsids 177
   mammals 189, 210–43
   skulls 129
herds 132, 140, 142, 147, 148
Herrerasaurus 116
Hesperocyon 202
Hesperornis regalis 172
heterodontosaurs 140
Heterodontosaurus 140
Hipparion 223
Hippidion 223
Hippopotamus 231
hippopotamuses 207, 210, 211, 222,
   230–1, 232
Holoptychius 25, 58
Homalocephale 141
Homalodotherium 221
hominids 244–5
hominoids 242–3
Homo erectus 9, 37, 245
Homo habilis 244
Homo sapiens 37, 242, 243, 245
Homo sapiens "Cro-Magnon" 245
Homo neanderthalensis 37, 245
Homunculus 241
hoofed mammals 189
   camels 234–5
   early rooters and browsers 210–11
   giraffes, deer and cattle 236–7
   horses 222–3
   oreodonts and early hoofed browsers
      232–3

rhinoceroses 228–9
   South American 216–21
   swine and hippopotamuses 230–1
   tapirs and brontotheres 224–7
horns and antlers
   early horned browsers 232–3
   giraffes, deer and cattle 236–7
   horned dinosaurs 156, 160–3
horses 36, 37, 210, 222–3, 228
Hovasaurus 87
Huayangosaurus 120, 121
humans 9, 37, 189, 244–5
hunting 128, 129
Huxley, Thomas 220
Hybodus 48
hydrothermal vents 10
hyenas 202–3
Hylaeosaurus 159
Hylonomus 74, 75, 78
Hypacrosaurus 147
Hyperodapedon 99
Hyposognathus 80
Hypsidoris 56
Hypsilophodon 142
hypsilophodonts 142–3
Hypsocormus 57
Hyrachyus 228
Hyracodon 228
Hyracotherium 222
hyraxes 211

I

Iapetus Ocean 19, 21, 22, 25
Icaronycteris 189, 197
ice ages 19, 20, 36
Ichthyornis dispar 172
ichthyosaurs 72, 74, 75, 82, 90–1, 94–5,
   96, 97
Ichthyosaurus 33, 90, 96, 97
Ichthyostega 24, 65
Ictitherium 203
Idricotherium 228
Iguanodon 113, 115, 138, 144
iguanodonts 144–5
Ilingoceros 237
Imagotaria 207
insectivores 196–7
insects
   evolution 27
   flying 120
   pollinating 156
   survival of 167

invertebrates 17, 22
Ischyodus 49
Ischyromys 238

J

jackals 202, 203
Jamoytius 22, 44
jawless fish 20, 21, 42–5
jellyfish 15
Jurassic Period 9, 32–3, 72, 110, 120–1,
   169

K

Kamptobaatar 34, 35
kangaroos 192, 193
Kannemeyeria 184
Kanuites 205
Karaurus 71
Karoo strata 28
Kennalestes 35
Kentrosaurus 154
Keraterpeton 68
koalas 192
Kritosaurus 148
Kronosaurus 91
Kvabebihyrax 211

L

Labidosaurus 78
labyrinthodonts 64
Laggania 18
lagomorphs 238
Lambeosaurus 147, 153
land, life on 21, 25, 28, 31
landmasses 11
Lariosaurus 89
Late Cambrian Period 18–19
Laurasia 33, 121
Laurentia 22, 25, 27, 28
Leaellynasaura 143
legs, dinosaur 113
lemurids 240
lemurs 189, 240
leopards 204
Lepidosauromorpha 76
Lepidotes 54, 96, 97
lepospondyls 64, 68–71
Leptictidium 197
Leptoceratops 160
Lesothosaurus 140
Lexovisaurus 154

ACKNOWLEDGMENTS

(t=top, ... front cover)

5 Tim Bewer/Getty ... 7 Herding Dohloff/Science Photo Library, ... Louise K. Broman/Science Photo Library, br Dirk Wiersma/Science Photo Library, gcr Detlev Van Ravenswaay/Science Photo Library, 10c Noaa Pmel Vents Program/Science Photo Library, bc Mike Hollingshead/Science Photo Library, 11 main Babak Tafreshi, Twan/Science Photo Library, Richard Bizley/Science Photo Library, Bildagentur-Online/Mcphoto-Schulz/Science Photo Library, Mark Garlick/Science Photo Library, Paul Wootton/Science Photo Library, 12cl Bernhard Richter/Shutterstock, 13tr nobeastsofierce/Shutterstock, 14cr Ken Lucas/Visuals Unlimited/Corbis, 17cl Marques/Shutterstock, tr Alan Sirlnikoff/Science Photo Library, 18tc Frans Lanting, Mint Images/Science Photo Library, 20cl, 23cr, tl Sinclair Stammers/Science Photo Library, 24cr David Fleetham, Visuals Unlimited/Science Photo Library, 26cr Ken Lucas, Visuals Unlimited/Science Photo Library, cl Herve Conge, ISM/Science Photo Library, 28cl Stepehen J. Krasemann/Science Photo Library, 31tl Natural History Museum, London/Science Photo Library, tr Thomas Wiewandt, Visual Unlimited/Science Photo Library, 32cl Linda Bucklin/Shutterstock, 35cr Natural History Museum, London/Science Photo Library, 37tr Pascal Goetgheluck/Science Photo Library, 38-39 Jaime Chirinos/Science Photo Library, Background Sukharevskyy Dmytro (nevodka) /Shutterstock, 62-63 John Sibbick, 72-73 John Sibbick, background Photobank gallery/Shutterstock, 122tr Julius Csotonyi/Science Photo Library, bl Michael Rosskothen/Shutterstock, 123cl Natural History Museum/Science Photo Library, 124cl Dorling Kindersley, br Friedrich Saurer/Science Photo Library, 125t Dorling Kindersley, b Julius Csontonyi/Science Photo Library, 126cr Andreas Meyer/Shutterstock, 126t Andreas Meyer/Shutterstock, 127t Jaime Chirinos/Science Photo Library, 136c Linda Bucklin/Shutterstock, 137t Linda Bucklin/Shutterstock, b Michael Rosskothen/Shutterstock, 154bl Sofia Santos/Shutterstock, 155t Linda Bucklin/Shutterstock, b Leonello Calvetti/Shutterstock, 162b Michael Rosskothen/Shutterstock, 163 Linda Bucklin/Shutterstock, c Leonello Calvetti/Shutterstock, b Linda Bucklin/Shutterstock, 166-167 Mark Stevenson/Stocktrek Images/Corbis, 168-169 Jaime Chirinos/Science Photo Library, 186-187 Christian Jegou Publiphoto Diffusion/Science Photo Library, 189bl Bildagentur-online/McPhoto-Schulz/Science Photo Library, 205tr Laurie O'Keefe/Science Photo Library